NATIONAL SUICIDE

NATIONAL SUICIDE

How Washington
Is Destroying the
American Dream
from A to Z

MARTIN L. GROSS

BERKLEY BOOKS, NEW YORK

THE BERKLEY PUBLISHING GROUP
Published by the Penguin Group
Penguin Group (USA) Inc.
375 Hudson Street, New York, New York 10014, USA
Penguin Group (Canada), 90 Eglinton Avenue East, Suite 700, Toronto, Ontario M4P 2Y3, Canada
(a division of Pearson Penguin Canada Inc.)
Penguin Books Ltd., 80 Strand, London WC2R 0RL, England
Penguin Group Ireland, 25 St. Stephen's Green, Dublin 2, Ireland (a division of Penguin Books Ltd.)
Penguin Group (Australia), 250 Camberwell Road, Camberwell, Victoria 3124, Australia
(a division of Pearson Australia Group Pty. Ltd.)
Penguin Books India Pvt. Ltd., 11 Community Centre, Panchsheel Park, New Delhi—110 017, India
Penguin Group (NZ), 67 Apollo Drive, Rosedale, North Shore 0632, New Zealand
(a division of Pearson New Zealand Ltd.)
Penguin Books (South Africa) (Pty.) Ltd., 24 Sturdee Avenue, Rosebank, Johannesburg 2196,
South Africa

Penguin Books Ltd., Registered Offices: 80 Strand, London WC2R 0RL, England

This book is an original publication of The Berkley Publishing Group.

The publisher does not have any control over and does not assume responsibility for author or third-party
websites or their content.

PRINTING HISTORY
Berkley trade paperback edition / September 2009

Library of Congress Cataloging-in-Publication Data

Gross, Martin L. (Martin Louis), (date)
    National suicide : how Washington is destroying the American Dream from A to Z / Martin L.
Gross.
    p. cm.
    ISBN 978-0-425-23137-1
    1. United States—Politics and government—21st century.   2. Political planning—United States.   I.
Title.
    JK275.G76 2009
    320.60973—dc22

                                    2009013501

PRINTED IN THE UNITED STATES OF AMERICA

10   9   8   7   6   5   4   3   2   1

Contents

INTRODUCTION

America had been mesmerized for almost two years by the dialogue of the presidential election. There have been continuous arguments and debates between the Republican and Democratic candidates, thousands of commentaries by the press, and endless personal attacks, all culminating in the typical quadrennial theater that has not advanced either the substance or the knowledge of our failing federal government.

It represents a sad commentary, one that has been standard for years, but is now worsening rapidly.

The election has resulted in the naming of a new president and reinforced the prejudices of partisanship. But it has failed, as always, in improving the basic knowledge of the American voter, adding little or nothing to our citizens' woeful understanding of a dysfunctional Washington apparatus.

Today, just as after all prior presidential elections, American citizens are as poorly informed about the failed inner mechanisms of Washington as before. Instinctively, they remain part of the 74% of Americans who have lost respect for their government and its wasteful, inefficient, and hidden operation.

That condemnation and frustration will continue until, instead of being turned into political mutes by the parties, the candidates, and the press, the voters learn the truth about Washington. Only then will they be able to think intelligently about a government that is robbing its citizens of their treasure, their personal confidence, and their self-respect.

To that aim, this book is dedicated.

NATIONAL
SUICIDE

THE ROAD TO OBLIVION

Oversize Dysfunctional Federal Government, Faulty Management, Fiscal Stupidity, Fiery Partisanship, and Amazing Ignorance

America's politicians tend toward grand, hyperbolic statements about the federal government that often have no grounding in reality. In January 1996, in his State of the Union Address, then President William Jefferson Clinton stated brazenly: "The era of big government is over."

The assembled Congress cheered loudly, though they knew, of course, that this was a ludicrous comment. The statistics support the reality. In the 8 years of the Clinton administration, the federal national debt grew by $1.4 trillion and has never receded in its continual upward trend. The debt was $4.4 trillion in 1993, rising to $5.8 trillion in 2001 at the end of his administration.

In 2000, Americans elected another bold boomer, President George W. Bush, who several times expressed his desire to cut the size and cost of government, in opposition to the Democrats' historic tendency, as he said, to "tax and spend." Several times, he pronounced that it was his intention to balance the budget and cut federal spending. The reality once again was quite the opposite. He did cut taxes for most Americans, but the federal giant continued its brazen upward cost under his "compassionate conservatism," which finally meant overwhelming, unnecessary spending.

During young Bush's 8 years in office, the national debt grew by over $3 trillion, making, once again, a mockery of still another politician's word. Perhaps a third of this was the cost of the wars in Iraq and Afghanistan, but even domestic spending greatly exceeded that of Clinton, himself a master of largesse with the taxpayer's money.

The administration was controlled by a Democrat in 1993, then by a Republican in 2001, both with fiscal failures. In 2009, it once again returned to Democratic control, with even greater spending matched to fiscal distress.

Today, the term *billions* is a modest one as the federal government initiates a new vocabulary of "trillions" in deficit and debt. For 2009 alone, we are informed that the annual deficit will rise to $1.85 trillion, an alarming failure that will continue at almost a trillion a year for some time.

The nonpartisan Congressional Budget Office (CBO) estimates the deficit for 2010 as $1.4 trillion. According to the president's 2010 budget, in the period 2010 to 2019 the national debt would grow by $9.3 trillion, almost doubling that frightening obligation, and raising the debt to an astronomical $23 trillion, four times larger than in 2000.

Meanwhile, the national debt rises inexorably, second by second, some $5 million a minute, or $720 million—almost three quarters of a billion dollars—every day. By 2010, it will increase the national debt for each American family of four to $160,000.

Not only is the era of big and growing government alive, but it is comfortable and jealously protected by both political parties. Today that government, which is living and expanding on more borrowed money, has in fact a stronger, more overwhelming, more frightening destiny than ever before.

America has adopted a spending pattern similar to that of a spoiled profligate child of a wealthy man who looks to his parents to even out his accounts. But in the case of the federal government, there is no parent to look to, and our wealth is not only suspect, but dissipating with every passing day.

Little wonder that the national debt, held by Americans, government agencies, and foreigners, has by the end of 2009 reached to more than $12 trillion, and will reach $13.5 trillion by the end of 2010. Even more frightening, there are some $57 trillion more in unfunded future obligations in Social Security, Medicare, and scores of loan guarantee programs—debt that America has no possibility of paying back under the present political and fiscal circumstances.

Most of the damage has been done in the last 30 years. In 1980, the federal debt consumed only 33% of the gross domestic product (GDP). Today it has reached 85% and in 2010 will reach 97% of the GDP, and 100% soon after.

We have been warned that we are indebting our children and grandchildren, which is true. But we forget that we are forcing debt on the current generation as well through higher interest payments, money lost today supporting the ever growing federal debt.

The danger to America's future is encapsulated in one statistic: the amount of interest we must pay annually to carry that national obligation. In 1988, it was $214 billion a year. By 2008, it had reached $451 billion. By the end of 2010, our wasted interest payments will have reached some $550 billion a year, a fortune almost equal to our entire Social Security and defense budget. By 2019, the interest payment on the national debt will rise to more than $1 trillion each year.

We are reminded of Thomas Jefferson, who warned in a letter to a friend that he considered "public debt as the greatest of the dangers to be feared," then summed up his philosophy: "I wish it were possible to obtain a single amendment to our Constitution . . . taking from the federal government their power of borrowing."

The announced figures of the annual deficits of the last two administrations are grim enough. But now a true audit of the government's books concludes that, as we suspected, the figures have been doctored all along. Things are actually considerably worse than Washington has been admitting. Day-to-day government accounting, it has been revealed, is a highly "creative" operation, using the negative definition of the word.

The Official Budget of the United States, which Washington reports, involves only cash expenditures. It does not take into account accrued liabilities, whether for pensions for military and civilian employees or all internally borrowed monies, as per billions taken yearly from the Social Security fund, for which the government receives only an IOU.

All this peculiar accounting is designed to make it look as if the United States were solvent, which of course it is not.

For years, Washington has been using this devious cash method of keeping books. Instead, an audit of government finances, conducted by the U.S. Treasury, uses the accrual accounting method required of all corporations, nonprofits, and local and state governments with expenditures of over $1 million.

What does this audit show?

That the annual deficits are much larger than Washington has been admitting, losses that are bringing us closer to the tipping point of total fiscal irresponsibility and eventual mayhem.

Take the year 2005, for example. Instead of the announced deficit for the Bush administration, for instance, which was ostensibly $318 billion, the Audited Federal Budget shows a deficit of $729 billion. The disparity between the announced and audited budgets of the final 4 years of the Clinton administration is even greater. Instead of his supposed much heralded "surplus" of $559 billion, the true figure was actually a deficit of $484 billion, a truth spread of more than $1 trillion. The reality is that there never was a surplus. It was, instead, a well-publicized manipulation of accounting procedures.

As Congressman Jim Cooper (D–TN) put it, "We've been hiding the bottom line from the American people. It's not fair to them, and it's delusional on our part."

Not only is the work of America's politicians, especially in Washington, one of "delusion" but the actions of the political class, in their mad compulsion for election and reelection at any cost, constitute the major reasons for America's increasing flirtation with self-inflicted failure—read "national suicide."

Once the soundest country in the world, we have now instead become a humiliated debtor nation. Recently, the new secretary of state traveled to China to convince them to buy still more of our debt, of which they now hold almost a trillion dollars.

The cost of government rises inexorably as Washington

continues its uncontrolled orgy of spending, often without reason or value, as we shall later see in detail. In just one decade, the size of the annual national budget has doubled, from $1.8 trillion to $3.6 trillion.

Washington inexorably spends a greater and greater percentage of the gross national product (GNP), depriving the private sector of its engine of growth. In 1935 under FDR, whose administration had been considered the pinnacle of big government, and in the midst of the New Deal, the cost was actually only 10% of the GDP, less than half the present expenditure.

Today under President Obama's 2010 budget, the cost of the federal government has risen to a record astounding 25% of the GDP, compared with 18% to 20% for most of the past 30 years. State and local costs have been rising along with Washington's, and by 2010, the price of all government will reach an astronomical 41% of the nation's total income.

In fact, the 2010 budget is a 20% increase over the previous year. Subtracting the cost of the wars and the alternative minimum tax (AMT) patch, it is still a 15% percent rise, an unsustainable burden not only on the economy but on the morale and psyche of the beleaguered American citizen.

The statistics tell us a great deal, but do not explain all the serious problems involved in big government. As budgets rise, government eats up both the fiscal and the social oxygen, forcing the public to bear the increased burden that politics directly has on our lives. As the mammoth Washington machine grows and changes, government, and especially politicians, become too important in our lives.

Their eccentric gyrations, once virtually ignored by the American public, are now often economic life and death sentences for citizens, not only through taxation but through the effect of big, wasteful, and inefficient government on the economy, on our jobs, and on our very way of life. In the circus created by Washington, no one is immune from its deleterious effects, to the point at which politics is replacing philosophy as a way of viewing life, all to the detriment of an intelligent, thoughtful society.

The unfortunate reality of the dysfunctional federal government is that it is an anomaly in this era. America is the most developed nation in the world, with the greatest potential for the creation of wealth and the most diversified system of social advancement and opportunity, one that frees every segment of its citizenry. But its federal government is a retrograde affair, an inefficient, even crazy-quilt, operation that bears no relation to 21st-century sophisticated economics and potential efficiencies.

Further, America is justifiably the world's great engine for change and improvement, creating a landscape of opportunity and accomplishment that places all its citizens on an escalator of social class. But Washington, its politicians, its bureaucracy, and its strange methodologies, is more consistent with 19th-century mercantilism than it is with modern economics and efficiencies.

America is caught in a time warp between its private profit-making ingenuity and its governmental narrowness and ignorance.

The villain is politics, which in modern America has turned into a morally corrupt machine for retrograde government rather than that of the great Enlightenment that gave birth to this amazing nation.

It might be said, without fear of intelligent criticism, that America, the greatest nation in the history of the world, has now reached a point in its mature development in which its federal government has become the most dysfunctional central operation in the fully developed world. It has morphed into a grave threat to America's stability and its place as the leader in the world, both geopolitically and economically.

Besides the narcissism of politicians, another aspect of the spread between the promise and the reality of the federal government is the ignorance of many of America's politicians, within both the White House and the U.S. Congress. They must master the political lingua franca to become elected, but most know little about governing, either before or even after their spell in national office.

In Congress, they seem acquainted only with the narrow work of their subcommittees and fail to understand the cumulative impact of operating legislation going back a generation or two, legislation that affects, and often cripples, the fiscal health and future of our government.

I discovered this political propensity for ignorance firsthand. As the author of *The Government Racket: Washington Waste from A to Z*, and other bestsellers on the political and intellectual deficiencies of the federal government, I testified six times before various U.S. House and Senate committees on the question of waste and spending.

I was often praised for my insights, but simultaneously I witnessed a display of abject ignorance by the members of Congress.

One example stands out in my mind. The subject was the question of government welfare, or charity, for America's poorer citizens, those below the poverty line.

In the administration of President Clinton, the press and the public had made much of the fact that Clinton and Congress had supposedly "reformed" welfare. The unpopular program, then called Aid to Families with Dependent Children (AFDC), helped support unmarried low-income mothers and their children.

Finally, after 30 years, the program was reformed toward work to great fanfare, effectively reducing the welfare rolls by some 40%. It saved little or no money because of the extra cost of job training and other benefits, but it should be applauded because of its intangible social gain.

But what should not be applauded was the shocking ignorance displayed by members of Congress about welfare in America. Most Americans support charitable activities of the federal government on behalf of the poor as an expression of Judeo-Christian morality. But they do not support it when it is not only excessive but virtually secret, ineffective, and poorly spent and directed and of much less benefit to the poor than it should be.

When I stated to Congress that the accumulated welfare legislation and its yearly budget was now so massive that it threatened federal fiscal bankruptcy, I received shocked and skeptical looks.

They pointed out that AFDC represented less than 1% of the entire federal budget. True, but when I explained that AFDC was only a minuscule portion of a carefully hidden, unpublicized giant welfare budget known to few politicians, they became restless, even angry. Obviously, they did not understand the truth— that the unknown welfare programs were swallowing up much of the nation's income.

"How do you know that?" they asked.

I then produced the evidence. There is no category in the

federal budget for "welfare" or "government charity," so this money cannot be tracked down and truly divulged or examined.

But there is, quite by accident, a virtually unknown document that catalogs it all. It is a 250-page volume titled *Cash and Non-Cash Benefits for People with Limited Income*. It was not compiled by one of the many large cabinet agencies involved in some form of welfare or by the Office of Management and Budget (OMB). It was the work of an unknown bureaucrat, Ms. Vee Burke, in the small Congressional Research Service (CRS).

Every 2 years she produced this volume for the benefit of those who wanted to know the true cost, which as we shall see, is hopelessly massive. Burke has since retired, and, without her, that document is apparently no longer being issued.

Without that document, it would be impossible to find the reality. The enormous sums involved are hidden within six different cabinet agencies and scores of separate, unrelated welfare programs, all without anyone in charge. There is no computer input or access to how much any one American is receiving from the government or from how many different programs. It would seem that the government is ashamed, rather than proud, of the broad spectrum of welfare sponsored by Washington and paid for by working taxpayers.

And ashamed they should be. Instead of revealing and debating the facts with the public and through the press, those few knowledgeable politicians in Congress and in the White House have been hiding the truth from their colleagues and from the American taxpayers, who are bearing the unusual burden.

The CRS welfare report shows that together with state welfare, mainly Medicaid, mandated by Washington, the cost of welfare exceeds almost all the major federal agencies, including

Social Security and Medicare. Congress has passed 85 different, expensive welfare programs over time that are still in effect, some since New Deal days.

The cost, including state welfare programs, is massive, now reaching at least $700 billion a year. That enormous figure is extrapolated from the 2002 CRS report figure plus a 4% annual increase, surely a conservative number if we use only the Bush administration's typical 7% increases as a guide.

Even that large percentage rise has been surpassed by the new administration. The 2009 Omnibus Bill, which cost $410 billion, was an 8% increase over the prior year, $32 billion in greater spending. This indicates that the $700 billion welfare estimate is understated, perhaps by $100 billion or more.

It is not surprising that that fortune is draining the Treasury like no other cabinet expenditure. It is larger than Medicare (not a welfare item), which costs $425 billion and Social Security (also not welfare), which runs over $662 billion. It is even larger than the Defense budget.

The programs cover almost-free care for medicine, housing, and food plus cash and dozens of other free benefits, including such strange concepts as money to weatherize your home and money to educate migrant workers. (See "Welfare" on p. 305.)

The startling aspect of this generosity is that the number of those below the official poverty line—some 37 million Americans— has risen, not lowered, since 2000, despite the government's having cumulatively spent several trillion dollars on the poor. This is especially strange because, as we shall see, granting the same amount of money outright to the poor would eliminate all poverty in America for all time, with hundreds of billions left over.

Philanthropy is one aspect of an effective, solvent federal

government. But governing sagely so that the nation can continue intelligent welfare short of bankruptcy must be the first priority. In this case, both parties have reversed the priority by keeping the facts secret and indulging in unexamined, massive expenditures.

The result is that by relying on political motivation, rather than good government, Washington has defaulted on its responsibility to the national commonwealth.

This raises a touchy but significant problem in the American political system. Congressmen are of course adept at raising money, easily learn how to handle constituent service, and execute the committee work assigned to them.

But what few of them know is the inner workings of the federal government, especially its complex inventory of programs and legislation. Most have little idea of the present status of programs they and their predecessors have passed over the past two generations and the fact that they are currently costing the taxpayers a substantial fortune. Neither do they know how these programs are presently being managed by the executive branch, their coequal partners in governing. Nor are they aware of which programs should be continued or modified or completely eliminated.

I believe that in the 2 months between their election in November and being sworn in the following January, indoctrination classes, at a high level, should be conducted for all elected officials by three knowledgeable federal organizations—the Congressional Budget Office (CBO), the Government Accountability Office (GAO), and the Office of Management and Budget (OMB).

Knowing the "secrets" of the often-hidden Washington apparatus would surely slow them down in legislating still more money once they learn what is happening to the government programs they have already established and often forgotten.

An unrestrained federal government and the politicians who run it are at the core of many of the nation's most severe problems and dilemmas rather than, as the practitioners proclaim, their solution.

It is now a growing tradition in American government that politicians—of both parties—will distort brazenly, inflicting their often misguided will on citizens while the government evolves into a dumb, inept species that threatens the sanctity and survival of the nation. Unchecked and unreformed federal policies, plus rampant Washington spending and disorganization, are surely pushing the nation toward first bankruptcy, then potential national suicide.

The great contrast of the American civilization is between the family-oriented, patriotic, hardworking, generally prudent American citizens and their federal government, which in the common parlance is correctly viewed as out of control. Washington is engaged in political demagoguery and false theories and is unable to meet either its obligations or its extravagant promises to the people.

Worse yet, America's politicians have evolved as the enemy of the middle classes, especially its most productive and successful citizens. Their generosity to the poor, no matter how poorly performed, is rewarded by the media as signs of true Judeo-Christian concern, and their support of the rich provides politicians with an unlimited amount of campaign contributions, the mother's milk of their profession.

The poor and the working poor pay almost no federal income taxes to the IRS, obligated for only the 7.65% Social Security and

Medicare payroll tax, which 25 million Americans get back each year through the Earned Income Tax Credit. The lower-earning 50% of Americans finally pay only 3.5% of the total IRS taxes, while the rich, the top 1%, pay 33%. The middle classes, as always, disproportionately bear the major burden.

They are not only overlooked but are punished from time to time by what can only be classified as extreme ignorance and indifference to their needs by the insensitive political class. In fact, political action toward the middle class is often accompanied by flagrant deception.

A grating case of violating the government's contract with middle-class taxpayers is the so-called tax reform of 1986, in which the maximum rate was lowered to 28%. This was a step forward, but taxpayers were told that in return they had to forgo two vital time-honored deductions: the state and city sales taxes on all purchases, including large items such as cars, and also the deduction for interest on loans, including their punishing high-interest credit cards.

They did that willingly, expecting to save on the lowered IRS rate. But not long after, the government, which does not honor commitments from one year to the next—depending on political winds—violated the new rule and has since returned to the 35% rate. By 2010, that top marginal rate will rise to almost 40%.

Meanwhile, in 2009, the promised relief for middle-class taxpayers was announced—a mere $400 a year per person, $7.70—less than $8—a week, more an insult than a tax reduction, especially after glowing promises.

And never, never has there been a return by Washington of

the once-beloved deductions for sales taxes and loan interest, a continually growing cost to taxpayers. (See "Taxes" on p. 278.)

All politicians talk about their concern for the middle class and how much they wish to help these beleaguered citizens. But the reality is quite the opposite. The reason politicians concentrate on the middle class is actually a selfish, skeptical one. The middle class pays some two thirds of all income taxes, making them the golden goose of politics, the place where true revenue resides. Every small increase in middle-class taxes reaps giant rewards for Washington and its politicians—thus the reason for so much rhetoric and so little true concern.

Basically, taxation in America is a concerted attack by Washington on the middle class, and the major reason for that group's steady financial decline.

The result is that over the years, they have been drained to extremes with regular yearly increases, for example, of 6% in FICA taxes, with IRS deductions taken away as income rises, with AMT penalties, with extra Medicare taxes for the successful but hardly rich. The true heroes of the middle class are Reagan, who cut the marginal rate to 28%, and, more recently, George W. Bush, who gave $2,000 a year in tax relief to a median family of four.

What we need is for politicians to stop promising real aid to the middle class and delivering pennies. We need to demand a program that will cut their taxes at least 20% immediately, accompanied by an equal cut in government. (See "Conclusion" on p. 324.)

One easy way to try to restore balance is to return to the personal exemption of $600 in 1950, inflation adjusted to $8,400 instead of the present $3,650. This will give a family of four

$33,600 in exemptions, double what they now receive. At a marginal tax rate of 25%, it will cut middle-class family taxes by some $4,000 a year, the minimum that a reform should deliver.

Long-term capital gains is another tax that the middle class, which includes the bulk of the 100 million investors, needs to have adjusted. Recently it was raised to 20% from 15%, a one third increase. Instead, in the fiscal crisis, it should have been lowered to 7.5%, or even to zero, for 1 year. Through their various retirement funds, 401(k)s, and IRAs, many working Americans have lost around half of their liquid wealth, money saved over decades, even a full generation.

To stimulate the stock market so that the lost money can eventually return requires a low capital gains tax, the métier for market progress. Instead a confused and shortsighted Washington recently put in an increase in that crucial tax.

It is unfair for Congress and the president to constantly alter the rules of the game every 2 or 4 years, whipsawing taxpayers with changes in capital gains rates, marginal tax brackets, exemptions, deductions, and other factors vital to their existence. What is normal in American politics, but upsetting to taxpayers who financially support Washington, is that the overpoliticized system makes it virtually impossible for taxpayers to plan from year to year, often having to adjust to major shocks in their fiscal planning with each election.

Politicians are transient, but the public is not. The public commonwealth is almost always ignored by our politicians, who seek ideological praise, notoriety, and power for their actions rather than provide a constant base of rules for the confused citizenry. It is a violation of trust, a fact that is almost never considered by politicians, whose internal codes of honor need to be self-examined and externally graded.

A sociological reality for America today offers up a difficult conundrum that we have not seen fit to face. It is that half of Americans who pay almost no income tax now have the political power to tax the other half and feel no compunction to reduce the size of government and its excessive expenditures. This makes pragmatic sense because they are often recipients of government largesse, while the other half pays the bill.

This of course feeds the unfortunate class war, which in historic terms is a reversal of the early American story. It could promote a rallying cry of the taxed class, the reverse of the colonial call into a new slogan: No Representation Without Taxation.

Another major inequity that bedevils the middle class is the fact that taxation is not apportioned geographically to take into account regional differences in earnings and cost of living.

A couple making $120,000 a year in the New York Metropolitan area—say a nurse and a fireman—are often in the top 35% tax bracket. Meanwhile, the same couple in Alabama might be paid less, but be equally well off because of a lower cost of living and end up in only the effective 25% federal marginal tax bracket.

Another case of government betrayal is the alternative minimum tax, which was designed some 40 years ago when it was revealed that 155 Americans who made over $200,000 a year had not paid a single penny in federal taxes. It was all quite legal and was due to a deficiency in the tax code. (See "Alternative Minimum Tax" on p. 55.)

The revelation sent a shock wave through Congress, which quickly changed the tax law, hoping to ensnare this clever handful—

only to punish millions of innocent Americans with extra taxes they never incurred.

This second unfair income tax eliminated portions of legitimate deductions such as capital gains, child credits, high state income and property taxes and others, turning deductions once heralded by politicians as essential to the middle class into tax liabilities, flipping the IRS code upside down.

Not only were the 155 never caught—in fact, the number grew—but the crazy net also entrapped millions of innocent middle-class people. By 1967, the AMT punished 618,000 taxpayers. By 2006 it ensnared 4 million, and by 2008, that iniquitous financial maw would have swallowed some 17 million Americans if not for the expensive $30 billion "patch" that kept the AMT from growing, if not receding, at least for 12 months. In 2009, the crude patch became infinitely more expensive, now requiring $70 billion to relieve more than 20 million Americans from suffering that onerous, unfair levy on the middle classes.

The cause? Stupidity? Perhaps. But more likely it is a case of pure chicanery on the part of politicians of both parties, who never indexed the original law and its exemption for inflation.

They claimed that they made a mistake but more likely it was purposeful, and they were lying to taxpayers. The AMT went through 10 sessions of Congress and nine presidential administrations without being adjusted for inflation. Obviously, that was a plan, not an oversight. The reason was not ignorance or a mistake but that politicians saw the AMT as tapping the giant cash cow of upper-middle-class Americans, creating a steady stream of billions for politicians to spend as they saw fit.

This reprehensible tax is still active and will take $1 trillion more from innocent, unsuspecting taxpayers in the next 10 years unless Congress and the president decide to spend many billions to repeal this supposed mistake.

Americans are a good and naive people, subject to trust, often against their own interests. But what Americans do not know—though they are beginning to suspect—is that politicians are not like other Americans.

Citizens are quite adept at governing their own lives and distributing their incomes logically for maintenance, for investment, for vacations, and for the education of their children. Politicians, on the other hand, are much less adept at governing. They see the federal government's income as an opportunity to allot money to gratify their ideology or their ambitions and to use their power to buy votes with the public's own funds, which are often then misspent.

When politicians are liberal, the money is usually allocated to the poorer. If conservative, more goes to corporations and the military, to the 100 million investors in the stock market, and upper-middle-income Americans. Supposedly, that all balances out over time, and although illogical, those special interests purportedly substitute for good government. But, of course, they do not.

Instead, the country is pulled first one way, then another, depending on who is in power. The citizens in the middle, which includes most Americans, are always confused and always lose out.

This system of negative governance is highly detrimental. But it is worse when politicians of both parties agree that the target is so valuable that buying the votes deserves a bipartisan, if expensive, push.

That is what happened in the 2008 farm bill, which cost

taxpayers—mostly city folk—almost $300 billion. President Bush vetoed the bill after it passed in Congress by an overwhelming bipartisan vote in May 2008. But the desire to please farmers was so strong that the politicians of both parties in Congress easily overrode the veto and made it law. (See "Farmer Subsidies" on p. 154.)

The bill is a travesty, even by traditional special-interest logic. Government dole, tradition dictates, should be based on supposed need in order to sell it to the gullible nation. In 2008, however, farmers had never been as successful. The foolish subsidies of ethanol from corn and other crops for biodiesel has helped increase the price of many farm commodities, making federal help for farmers totally unnecessary.

Then why the farmers?

The reason is a simple one: politics, the ultimate villain in the story of government failure. The major farm states have considerably less population than the urban and suburban states, but they have enormous political power. Thinly populated South Dakota, for example—as a result of the major compromise of the 1789 Constitutional Convention—has the same number of senators (two) as say New York with only a twenty-fifth of the population.

Because farm states are heavily overrepresented in the U.S. Senate, they automatically become the bosom friend, and election target, of vote-hungry partisans in both parties. Corralling the vote of the farm states puts either political party way ahead in controlling Congress and in the electoral college for presidential elections.

Congress has long been the target of American humorists. Will Rogers and Mark Twain made them the butt of jokes, ostensibly good-natured ones. "Fleas can be taught nearly anything that a Congressman can," Twain once remarked, then later said, "It could probably be shown by facts and figures that there is no distinctly native criminal class—except Congress." Will Rogers dismissed our deliberative legislative bodies with a simple put-down: "Congress is the best that money can buy."

The character of members of Congress varies greatly, but public opinion, particularly today, is highly suspicious of their integrity.

Part of it is due to the question of "pork" (see "Earmarks" on p. 135), in which anywhere from $20 to $60 billion a year is taken out of the federal treasury and spent in members' own localities, a political trick that I helped expose many years ago in my first critiques of Washington. Earmarks have steadfastly been under attack by the wrath of Citizens Against Government Waste and such legislators as Senators John McCain of Arizona and Tom Coburn of Oklahoma, but "porkers" still maintain their morally deficient power in Congress.

This trick, made more famous recently by the Alaskan $220 million "bridge to nowhere," was never envisioned by the Founding Fathers, who worked hard to separate local, state, and federal matters in the Constitution. Now, however, it is regularly used to supposedly increase the popularity of members of Congress, especially when their constituents are civically brain-dead.

Jefferson warned against the diversion of money from the nation's capital to localities, which is the essence of earmarks. The fight for what later became known as "pork," Jefferson warned, would set off a "scene of scramble for who can get the most money wasted in their state."

The character of federal legislators is increasingly under examination as they use their national office—which was once considered the height of national service—as a mere stepping-stone to a "higher" plateau, that of overpaid lobbyist.

There is nothing inherently wrong with lobbying. In fact, the Founding Fathers specified that citizens should have the right to petition the government for redress of their grievances. The problem today is twofold: the concentration of vast sums in the hands of lobbyists, which are used to influence legislators through campaign contributions, and second, members of Congress too often seek lobbying as a second career instead of continued public service.

Increasingly, members of Congress—both House and Senate—are leaving voluntarily what we once thought was an excellent career to exchange their $165,000/year job, with its inherent honor, for a lobbying post on K Street for $500,000 and often much more.

No one is more effective at lobbying for special interests than a former member of Congress who just a short time ago held hearings on the very subjects he or she is now being paid handsomely to lobby. Occasionally in the past, a defeated Congressman who preferred to stay in Washington capitalized on his experience by converting to a lobbyist. But today, there has been a tidal wave of members voluntarily leaving their jobs in Congress to cash in, a reaction that says a great deal about their lack of dedication to the civic ideal.

A recent study showed that of the 198 members of Congress who left during the previous 6 years, 86 became lobbyists, some for as much as $1 million a year. The list is an A one of outstanding legislators who once filled our television screens. The list includes Fred Thompson, former Republican candidate for president, J. C. Watts, an outstanding Oklahoman and former football player, maverick Democrat Zell Miller, Senator Tim Hutchinson of Kansas, Senator Ben Nighthorse Campbell of Colorado, and longtime Senator John Breaux of Louisiana. Appropriations Chairman Bob Livingston left Congress in 1999, only to build a multimillion-dollar lobbying firm.

One recent congressional retiree, Gerald Solomon of New York, became a lobbyist on retirement (with General Electric as a client) and a part of a prominent lobbying group headed by former Senator Paul Laxalt (R–NV) and Senator Russell B. Long (D–LA).

There is no partisanship when it comes to lobbying and money.

Some former national leaders prefer not to register as lobbyists as required by law, and skirt the issue by becoming "advisers." This includes the top Republican, Bob Dole, former majority leader and nominee for president, who received $1 million for advising Dubai on its proposed port ownership, and former Democrat Senate Majority Leader Tom Daschle, who reportedly made a similar amount advising a Washington firm.

The new administration had made its anti-lobbying effort an important part of its supposed cleanup of Washington's soiled ethics. But in reality, the power of lobbying and influence, the so-called revolving door, continues to show itself unbroken. The new number two man in the Defense Department was a lobbyist for Raytheon, a large defense contractor, along with several other former lobbyists who were given "waivers" by the new administration in order for them to receive important government positions. Before he dropped out, Daschle, though a former adviser and not a registered lobbyist, was nominated as secretary of HHS in 2009, despite having earned large fees from healthcare companies he would be regulating.

The participation of former government officials and legislators as lobbyists worsens the political arena, for it distorts the operation to "redress grievances" by adding large amounts of money to the process. The government presently permits lobbyists not only to try to influence legislation by sound advice, which is their right, but to donate large sums to legislators' campaigns, what could easily be seen as a not-so-subtle form of bribery.

This practice, in which hundreds of billions of the people's dollars can be involved in a single piece of legislation, should not be permitted in a democracy. Just in the first 6 months of 2008, registered lobbyists donated $140 million to members of Congress, an excessive form of persuasion.

The Washington environment has never been worse for the quiet, contemplative atmosphere needed to make sound solutions to the nation's problems. The air is poisoned with greed and the need for millions in often soiled contributions to operate an effective campaign in this era of immediate communications. The media is also to blame for creating a political circus that enhances the ferocity of battle between the increasingly leftward Democratic Party and the reactive right wing Republicans.

Together this increasingly heated ideological struggle distorts the effort to be creative on behalf of the national interest and contaminates the solution-making power of not only Congress but the presidency as well.

The result is that America is living in an environment of poor decision making and bad public policy supported by both American political parties. In fact, it would not be an exaggeration to state that most of our dire national problems today, and in the future, stem from the policy errors of the federal government.

An example is the worst financial crisis since the Great Depression, the mortgage-related credit debacle of 2008 to 2009. This brought on a recession with massive losses in the stock market and the end of such once-classic firms as Bear Stearns and Lehman Brothers, the nationalization of AIG, the forced merger of Merrill Lynch with Bank of America, and the government takeover of Freddie Mac and Fannie Mae, plus the threat of a banking fiasco of frightening proportions. Thus far it has cost the government an additional two trillion dollars, with the surety that more will have to be spent to calm the financial waters.

It all began with the piercing of the housing bubble, with its attendant home foreclosures, the near-destruction of the housing market, and loss of trillions in equity to homeowners. In addition, there were some trillion dollars in losses by banks and brokerage firms, which invested excessively in subprime mortgages. Not only did it infect the economics of America but the mortgage securities were sold worldwide, from Shanghai to Berlin, where banks and economies also suffered the economic blow.

The press has singled out the obvious villains: the mortgage brokers and bankers who sold the public near-fraudulent mortgages that homeowners couldn't afford to carry, thus causing defaults, foreclosures, and housing mayhem. It has also castigated the regulators, who either were ignorant or looked the other way.

This much is known, as was the necessary intervention by the federal government to head off a severe recession and save brokerage and mortgage firms and banks nearly destroyed by the crisis. There the government acted correctly after the fact. But what is generally not known is that the major villain in this stark scenario, and the basic cause of the economic debacle, was our own federal government.

It was Washington, our Congress, and three presidents and their often distorted political instinct that created the fiasco in the first place, another case of bad federal policy.

There is the acknowledged error by the Federal Reserve in bringing interest rates down excessively in 2005 and 2006, as low as 1%. This, combined with flooding the market and the banks with cash, led to a euphoric credit market and too-easy loans, thus overstimulating home buying and building.

But perhaps the gravest contributor to the credit crisis was legislation sponsored and passed by the federal government itself. At its core was a then-unknown law engineered by Congress and the White House under Jimmy Carter, then expanded by both active boomer presidents, William Jefferson Clinton and George W. Bush.

What were the federal laws that triggered the housing bubble and subsequent crash?

The name of the original bill is the Consumer Reinvestment Act (CRA), first signed into law by President Jimmy Carter in 1977 and designed to provide more housing for low-income, mainly minority, Americans. It was then amended and greatly expanded beyond minorities in 1995 by President Clinton and in 2005 by President Bush, virtually forcing large banks and lenders to loosen their credit standards—under penalty of law—for all poorer Americans, minorities and otherwise.

The CRA stimulated, even forced, the banks through oversight and threat of punishment, to provide very low subprime loans to people, many of whom could not afford to maintain a house on their own. To make home ownership almost universal, the CRA forced banks to give home loans to millions of poorer Americans, often with no down payment and with virtually no income verification. If the banks were found wanting in granting mortgages to the poorest, they were warned they would not be permitted to open additional branches or merge with other banks.

The CRA program, as amended and greatly expanded by Clinton and Bush, also arranged for the paper securitization and worldwide sale of those subprime loans, which was the trigger that detonated the crisis.

The CRA, sponsored by three presidents and the U.S. Congress, was, in truth, not a piece of financial legislation but a massive social work project—to bring the American Dream to everyone, whether he or she could afford it or not.

It was well intentioned, but, of course, it ended in disaster. It was another massive federal project that confused philanthropy with economics. It was not fully thought out or properly financed by the nation's increasingly aggressive politicians.

I experienced the result indirectly through a relative, a 22-year-old male without a steady job or a regular income who obtained a 100% mortgage to buy a house in Florida, which was, of course, foreclosed.

Bad policy decisions emanating from Washington weaken the American fabric, little by little, driving us first toward national chaos, then toward national suicide. One poor decision, which has especially been true during the last 16 years under Clinton and the younger Bush, will surely lead America into dire cultural and financial straits not yet imagined. It is the extraordinary invasion of illegal immigrants.

Democrats under Clinton encouraged illegal immigration, contemplating eventual amnesty and new Democratic voters, especially among Hispanics. Republicans, under the younger Bush, represented the wishes of business to seek cheap labor and to pressure downward the wages of Americans through competition with low-earning illegals. In addition, Bush had a favorable experience with Hispanic voters in Texas and thought he could convince them nationwide to become Republicans, which has proven to be more fantasy than reality.

Without a powerful angel in Washington to enforce either the border or the law, America was—and is—swamped with poor, mainly uneducated Hispanic immigrants, mainly from Mexico and Central America, choking our schools, our hospitals, and our social service agencies. My local hospital, one of scores, has just become a medical center for illegals after they forced the closing of the main hospital in a nearby area heavily populated by nonpaying, noninsured illegals, people whom the hospitals must treat without payment, by federal law.

Much has been discussed about what to do with 20 million illegals. But while Washington continues to talk, illegals are settling the issue for themselves—in the bedroom. When a child of an illegal is born, he or she immediately becomes an American citizen through a misinterpretation of the 14th Amendment of the Constitution. This false birthright stems from the 1866 amendment to grant citizenship to the freed slaves, but it has strangely been used—without contest in the Supreme Court—to give the same honored privilege to children not only of foreigners but of illegal foreigners at that.

The present illegal adults will eventually die off, probably without ever becoming citizens. But not before they have given birth to at least two additional generations, each creating upward of four children. This is a geometric population time bomb, which could eventually create first 40, then 80, then over 100 million new American citizens descended from the present illegal parents and grandparents living in the United States.

Most believe that it will require a constitutional amendment to correct the situation, but actually in drafting the amendment, room was left to Congress to change or even cancel it. Bills are now in Congress to do just that, but thus far nothing is being done. (See "Baby Citizens" p. 61.)

There are, of course, millions of legal immigrants to America. But as citizens view the immigration situation, it strikes them that most of the new Americans are from the third world, and not from Europe, as were prior immigrants. Rumor has it that Europeans don't want to come here, but that is a canard. The reality is that they very much want to emigrate here, but are rebuffed by a Washington that is strongly biased against Europeans.

Several million Europeans, from virtually every nation on the Continent, apply for 55,000 green cards drawn by lottery every year, each one seeking permanent residence here. A few thousand make it, but others are turned down and never become new Americans. They are in essence restricted by the immigration law of 1965 passed by Lyndon Johnson, one that totally changed the demographic face of America.

The bill, the Immigration and Nationality Act of 1965, changed America more than any other piece of legislation in the last 100 years. Simply by mathematics, it eliminated the national-origin immigration quota that favored those of European stock because they were the founders of America and made up a great majority of the American population. They were also the ones who set the tone of the culture, one that has been extraordinarily successful.

That new law eliminated immigration quotas based on national origin and substituted "family reunification" as the modus operandi.

For example, if Irish Americans made up 10% of the American population, the old law gave Irish immigrants 10% of the immigrant visas. But that was discontinued by the 1965 law, which now makes it almost impossible for Europeans to emigrate here legally.

I recall a young French woman, a university graduate and a hostess on a transatlantic cruise ship, who told me that she had applied for an immigrant visa 5 years earlier and had been turned down because she had no family here to be reunited with. She was told her best chance was to marry an American, which explained her working on an international cruise ship.

Like myself, Americans of European stock are mostly long separated from their European ancestors by a span of time that is generational. (My grandfather came here from Hungary in 1893, and I have no contact with anyone there.) But the family of recent immigrants, as from Mexico, are still alive. The 1965 law enables them to bring their immediate family members here, which has accelerated greatly the immigration of non-Europeans, drastically changing the ethnic mix of America.

In debating and supporting the 1965 law, Senator Edward Kennedy claimed that "the ethnic mix of this country will not be upset." Of course, he was wrong, and that mix has changed enormously as a result of this law.

A *Boston Globe* article on immigration quoted Simon Rosenberg, president of the New Democratic Network, as stating that the act is "the most important piece of legislation that no one's ever heard of," and that "it set America on a very different demographic course than the prior 300 years."

Quite true. That change in immigration has created a nation of many diverse minorities, which in a generation or two will achieve majority status, with all the wrenching fiscal and cultural change that it implies.

Washington doesn't always make bad decisions. Some are noteworthy for their social value. But in most every case, the initial power and great value of these programs diminishes as they become abused by politicians. As the programs mature they become, as they are now, fiscally untenable. Their poor fiscal design eventually becomes evident as politicians overpromise. We then have to drastically lower our expectations for the succeeding generations or destroy the future of these programs, and with it the American sense of security.

Their assets have been robbed, or expended too generously by politicians seeking votes. They have become gravely weakened fiscally with little hope of their ever being restored to their original power and stability.

This is the case with three popular programs that now face fiscal defeat: Social Security, Medicare, and Medicaid, one developed by FDR and the other two by Lyndon Johnson.

These three now eat up almost 50% of the typical national budget. Worse yet, they have been so abused by Washington that one of them, the Social Security fund, is running out rapidly. The current Social Security surplus (more money now comes in than goes out) is robbed yearly and spent on items other than retirement benefits by politicians. For example, $209 billion was taken from the Social Security funds in 2009 and spent elsewhere, a tactic used to falsely hide much of the budget deficit.

And there is not, and never has been, a "lockbox." As we shall see, it is best labeled "The Great Social Security Heist," a caper pulled off by your friendly politician.

The result? We were informed that by 2017, there will no longer be a Social Security surplus, meaning that more money will be going out than coming in. But in 2009, a year was taken off that deadline, which has been reduced to 2016. That, plus the fact that over $2 trillion of retirement funds has already been spent elsewhere ($4 trillion by 2017) by our politicians, is creating a desperate situation. This will soon come to a head because there are 77 million baby boomers awaiting their monthly checks, along with their Medicare benefits. To make it truly whole would require raising taxes some 50%, to a level of extortion.

Already, the age of retirement has been extended to 67, with the possibility that it will reach 70. Many who have paid in all their lives will have passed away before they are eligible and will be robbed of benefits. Others will have to wait too many years after stopping work to retire and will be pressed financially by the age clock. And a once-magnificent program, beloved by Americans, will be hopelessly warped by the lack of foresight and the economic ignorance and duplicity of America's politicians.

The actuarial basis of the program has been destroyed. When it was inaugurated in 1933, there were 16 workers for every retiree.

Now the proportion is 1 to 3 and becoming lower. Even presidents and members of Congress who have attended at least their local community college should know that maintaining benefits at the present level is a statistical impossibility.

Medicare is in a worse position than Social Security. In 2008, less was taken in by the hospital Part A insurance than was paid out. The year the fund is tapped out has now been moved up from 2019 to 2017. The current costs are some 10 times what was anticipated when they were passed in 1965, a political technique called "low balling," which has been perfected by politicians and bureaucrats to advance their favored projects. (See "Low Balling" on p. 209.) We now face future liabilities from the newest entitlement, the Medicare R_X program, whose unfunded liabilities will eventually exceed that of Medicare itself.

We face grave problems with higher medical costs, which increase at twice the rate of inflation each year, and a gnawing, ever-present problem—that of Medicare and Medicaid fraud by doctors and hospitals. The HHS estimates Medicare fraud at some $20 billion a year, but anyone familiar with the program knows that a more reasonable figure would be closer to $100 billion. (See "Medicare Fraud" on p. 215.)

There isn't enough money in the Treasury, now or in the future, to maintain these three programs at the present profligate level, thanks to politicians who mortgaged the nation's future for their politically extravagant present. Now, the chits are coming home for payment, and the money is not there.

The original oracle, Jefferson, summed up this federal shell game with one pungent comment in a letter to James Madison during the writing of the Constitution in 1789: "No generation has the right to contract debts greater than can be paid off during the course of its own existence."

But, say supporters of the federal government, with all its ills, at least our taxes are lower than those in the semisocialized nations of Europe. That is true on the surface, but in reality, Americans are more painfully taxed than almost all European nations. Some 32% of America's GDP goes to taxes, versus 39% of the European Union's GDP. But those numbers fade in importance when examined in detail.

First, that 32% will rise considerably after the Bush tax cuts are eliminated by 2010. Second, because of deficits, spending by America's many governments is much higher than its tax receipts. In fact, the new 2010 federal budget indicates that all spending, federal, state, and local, will now eat up 41% of the GDP, a new record and larger than the European tax base.

Direct income tax, which takes money immediately out of our paychecks, is generally less in Europe, which makes up the difference in voluntary taxes, the value-added consumer taxes paid on most purchases. However, if America were to adopt a VAT tax, it would not be beneficial because it would surely be *added* to the IRS tax and not be instead of it.

Another stark difference in favor of the Europeans is that their corporate taxes are lower, while America and Japan have the highest in the world—over 39%. This, of course, dribbles down to consumers, to their punishment.

Most Europeans have very low local and regional taxes, while in America those taxes can be extravagant. In fact, in Europe the schools are almost all paid for by the central government, while in America, ever-rising local property taxes pay for schools, taxes that are becoming onerous for the average homeowner. Those property taxes, which are rising twice as fast as inflation, force the local homeowner to unfairly pay the lion's share of the cost of schools or lose his or her home for failure to pay.

I recall that in 1953 I bought my first home on Long Island for $10,000 and paid a nominal sum, less than $300, in local property taxes.

The property taxes on that same home are now $13,000—including $9,000 for the schools, a travesty of common sense. And just as income taxes are compulsory and VAT is paid voluntarily, the property tax is compulsory. If you don't come up with it in cash every 6 months, you lose your home. Morally, it is more confiscation than taxation.

Another factor makes the initial 39% to 32% comparison a false one. Europeans pay almost nothing for their healthcare, while Americans pay with out-of-pocket after-tax money some 50% of the almost $2 trillion medical bill. And in Europe, university education has only a nominal cost, while Americans pay $15,000 a year in state colleges and over $35,000 a year in private schools. In addition, most Europeans receive very high long-term unemployment benefits and guaranteed monthly paid vacations, a rarity in America—except for privileged, protected federal government employees. (See "Bureaucrats" on p. 79.)

Together, these benefits tip the net tax burden heavily against America. In fact, net net, America possibly has the highest effective tax rate of all countries except those in Scandinavia, which provide cradle-to-grave security.

No, the governmental system in America is stacked heavily against the working middle class and vigorously supports both the poor and the rich. This, of course, does not mean that European lifestyle is better than ours but just that the idea that we are taxed less is a myth. In fact, because much of the Europeans' taxation is a voluntary VAT, Americans feel the tax bite more acutely.

The basic problem with our federal government is that it no longer strongly resembles the brilliant organization laid out by the Founding Fathers in 1789. That was a federal plan, which meant that the central government would have specific duties and the states and localities others.

The Great Compromise was, on one side, the result of the philosophy of Alexander Hamilton along with John Adams, who both sought a relatively strong central government, even though the present dysfunctional, overblown Washington apparatus would be distasteful to them. On the other side was Thomas Jefferson, who hailed the direct rights of the states and the people.

Thomas Jefferson and James Madison favored the power of the states and localities rather than the federal government, an idea that many now fear is illogical in the modern world. But both sides of the argument feared what has occurred—a central, too large, incompetent federal government incapable of and unwilling to meet the needs of the people within a prudent framework and without excessive debt.

Jefferson was echoing the thoughts of his friend James Madison, considered the drafter of the Constitution, who warned that a potent federal government would include the threat of a "tyranny of the majority" in Washington. Today that tyranny is one of excessive power, excessive intrusion, and excessive amounts of money poorly spent with the threat of national bankruptcy and all that attends. Madison warned that he was "uncomfortable in pressing for a national government that could possibly be taken over by a unified majority position." Read: "The United States, circa now."

The Great Compromise between the two forces, the Federalists and the Jeffersonian Republicans (ironically, now Democrats), was installed in the form of the 10th Amendment to the Constitution, the last item of the Bill of Rights. That amendment was designed to limit the federal government's power through a simple statement: "The powers not delegated to the United States by the Constitution, nor prohibited by it to the States, are reserved to the States respectively, or to the people."

Jefferson and Madison saw the 10th Amendment as the firewall between Washington and its potential excesses. Unfortunately, that sacred amendment is now a discarded piece of historic paper, having been violated many thousands of times. Today it is virtually meaningless in the forced dialogue between the federal government, the states, and the people.

The abdication of the 10th Amendment began heavily under FDR when he rearranged the relation of the federal government and the states to create a new system that would attempt to heal the agony of the Great Depression directly from Washington. FDR went so far as to attempt, but failed, to "pack" and enlarge the Supreme Court so that they could no longer interfere in his plan to bring total power to Washington.

The emergency has been over for 70 years, but the concentration of power in Washington has proceeded almost continuously since. Sadly, much of it has been based on deficit spending and future mandates intended to temporarily shore up reality to meet the exaggerated promises and reputation of the central government.

And in the process, federal taxes today have risen more than twofold, inflation adjusted, per capita, than those under the supposedly wild-spending FDR's peacetime New Deal—over 20% of the GDP today, and much more after 2010, versus 10% in 1935.

Today, the normal relations between Washington and the states has been shattered. The states are still the best avenues for trying new solutions to our problems, as per healthcare advances made by various governors. But in this new unconstitutional relationship, the states may have the innovative ideas, but Washington, which takes the great lion's share of the overall taxes, has the money. The result is often national paralysis, as we shall see, along with a propensity toward national suicide, as we find it fiscally impossible to deal with our challenges.

What is the design of the present Washington government?

Actually, there is none. No one can draw an organizational chart because it grew like Topsy, without plan or foresight. Under the Founding Fathers, there were 5 cabinet agencies, all with clear missions. Under President Harry Truman, it was expanded to 8, but still within reasonable control and function. Today, there are 15 cabinet agencies, most without clear function or organizational design, the result of 60 years of haphazard and uncontrolled growth.

Unlike the central governments of other developed countries, Washington's organization is unique in that form does not follow function. Instead of following a true definition, this government is mainly a collection of many thousands of programs passed by Congress, which are placed, often willy-nilly, into specific cabinet agencies, which may or may not be the logical choice.

There are, incomprehensibly, exactly 1,399 federal programs just for rural America.

A bureaucracy is then developed for each program by the president to execute Congress's wishes. But later Congress, and the executive branch itself, forget about the program, which grinds on year by year without a sunset date. Annually, un-reevaluated, often forgotten, it receives its usual allotment, plus regular increases.

It is not that central government is necessarily bad or ineffective, but rather that the American central government model is unique in that it was never intended by the Founding Fathers and has no reasonable model, either here or overseas.

This failure of form matched with function is common in Washington. Take the Department of Education, created in 1979 under Jimmy Carter. The department does not educate a single child, a violation of the organizational rationale of following a mission, a salutary trait of European central governments. In France, a memo from Paris to the schools changes the curriculum immediately, while a memo from Washington to the states creates a giant yawn and a request for still more misspent money.

Americans correctly prefer local control of education, for they do not trust Washington, as they shouldn't. But neither Washington nor the states have figured out a method of paying for education other than the present near-confiscatory property taxes. The solution is probably consumption taxes run by the state and the federal governments, plus the use of the $60 billion in support from Washington, money now uselessly eaten up by the incompetent Department of Education.

The Department of Defense educates military children, and

the Department of Interior educates Native American children. Not only is the Department of Education without direct function but it spends $60 billion a year on invented tangential and ineffective programs. Between 2002 and 2004 under President George W. Bush, the agency's budget rose 70%.

That increase, however, is modest compared to the $81 billion additional for education being spent as part of President Obama's stimulus bill, the American Recovery and Reinvestment Act.

"Spend funds quickly to save and create jobs," stated a five-page document sent to state education officials from the Department of Education in March 2009, adding that they must be sure to keep receipts. The astronomical sum is supposed to "improve school achievement through school improvement and reform," a hollow, meaningless effort.

In fact, never in the history of Western civilization has so much money been spent in so short a period of time and been totally, absolutely wasted.

Just as No Child Left Behind, President Bush's $24 billion program, failed, devolving into useless testing and research, so the $81 billion will equally be wasted as long as the state-controlled educational establishment continues to support the present failed K–12 system—one based on low curriculum, inferior teachers, principals, and superintendents who initially come from the bottom third of the high-school class. To that we must add inferior training, false degrees, and an emphasis on a subject called Education, which does not exist, instead of a true academic curriculum.

They have no desire to improve the quality of education, only to maintain their control of the profession, something Washington only aids and abets with its cash. (See "Education" on p. 142.)

The structure of the American government fails us because since 1933, we have sought to imitate the central governments of Europe, but without the necessary underlying design. In education, for instance, the Constitution leaves that function to the states, but Washington ineptly tries to take over much of the function through the persuasion of money. But because the function of education is not designed to be national, Washington's efforts naturally fail, and miserably so.

The present design of the federal government is so inept that overly ambitious individual cabinet departments aim to imitate the entire national government. With the help of both Congress and the presidency, they extend their grasp into areas that no one had anticipated or even understands.

That is the case of the Department of Agriculture, for example, which tries to serve farmers, the suburbs, the exurbs, and rural areas and operates as well in juvenile delinquency, in food welfare, as a rental and housing agency, as a forest service, as a utilities operation, as a bank, by supporting renewable fuels such as ethanol, and for a multitude of tasks that go far beyond agriculture and now cost the American people some $90 billion a year.

A review of the organizational chart of the Department of Agriculture, as we shall see, is a lesson in chaos and an expensive one at that. (See "Cabinet Madness" on p. 85.)

Ironically, it provides little to the family farmer, for which the department was originally intended. Instead of the 7 million farms that existed in 1933, there are now only 2 million farms, with only 1 million full-time farmers. The so-called family farm has virtually disappeared. Most farmers work sizable properties; those who raise corn for a living typically own over 2,000 acres.

It is not the small family farm, as originally intended, that receives most of the government largesse. Instead, the Department of Agriculture is the center of enormous corporate welfare for the farm belt. Of the 2 million farms, less than 3% of them are responsible for 50% of the farm crop and are the recipients of most of the distorted multibillion-dollar government subsidies.

The recent aim of the new administration to cut out wealthy farmers from gaining subsidies is a hopeful program—if actually enacted over congressional opposition.

Under Washington's haphazard system, legislation is too often duplicative, over and over again. In Europe, under the parliamentary system, the minister of labor is responsible for job-training programs. As with ministers in other areas of parliamentary central government, he or she is both a legislator and executive. These ministers are involved not only in passing the law but in executing it as well. Therefore, there is no rational reason to pass the same or very similar laws again and again.

But in America, with the new, muddled separation of powers, Congress passes laws and the president executes them. The main interest of representatives is in passing legislation that will gain them publicity that shows their concern for the citizens. There is little concern or understanding about how the executive branch is enforcing their legislation or how much it will eventually cost or how it fits in with prior bills passed by Congress any time within the past two generations.

The result? There are 160 different job-training programs run by the federal government, parceled out to scores of different agencies, all with little or no coordination. All but the latest ones are only faintly remembered or evaluated. This steady duplication of over 1,000 programs is one of the great scandals of the federal government and one of its most expensive. (See "Duplication" on p. 128.)

Not only is the federal government intrusive of the public but often it is detrimental to the welfare of the states and localities as well. One prime example of this intrusion is unfunded federal mandates, in which Washington rules and the states pay. They exist in education, Medicaid, highways, motor vehicle departments, and other normal state functions and are increasingly spreading into other areas. They add billions to state budgets, forcing states to perform duties for Washington for which they receive nothing but citizen pain in return.

This sleight of hand by Washington is growing because of the daily violation of the 10th Amendment, planned as a bulwark against the "tyranny of the majority" in Washington, which today is a near-defunct document. By palming off obligations to the states without payment, Washington is responsible for higher and higher state taxes, especially local homeowner's property taxes, the fastest rising taxation in America, most in violation of the Constitution. (See "Unfunded Mandates" on p. 291.)

The present situation in Washington is untenable. Legislation, as we have seen, has piled up in such quantity that it is virtually impossible to even catalog it correctly. There is almost no evaluation of current programs that have outlived their usefulness and are no longer necessary. (See "Questionable and Unnecessary Agencies" on p. 257.)

There are scores of these agencies, spending billions each year. One classic case is the Rural Utilities Service (RUS), which goes back to the New Deal, in 1933, when many farms were not electrified. The agency gave loans directly from Washington to cooperatives and guaranteed other loans from banks so that farms could have lighting. In fact, the agency did a good job, and the results are that today farms and rural areas are well electrified.

But once the job was done, the agency did not close down but was instead expanded beyond its mandate. It became sloppy and wasteful to the point at which the present law permits the so-called rural groups to borrow vast sums to light up not just farms and rural areas but to serve suburbs, sizable towns, and even large metropolitan areas. According to one recent study, only 28% of RUS loans have gone to rural areas. Meanwhile the service's new functions have not only been misguided and probably illegal but also expensive. Of the last $14 billion in RUS-disclosed loans, the government has lost over $3 billion in defaults.

Outside of class distinctions, there are still two Americas, which are as disparate as possible. One is the private sector or civilian population of families and individuals; the other is the federal government. One is efficient and successful, while the other is retrograde, overly costly, hopelessly inefficient, and threatens the future of the private sector and the future of America.

Washington has set America on a suicidal path, one that must be reversed by reorganizing and eliminating much of the federal government and its costly, antiquated, politically rather than functionally based systems.

The private sector has taken America through difficult times, including several recessions and the competition of foreign governments and their often unfair trade practices. (See "China" on p. 91.) That private sector has adapted through ingenuity, innovation, and brilliant accommodation to an often harsh reality. It has retained and often expanded the highest standard of living in the world.

The federal government meanwhile operates without logic or innovation and performs as if it were in the 19th century instead of in a 21st-century competitive environment.

The villain, of course, is the American politician, a narcissistic entity whose goals are too often manic ambition, fame, and publicity, all resulting in election and reelection. That selfishness includes a lack of courage when it comes to fighting special interests against progress and a betrayal of the people's vital needs.

A case in point is the failure of Washington to create more electrical energy for the nation through the use of nuclear reactors, mainly because of the antinuclear lobby that legislators fear. Meanwhile France, which has no oil, moved ahead productively on nuclear energy and creates 80% of its electricity from that pollution-free source. Politicians have many masters other than the people, especially the media, which falsely publicized the supposed danger of nuclear energy even though in its 60-year history there has never been a single fatal public accident.

This cowardice by politicians has helped create the present dangerous economic crisis in oil. For 30 years, our politicians have foolishly thwarted oil companies from increasing domestic production, as exemplified by Alaska. (See "Alaskan Oil" on p. 50.)

One conundrum remains unexplored. Why should the American people tolerate this dysfunctional government and its danger to our successful existence? There are many answers.

One is perhaps the rise of ideology as a focus of life. Politics and one's supposed good intentions as executed by the federal government have become misplaced symbols of morality. Politics has replaced philosophy in the public arena. In this emphasis on ideology, one confuses one's identity and one's life force with one's politics, as if the two were synonymous.

Though the direct cause of America's governmental ills is, of course, the politicians on both sides of the aisle and the presidency itself, we should not absolve the American public from its share of the blame. Over the last generation, Americans have increasingly enjoyed big government and all the largesse it seems to provide—until the balance sheet explodes. Benjamin Franklin once warned us that when Americans learn that they can vote themselves money, the republic is finished.

His dire prophecy may soon become fulfilled.

This love of the seemingly endless cornucopia of blessings from Washington is especially true among young voters, who despite college degrees, are usually poorly educated in history, government, and economics. However, increasingly—before they enter the pragmatic adult existence—they are becoming addicted to large, inefficient central government in Washington as the quick, easy answer to all of society's problems.

Too often they see the supposed good intentions of government as signs of tolerance and the fight against poverty, two of their important goals. However, they continue their support for big government without examining the actual facts of Washington's many abject failures and its negative effect on their future lives, their remaining half century on earth.

Even more destructive is their view of the federal government as an entity that actually creates money, rather than the accurate view of Washington as a collector of taxpayer money, too often spent without intelligent thought.

Americans were long a skeptical lot, unused to the vagaries of European politics and its continual class warfare in which socialist and communist movements, alternating with periods of fascism, roiled that continent for hundreds of years. Americans were virtually immune to those tendencies and took their politics less seriously, creating major political parties whose differences covered a narrow spectrum of ideas, which were often not overly significant.

Class warfare was a foreign idea but one that seems to have lately gained unfortunate power in the American political world. Older citizens remember a calmer era when it was difficult to discern the ideological difference between the Democrat Harry Truman and the Republican General Dwight Eisenhower, in either domestic or foreign policy. The nation then had a pragmatic sense that made the Republic secure and prosperous. Although there have always been differences of opinion, that did not automatically disqualify the opposition as evil, or stupid.

The nation survived with either party in power. But today, in this new Age of Ideology, rancor is the order of the day and class warfare has become standard operating procedure. It may satisfy the new sense of ideology and false spirituality, but it does little to secure the nation's present, or future.

The current reality is that the size of the federal government is beyond excessive, and its quality registers as a failure. It weakens the dollar, puts us in debtor positions to foreign nations, and destroys the economic balance between government and the private sector, leading to grave financial distortions, then to potential chaos.

The government, in cost and parameters, needs to be cut immediately by at least 20%, creating a new model of responsibility that I will offer in this volume. To accomplish this reduction of

$600 billion a year in expenditures and the return to prudent government, we must set up a large series of changes that could permanently eliminate the typical nonemergency deficit and start to pay off the national debt.

This must involve a strong revolution in the organization of a confused Washington. There must also be a new design of cooperation between Congress and the executive branch, one that eliminates the errors caused by the excessive separateness of the two bodies of government—once a boon, now a travesty. We must somehow redesign the relations between Congress and the president so that before any legislation is proposed, passed, and signed into law, both segments of government agree that the legislation is affordable, nonduplicative, has a sunset provision, will be subject to reevaluation every 4 years, and does not increase the national debt.

This will require a structural change in the management of the nation, including the development of a management corps outside the political system, much as towns often hire city managers to avoid the negative input of politics in their fortunes.

Excessive ideologically driven politics, as we are beginning to learn, can be the death knell of democracy. Unreasoning politics driven by ideology dampens the ardor for the American Dream and strikes at the usually optimistic core of the culture. It even elevates reckless and ineffectual spending to undeserved heights, as if easy intentions and excessively large national budgets were the measure of one's morality.

In the current American ideological contest, played out on 24-hour television news, we see the centuries-old arguments of Europe being reincarnated on American soil, much to our disservice. The secret of America was not necessarily unity on all subjects. Instead it was a sense of patriotism—now sharply eroding—that insisted that country was above party, that nationalism was more central than ideology. But politics has now become an ugly contest, the exaggerations of increasingly hostile politicians.

Equally important, scores of major programs that once seemed to be vital often lose their rationale over the years and should be closed, as we shall see. Still others should be returned to the states, which can better administer them, at a lower cost.

The cabinet agencies require a reorganization and a severe consolidation that politicians will resist but that are essential for the continued operation of Washington.

In individual chapters, organized A to Z, I will describe the many failures of the federal operation and offer needed change. But then, in "Conclusion: Instructions for the President," I redefine and redesign the federal government so that it can be reconstructed as a boon to the country rather than being the core of the headlong drive toward national suicide.

In doing this, the hope is that this volume will enhance the future sanctity and health of America and provide a scheme for the reversal of the present senseless federal operation. The added hope is that the American citizen, now a subject of Washington, will once again become its ruler.

Join me in this investigation, one aimed at restoring the wounded dignity, security, and power of the magnificent American republic, one that has vigorously promoted human decency and freedom not only for the United States, but for the entire world.

A

ALASKAN OIL

IS ALASKA A STATE OR A COLONY?

Alaska is the largest state in the union, some 2.5 times the size of Texas. It also holds the nation's largest concentration of oil.

Observers are always moaning about not having enough domestic oil production. Meanwhile Alaska has the potential of a smaller Saudi Arabia. But Washington refuses to drill there, a case of folly and suicidal impulses that is perhaps unprecedented in any rational sovereign nation.

One survey a few years ago by the U.S. Geological Service raised Alaska's oil reserve to 50 billion barrels. But the strongest evidence for Alaskan oil is that in 1989 that reserve was calculated at only 13 billion barrels.

In 2008, that same agency sharpened its predictive pencil after a 4-year study and came in with a new estimate of the glut of oil that lies in the water just off the coast of Alaska, totally in our territorial control.

They found, says the agency, that there are some 30 billion

barrels of new undiscovered oil there, about a third of all the potential of the Arctic zone—plus over 1,000 trillion cubic feet of natural gas. In fact the Arctic's potential gas reserves are equal to that of Russia's proven reserve, the largest in the world.

When the full exploration is done—if Washington ever permits it—the Alaskan reserve of oil should reach to well over 100 billion barrels, making Alaska the Middle East of American petroleum.

Alaskan oil, especially in its North Slope, bears an excellent geological comparison to its two oil-rich neighbors—Russia to its west and Canada to its east and south. Northern Alaska and the continental shelf of the Arctic Ocean make up an oil-rich area the size of California. This treeless region has already produced 15 billion barrels of oil to date, but is still only lightly explored.

The problem, as usual, is Washington.

The federal government has been indifferent to, even ignorant of, the importance of Alaska in the scheme of America's desperate need for self-sufficiency in oil production. At present, we send billions of dollars each year to foreign nations for imported oil, money that would change the economic balance of America for the good—if we could keep the cash on our shores.

This is not a new problem. It has existed ever since Alaska became a state in 1959 when Washington selfishly expropriated most of the landmass for itself. It left only 29% of the acreage, the only land now available for oil production, to the state. Alaska has since done an excellent environmentally safe and effective job of drilling and producing oil. It has done it so well that every Alaskan recently received some $2,000 in oil royalties from the state.

And what has Washington done? As usual, nothing. Not a teacup of oil has been produced in the Alaskan land controlled by Washington.

The unfortunate irony of the situation is that the best oil fields in the North Slope of Alaska—the Arctic National Wildlife Refuge (ANWR) and the National Petroleum Reserve, both federal government controlled—have been sitting there fallow since their discovery a generation ago.

Is Alaska actually a state or is it a colony of Washington, which apparently is in firm control of Alaska's economy, at present and in the future?

The best current oil-producing area in Alaska is the one at Prudhoe Bay, fortunately discovered on state land. It is also one of the most productive oil fields in the world. It is so productive that, despite a decline in its output, it still produces 17% of all America's oil, which is easily shipped to the West Coast via a 1,600-km pipeline, which was finally constructed over grave opposition.

Unfortunately, that production is decreasing yearly, and the pipeline has room for 1 million more barrels of oil a day.

That environmentally sound oil field on state-controlled property is very close to the two undeveloped federal oil lands nearby, whose production is urgently needed. All three are on the coastal area, which is very rich in oil. One of the reasons they have not produced oil thus far is that Congress is afraid of the environmental movement and prefers to punish America instead of contesting that unpatriotic lobby.

"The ecology movement keeps talking about the pristine beauty of the North Slope and that oil development will ruin it," says Ken Boyd, former director for oil and gas in the Alaska state government. "The reality is that much of the North Slope, and especially the oil-producing areas, is one of the ugliest places in the world; a flat miserable plain that is tundra-like. And besides, the state has done an excellent job of handling the local ecology."

The area holds enormous oil deposits that could easily quadruple our Alaska production and double our domestic oil supply. There is little doubt that if Washington ever permits the oil companies to exploit the North Slope—along with Rocky Mountain shale and offshore ocean drilling, including the waters off the North Slope—we can make America self-sufficient in oil, perhaps within the decade.

The North Slope oil is tightly concentrated. The Prudhoe Bay region, for example, is not much larger than New York City. Its flow rate almost equals that of the Middle East with no pump jacks required to get the oil, which flows to the surface under natural pressure.

Frustrated by the Luddite behavior of Washington, the leaders of Alaska continue to explore and produce more oil on state lands. Concentrating on the area between the ANWR and the National Petroleum Reserve, the Alaskan state government has encouraged commercial oil exploitation, including the discovery of 500 million barrels of oil at the Alpine field and 100 million barrels at a nearby site.

In July 2008, the federal government did release 2.6 million acres of federal lands to exploration, but only because of the needs of the Alaska pipeline. At its height, the pipeline handled some 2 million barrels of oil a day from Prudhoe Bay. But it is now down to less than 1 million. If production erodes further, the viability of the pipeline is threatened. So Washington reluctantly acted to try to increase daily production and flow.

The future of Alaskan oil and America's independence in oil requires that Washington shed its usual narrow, parochial, selfish instincts. It needs to open exploration and production of oil in not only the North Slope but in all of Alaska's giant landmass and offshore waters. Unfortunately, Washington politicians—not the Alaskans—control that production, much to the despair of America.

There is one easy way to defeat Washington's suicidal instincts. All we need do is to return the mineral rights to the land unilaterally taken from the Alaskan people in 1959 and then watch as the state, not the federal government, intelligently works to defend the energy interests not only of Alaska but of all of America.

No, Alaska should no longer be a colony of the federal government.

Perhaps the state should be given back the great majority of its land taken by Uncle Sam in 1959 and do with it what it wants. That will surely make Alaska better managed than it is now by the far away, remote controlled, insensitive place called Washington, and, simultaneously, it could eventually free America from our dependence on foreign oil.

A

ALTERNATIVE MINIMUM TAX

A Trillion-Dollar Mistake or, More Likely, a Giant Political Lie

In August 1967, Lyndon Johnson's secretary of treasury, Joseph Barr, while testifying before Congress on the following year's budget, electrified his audience with the simple pronouncement that there were 155 American individuals who made over $200,000 a year but who didn't pay a single penny in federal taxes.

This revelation sent a shock wave through Congress, then, via the press, throughout the nation. It was made clear that these were not tax cheaters but only wealthy people who used the tax law, including tax-free municipal bonds, various legal deductions, and large donations to charity that resulted in a tax-free existence.

Congress was moved to action, although that later proved to be irrational and self-defeating.

The result is what became known as the alternative minimum tax (AMT), potentially the most onerous tax policy ever imposed on Americans. It is a second income tax, but, strangely, not one

based on increased income. Instead, it is based on taxpayers taking legal deductions that Congress has passed to maintain the
middle class.

Because it contains an exemption of $66,000, it mainly en-
snares the upper middle class, but yearly dips down into the ranks
of more and more Americans.

Designed to punish a handful of millionaires, it now threatens
millions of innocent middle-class Americans with billions a year,
and rising, in extra AMT taxes. In effect, this tax surcharge turns
the IRS code upside down by reducing or eliminating the once-
sacred deductions on your IRS 1040 returns.

If left unchecked as is, the AMT will cost American taxpayers, with as low as a $50,000 adjusted gross income, a 10-year total
of $1 trillion.

In 1997, the AMT punished 618,000 taxpayers. By 2006, it
penalized 3.5 million. By 2007, some 17 million Americans were
set to pay the onerous tax and were only temporarily saved from
the AMT by a "patch," which cost the government $30 billion
that year alone.

Each year, the patch becomes more expensive, as millions
more citizens are threatened with the punishing tax. In January
2009, the Senate Finance Committee approved a much larger
patch because those affected grew to 20 million strong. The 2009
cost, an enormous $70 billion, indicates there is much more tax
punishment to come each year from our politicians.

A Department of Treasury memo to the deputy assistant secretary dated March 7, 2005, lays out the specter of abnormal taxes
aimed at the middle class. It states that some 17 million more
Americans will have to pay the AMT by 2007, and by 2011
some one third of all taxpayers will be punished with the AMT.

By 2015, roughly 45% of Americans will be caught in its outrageous web.

Which deductions can taxpayers lose from this ludicrous Washington invention? The nefarious AMT, the most underhanded levy since the English tea tax of 1774, can even take away much of the home equity mortgage interest deduction. Having too many children and taking legit child credits can also get you in tax trouble.

Making money in the stock market or from the sale of your house, with long-term capital gains, is frowned on by the AMT. So are those once-wonderful tax-free municipal bonds, stock options, and high local property taxes in areas that pay teachers handsomely. So too is living in such greedy states as New York, New Jersey, or California where you are then penalized for paying their exorbitant taxes—instead of deducting them. The list of penalties for legit deductions is near endless.

The very tax promises of our government have been turned on their backsides. Those tax reliefs are no longer solely a balm but can become a curse. Most surprising, even the simple $3,650 a year personal exemption on your 1040 can push you into a punishing AMT tax bracket.

What happened? Did the AMT at least stop the tax-avoiding millionaires?

Hardly. There were only 155 happy tax-free millionaires when the law was first passed in 1969. By 1976, that number rose to 244, then to 1,467 by 1998. Eventually, says the IRS, 14,000 richies will pay no federal taxes under present tax legislation. As usual, the law of unintended consequences has caught up with Washington, creating not only failure but destructive action.

So if it failed in its stated, highly publicized purpose of curbing outrage over certain rich Americans, how come the AMT has hit so many nonrich Americans?

The explanation, says the federal government, is that they somehow failed to index the AMT for inflation, pushing more and more people into its maw each year. The exemption started at $10,000 and is now $66,000 for joint income taxpayers. But the true amount of the AMT deduction would be much higher if it had been indexed for inflation, and thus the AMT would affect only the truly rich.

The government excuse, made to sound as if it were an innocent mistake, is more of a blatant lie.

A freshman in economics 101 knows that a deduction is meaningless unless it is indexed for inflation. The government has thousands of economists who have gone beyond econ 101 and who knew just what they were doing—keeping the AMT unindexed to bring in more cash. We know this is the case because during the decades the AMT has been in effect, it has been modified a half dozen times and never was the original mistake—not indexing for inflation—corrected.

Besides, the AMT targeted more and more people because of real growth in the economy beyond inflation, which caused many taxpayers to fall into higher marginal taxes, the so-called bracket creep.

But because the AMT was originally designed to punish only the rich, who really cared?

In 1969, this was obviously an opportunity for a double hit—quiet the outrage created by the 155 tax-free millionaires and raise taxes on potentially millions of regular middle-class taxpayers in the process.

President Nixon inherited the problem of the supposed tax-free millionaires the following year, and a Treasury spokesman said it clearly: "I think the American people are saying something and the message is getting through."

In 1969, the result was a simple "minimum tax" that added a 10% surcharge to taxpayers who supposedly took too many legal deductions. The present law was born in the Revenue Act of 1978, which lowered capital gains and corporate taxes by $18.7 billion, but put in the AMT, designed to make up some of that revenue loss.

Did the law punish only the rich?

Hardly. Its grasp keeps widening every day. Estimates for the future are frightening. The Congressional Budget Office (CBO) says it may hit as many as 30 million taxpayers by 2014. The Brookings Institution believes it will ensnare 46 million, almost a third of all taxpayers, by then. Worse yet, it would increase the taxes of nearly every married couple making only $100,000 a year and filing jointly, hardly among the ranks of the rich, especially in such high-tax areas as New York and California.

The AMT also requires an enormous amount of preparation by accountants, which is estimated to involve 6 hours extra per taxpayer, at a cost estimated at $360 million in 1998, which is over a half billion today. The taxes have to be figured two ways, on the regular 1040 and on Form 6251, a 50-line AMT item, which calculates the tax minus some or all of the deductions. The taxpayer pays the larger of the two at a rate of 26% and 28% on the difference.

How have both the Republican (1995 to 2006) and Democratic (2006 to present) Congresses and the last two presidents (Bill Clinton and George W. Bush) tolerated this insult to America's pocketbook? In 1998, voters angry about the AMT finally pushed the Republican Congress to action. A repeal of the AMT passed both Houses, but President Bill Clinton vetoed the reform, stating that it was "a risky tax cut."

His successor, George W. Bush, did little more. His Congresses, both Republican and Democratic, were faced with a much larger problem because AMT receipts grew and the money brought in became more and more significant. They never passed a second repeal, showing that Congress, and presumably the president (as we saw with Bill Clinton), have only themselves and their desire for revenue, and never the taxpayer, at heart. And don't forget the original premise was a government lie.

The AMT is a sharp lesson for taxpayers.

It instructs them that when it comes to taxes, including the promise to only tax the rich, neither the Congress nor the president, whether Democratic or Republican, can be trusted with the people's money.

B

BABY CITIZENS

A FALSE BIRTHRIGHT FOR MILLIONS OF ILLEGALS

Americans are outraged—and justifiably so—by the invasion of illegals into our country, mainly Hispanics from Mexico and Central America.

There are an estimated 20 million illegals, and they seem to crowd out citizens as they take advantage of our benefits, even without legal status. They use our schools, our hospitals, and in many cases our welfare and social services, all at enormous cost. Equally important, they maintain their own Spanish culture, which is often at great odds with the culture that built and maintains our nation.

Thus they contribute to changing the character of American civilization. Illegals invest in a form of apartheid, quite unlike prior immigrants who created this nation by rapidly assimilating into the American culture. But the public outrage at the army of illegals is only the beginning of what is best described as a demographic bomb—one that is more explosive mathematically than even the critics of illegal immigration can imagine.

The failure to stop the invasion of illegals into America is a prime case of national suicide. It is the direct result of the unwillingness of the American political class to face the threat.

The result will be an upcoming demographic surprise that will eventually multiply geometrically the number and political power of illegals. It will be due to the fact that all children born to illegals on these shores are incomprehensibly considered citizens of the United States from the moment of their birth.

Thus without benefit of amnesty or going through the trials of learning English, taking a test, and waiting 5 years after making application for naturalization, the actions of their parents in the bedroom, rather than at the courthouse, will determine the future of America.

That is simply because under the present false interpretation of the 14th Amendment to the Constitution, progeny of illegals immediately on becoming 18, as full-fledged citizens, are able to vote. Meanwhile, from birth they are able to tap the enormous federal and state charity services of America.

In the cities of Los Angeles and San Diego, and in hospitals along the Texas and Arizona border, pregnant Hispanic women who come into the country illegally use our medical facilities to give birth at no cost to them. One federal official states that when the moment comes for their birth, they circle the local hospital until their water breaks and then enter to give birth.

The cost of these births is enormous, financially and medically, both initially and eventually. At Parkland Memorial Hospital in Dallas, a patient survey showed that 70% of the women who gave birth there in the first 3 months of 2006 were illegal immigrants, at a cost of $4,000 per child, paid for by state/federal Medicaid, Dallas County taxpayers, and the federal government.

Of course, the illegal parents paid nothing, for federal law requires emergency rooms to handle all patients regardless of their ability to pay.

A noninsured American with no money would have a much harder time than an illegal Mexican in dealing financially with the hospital administration. It appears that as an illegal foreigner in suicidal America, you receive totally free care that is much better than that afforded to an American. If an American lives outside Dallas County and cannot pay, the procedure is simple: The hospital will sue them.

For uninsured, poor Americans, the red tape is enormous and frustrating. But for Mexican illegals giving birth in our hospitals, nothing is too good or more easily obtained. They receive free prenatal care, including medication, nutrition, birthing classes, baby formula, and child care instruction. They receive, free of charge, car seats, milk bottles, and diapers. Parkland has even been forced to hire extra Spanish-speaking help to translate for their indigent illegal patients.

What do Americans believe we have done to poor illegal Mexicans to provide them—perhaps through misplaced guilt or a sense of national suicide—such munificence while regular Americans are not given the same largesse?

A secondary negative effect of illegal hospital patients is that they have flooded our facilities, bankrupting many hospitals, which have been forced to close. A report in the *Journal of American Physicians and Surgeons* notes that illegal aliens coming into the United States are forcing the closure of many hospitals.

According to this study, in California alone, 84 hospitals are closing their doors as a result of the rising number of illegal aliens and the cost of their nonreimbursed care. Politicians mention that there are 43 million in America without health insurance, but this report estimates that at least 25% to 50% of them are illegal immigrants. The problem is that under the Emergency Medical Treatment and Active Labor Act of 1985, hospitals are obligated to treat them without any reimbursement. The report stresses that illegals often harbor such fatal diseases as drug-resistant tuberculosis, malaria, leprosy, plague, polio, dengue, and Chagas disease, all long conquered in the United States.

The welfare and hospital costs of illegals have never been calculated, but they surely run into billions. According to the *Journal of American Physicians and Surgeons*, one family who came to Stockton, California, to work as fruit pickers is a case in point. The husband brought his wife and three children with him.

The wife gave birth here to their fourth child, born premature. It cost the San Joaquin Hospital $300,000 for treatment. The oldest daughter married another illegal and gave birth here. Then the adult mother had her fourth child.

The family now receives over $1,000 a month in cash from various government welfare programs.

Once illegals settle locally, in New York, Detroit, or any other American city, they continue to give birth again, at nearly double the fertility rate of American citizens.

Not only is it at great cost to those communities and to the state and federal governments but, even more important, they knowingly draw on a false constitutional concept that their offspring are no longer illegals but citizens of the United States—immediately on birth within our borders.

This is due to a misinterpretation of the U.S. Constitution, particularly the 14th Amendment, which was designed to confirm that black Americans, who had been here for hundreds of years and were freed by the Emancipation Proclamation, were and deserved to be citizens of the country. Passed by Congress and the states in 1866 after the Union victory in the Civil War, the 14th Amendment, designed to protect the freed blacks, states simply: "All persons born or naturalized in the United States and subject to the jurisdiction thereof, are citizens of the United States and of the State wherein they reside."

This so-called Citizenship Clause is unique in the civilized world, which mainly recognizes the newborn baby as being a citizen of the country of its parents. At one time in history, several European countries had the same faulty policy, but all have since moved away from it and have voted to end birthright of citizenship as being both illogical and harmful to their immigration policy.

Australia, at one time subject to the same ludicrous policy, has since eliminated birthright citizenship, as has the UK. Ireland had adopted it, but when it saw the negative ramifications, it voted in 2004 to eliminate the system. America is the only major nation that clings to this distorted policy.

In fact, it was never the true intention of Congress back in 1866 to grant citizenship to children of foreigners born here. The coauthor of the 14th Amendment, Senator Jacob Howard of Michigan, specifically stated that he meant it to exclude the children of aliens and foreigners. Even the children of ambassadors from foreign nations to the United States were excluded. Afterward, Congress drafted a bill to correct the confusion, but it died in committee. Most important, it was not the sense of the Congress when they drafted the 14th Amendment that it would extend to foreigners.

There is some confusion today among those who believe the words of the amendment are set in stone. That is not true. To rescind the supposed citizenship clause of the 14th Amendment, it is not necessary to go through a full and lengthy amendment process. Part of the 14th Amendment specifically gives that corrective power to the Congress. It states: "The Congress shall have the power to enforce, by appropriate legislation, the provisions of this article."

This article's true meaning was probably best expressed by Senator Reverdy Johnson of Maryland, who pointed out that the civil rights act of 1866, which had just been passed, best defined the meaning of the clause: "That all persons born in the United States, and not subject to any foreign power, are hereby declared to be citizens."

Because America's illegals, whether citizens of Mexico or elsewhere, are subject to a foreign power, that would eliminate all problems in regard to the clause. Using that correct interpretation, none of the babies of illegals born in the United States would be considered a citizen. Unfortunately, the clause has been misread.

The specific failure in the present interpretation is in the clause of the 14th Amendment that states that the persons involved in the claim of birthright citizenship must be "Subject to the jurisdiction thereof" of the United States. In the case of illegals, they are nationals of other nations, whether Mexico or Honduras or elsewhere, and are still subject to the jurisdiction of those nations and not to that of the United States. Therefore, the

14th Amendment does not cover any foreigners, aliens, or others who are either visiting or illegally trespassing on the soil of the United States of America.

Strangely enough, there has never been a full test before the Supreme Court of the citizenship clause in relation to illegal aliens. Actually, the place to argue this is in the U.S. Congress. Several attempts have been made in Congress to repeal the citizen birthright claim, but they all failed to even come to a vote.

The most recent was introduced by Nathan Deal of Georgia. The bill, HR 1940, would eliminate the birthright of illegal immigrants. Titled the Birthright Citizenship Act of 2007, it would legally nullify that section of the 14th Amendment.

Apparently, American politicians are insensitive to the will of the people and seem determined to maintain this abuse, despite pressure from their constituents. In the case of Republicans, it appears to be appeasement of employers, who enjoy the low wages of illegals and the pressure that puts on the higher wages of other American workers. In the case of the Democrats, illegals provide the possibility of future citizenship and more votes for their party.

In both cases, it is a crude and callous violation of the people's rights and needs by our politicians, a failing we, unfortunately, are becoming used to and tolerate—at least for the time being.

Those illegal babies falsely granted citizenship are known as "anchor babies" because it is felt that if illegals have a new citizen among them, they could not be deported. Whether or not that is true, the point is not significant overall.

What is significant is that those babies are the beginning of a giant demographic bomb that could gravely weaken the nation. The frightening truth is that 1 in 10 babies born in the United

States are anchor babies who now have citizenship. That number will soon rise to 1 in 5, which means 5 million illegal new citizens each year. That number will increase geometrically because the parents who have come here from Mexico or elsewhere will, during their lifetime, produce almost twice as many babies as other residents of America.

Those illegals who came here in their 30s will, before they pass away some 50 years later, be able to create two additional generations, all of whom will be citizens. These children, grandchildren, and great-grandchildren and *their* offspring will all be citizens, increasing the present 20 million illegals to upward of 100 million—all new American citizens.

That number, having doubled, tripled, or quadrupled over the next 50 years, will totally change the demography, the voting pattern, the politics, and the character of the United States.

Because Congress and the last two presidents supported this misinterpretation of the Constitution for selfish political reasons, they have placed America in the dire position of losing its national identity and bankrupting this nation in the process.

The lure of the United States is overwhelming to the poor, uneducated citizens of Mexico and Central America, who see salvation—correctly—within the borders of the United States. The lure is severalfold: First, they seek work and a decent standard of living at our expense. Second, they gain social welfare, hospitalization, and education not available in Mexico and Central America but all granted free to illegals at great expense and burden to regular U.S. citizens, who receive much less from the government and who pay for the privilege of being neglected in favor of aliens.

The greatest lure for illegals is the birthright citizenship, which means that when those anchor babies turn 18, not only can they vote, but they can petition the U.S. government to bring in their relatives from the old country, including grandparents and siblings, a process called "chain immigration" or "family gathering," which will further increase the number of illegal and unwanted immigrants.

It is not only a dire situation but a laughable (and sad) one that seems to confirm America's desire for national suicide in its willingness to change our national character by accepting those who refuse to integrate as well as previous immigrants. It is also a threat to our standard of living.

What can be done to stop this invasion and the false concept of immediate citizenship?

First, we can force a Supreme Court test, which has never been done. Or we can change the supposed law by a simple majority vote in the Congress—as voters in Ireland recently did.

A second step to eliminate the lure of America to illegals is to deny them employment. There is a bill presently drafted in Congress, called Secure America through Verification and Enforcement (SAVE) that can accomplish this. The bill not only beefs up the border patrol but requires all employers nationwide to electronically check out potential employees' citizenship and immigration status through a federal system called E-Verify.

Today, employers in two states, Arizona and Oklahoma, are required to use that system, after which all illegals detected are to be deported. If the federal bill becomes law, it will apply to all 50 states.

The bill is being held up in Congress. A discharge petition

has been drafted to get it out of committee and require a vote on the floor. A total of 218 members of Congress must sign that discharge petition for it to succeed. At present, 186 have signed. Of that number, 176 are Republicans and only 10 are Democrats. They need 32 more signatures, but there are only 22 remaining Republicans, which means they also need an additional 10 Democrats.

Hearings are temporarily scheduled in the Homeland Security Department, but there is no promise by the majority Democrats to bring the bill to a vote.

The next avenue is to eliminate the birthright citizenship clause entirely. This is less promising. It has been tried many times before and failed. The current bill, HR 1940, introduced by Deal, has 98 sponsors, hardly enough to force a vote or even a hearing.

The only hope for America to solve this unwanted illegal invasion that threatens the very existence of our nation as we know it, is for all citizens, Democrats, Republicans, and Independents, to angrily confront their members of Congress.

This is not a matter of exclusivity. For generations, America has been an antidiscriminatory haven for immigrants of every race and ethnic group. It is a matter of true diversity, of all residents of the nation determined to blend into the single model of our culture, something the illegals are not prepared to do, especially in seeking sanctuary here without the benefit of law.

Americans must not allow ourselves to be swallowed up by uninvited guests who may someday overwhelm the nation's magnificent heritage.

B

BILINGUAL AMERICA

Federal Taxes Support a Tower of Babel

When I was growing up, many of my friends' parents and grandparents were not fluent in English and a foreign language was spoken at home. In fact, my grandmother lived with us, and she spoke no English. While she was alive, until I was 6 years old, I spoke a halting, broken version of her language so I could communicate with her.

But at school, despite the Tower of Babel in various homes, not a word except English was spoken in our classrooms, unless it was in a formal class in French. I recall an incident in which two immigrant boys were whispering in their native tongue. Our instructor, whom I considered an older Anglo maiden woman (she was probably under 40) quickly hushed them with an angry stricture: "Boys. This is America. In this class we speak only English!"

One of the gravest sociological sins of this generation is that English is no longer sacrosanct.

If ever there was evidence that the nation, especially its politicians, its educators, and its jurists, who no longer first consider the self-interest of the country, is headed inexorably toward suicide, it is the bold campaign against the one indispensable unifying factor—the common, almost exclusive use of the English language.

It is that heritage that, decades ago, unified the children and grandchildren of immigrants—whether Russian, Italian, German, Ukraine, or Jewish—into a whole that made America, the land of immigrants, the greatest in history.

Today that chain of language unity has been broken, and there is doubt that it will ever return to its former glory unless there is a sharp change of sentiment by our leaders.

Good citizens become annoyed, even angry, when the telephone voice, or machine, at some corporation or store, inquires whether you want to speak English or Spanish. This is, of course, pandering to the large immigrant Spanish population, both legal and illegal, whose money, not whose assimilation, the businesses seek. The fact that it injures the commonwealth is of no interest to them.

In 1914 during a period of high immigration, President Theodore Roosevelt summed up the power of English as our unifying force, stating: "We have room for but one language in this country and that is the English language, for we intend to see that the crucible turns our people out as Americans of American nationality, and not as dwellers in a polyglot boardinghouse."

Who is to blame for ignoring this warning? Naturally, as in most cases of irrationality and debilitation of the national heritage, the villain is, once more, our politicians and the federal government in Washington.

As we shall see, the politicians who spend a fortune of tax-payer money supporting substitutes for the English language are the eventual villains. But the initial blame for the trend away from English belongs to the third leg of government, the judiciary. In this case, the villain is the Supreme Court of the United States, which is seldom sure where the national interest lies.

It all began in San Francisco, when the Chinese community, which had strongly resisted assimilation, was forced to integrate into the public school system. They decided that they would make use of the public schools, but only if the children could learn their ABCs in Chinese. In a rational land, that request would be laughed at, as it initially was by the school district and then by the federal district court and then the circuit court of appeals.

But the case came before the Supreme Court, in the form of *Lau v. Nichols*, which, on January 21, 1973, reversed the lower court decisions on the basis of the Civil Rights Act of 1964. The high court turned logic on its head by claiming the children's English deficiency was the result of school "discrimination."

The court, in effect, blamed the school district for the fact that the Chinese children couldn't speak English. But ethnic separation was the decision of the Chinese community for some 100 years. The court phrased this failure of the Chinese community in a positive framework, that the school had to dispense with discrimination and was required to teach them English. But the schools also had to make use of a California mandate that was then extended throughout the nation by the Supreme Court. That meant that both Chinese and English were to be the teaching languages, with Chinese the primary one, which is at the core of bilingual theory.

That decision that "English only" in the schools was a case of civil rights discrimination has since required all American public schools to establish bilingual programs. It set a precedent that today serves to keep immigrant students, mainly Hispanic, at the back of the class academically and as unequal in the job and professional marketplaces.

That wasn't the case when English was the absolute norm in all American classrooms regardless of ethnic backgrounds. The failure to demand English only in the classroom has resulted in disproportionately high school dropout rates for Hispanic students, while it stimulates pride in the Spanish culture, rather than the American English language culture in which they live.

It has also created an anomaly that is unprecedented in history: native-born American children who are not fluent in the English language.

The Supreme Court decision made bilingual education mandatory nationally, but Washington had already been involved in that peculiar educational regimen. The federal government first went into the bilingual business in 1967, when Senator Ralph Yarborough of Texas, targeting the Mexican American children of his state, offered an amendment known as Title 7, or the Bilingual Education Act, to the Elementary and Secondary Education Act of 1965 to provide assistance to local education agencies in establishing bilingual American education programs.

On February 12, 1969, Robert Finch, secretary of HEW, stated that prompt massive upgrading of bilingual education was one of the major federal policy imperatives and a new post, special assistant for bilingual education, was created.

The motivation was also antithetical, as are many federal imperatives, to the will and needs of most Americans. Its motivation, as one proponent commented, was to "cultivate ancestral pride; reinforce, not destroy, native languages; cultivate inherent strengths; and provide children with a sense of personal identification essential to social maturation." The problem was that all these initiatives were counterproductive in that they resulted in both the economic failure of millions of new immigrants and the destruction of American unity.

It all follows the new federal trend toward separation, not unification, of America, one that sets us squarely on the route to national suicide. What politicians advertise to minorities, whose votes they desperately seek, as being valuable for them is actually the worst possible remedy if those minorities seek success in the broader culture.

The result is that today, some dozens of languages are the primary instruction tool in thousands of schools. English, meanwhile, is taught as a second language for about 3 years, while the children learn their ABCs in Vietnamese, Spanish, Russian, Chinese, or a host of other languages. In fact, many schools stretch out the native language years beyond 3 because they decide the child is not ready to study English. That lag before English is taught as a primary tongue leaves many of the immigrant students disadvantaged, verbally and financially weak in society for the rest of their lives.

For those of us who remember the prior generations, not a single young immigrant had any difficulty picking up English, not only in schools but in the school yard.

This failed bilingual experiment has also taken place at enormous financial, as well as social, cost to the taxpayers. The present budget of the Department of Education shows that $730 million has been allotted to bilingual education in the year 2009, while much additional money is being spent by the states and local school districts, exceeding a total of $1 billion.

Culturally, the cost is even greater. One insight into the government's private view of bilingual education is that they seek to hide the activity from a generally angry public. I had trouble locating bilingual in the education budget until I learned that it is disguised as something called "English language acquisition," which is, of course, a euphemism for the exact opposite of the actual bilingual schoolwork.

Fortunately, there is a countermovement against this destructive federal program. In California, it was spearheaded by a Silicon Valley entrepreneur, who proved that a single individual can fight city hall, especially when the public is behind him. Ron C. Utz placed Proposition 227 on the California ballot in 1998 to promote English-only teaching in public schools.

After it passed with a 61% vote, the number of Spanish children learning in Spanish dropped considerably, down to 11%. Similar downgrades of bilingual education are being considered, or have passed, in several state legislatures. But the federal government in Washington continues its anti-English work unchanged, even raising the bilingual budget yearly.

There is an even larger fight brewing between the American public and the government powers who seek to weaken English as a societal bond. That battle is to create an environment in which English is the official language of every state and the national government, something many citizens falsely believe exists today.

In 1983, an American linguist and U.S. Senator from California, S. I. Hayakawa, proposed a constitutional amendment to make English the official language of both the federal and state governments. In 1999, proponents like Hayakawa and House Speaker Newt Gingrich seemed to be approaching success. When the House of Representatives finally passed a law mandating English as the country's official language, Gingrich happily declared, "Without English as a common language, there is no American civilization."

However, the bill faced opposition from several minority groups, especially Hispanic organizations and the American Civil Liberties Union (ACLU). The Senate refused to confirm the legislation. Since then, in virtually every session of Congress, a similar constitutional amendment is proposed, but each has failed. Senate Majority Leader Harry Reid of Nevada believes that such a law would be racist, but there seems to be no connection between language and race.

U.S. English, a nonprofit group founded by Hayakawa, continues to press for English as the official language, both in Congress and one state at a time. Today, the roster grows as citizens become increasingly angry at politicians who foist bilingualism on them. The states with official English laws now include Alabama, Alaska, Arkansas, California, Colorado, Florida, Georgia, Idaho, Hawaii, Illinois, Indiana, Iowa, Kansas, Kentucky, Massachusetts, Mississippi, Missouri, Montana, Nebraska, New Hampshire, North Carolina, North Dakota, South Carolina, South Dakota, Tennessee, Utah, Virginia, and Wyoming.

There are a few official bilingual states because of special historical circumstances such as English and Hawaiian in Hawaii and English and French in Louisiana because both were under other flags before becoming part of America.

The official English law, passed in Iowa in 2002, was recently challenged by a typical politician, its secretary of state. Eager to pander to any and all minority groups, he decided to offer voting ballots in Spanish, Vietnamese, Laotian, and Bosnian, even though only citizens can vote, and they have to show ability in English to become naturalized. Fortunately, an Iowa district court judge ruled that the state's official English law had been violated.

Several communities have passed similar pro-English laws, but perennial holdouts include two major American cities: New York City and San Francisco. New York City has made bilingualism in official work a masterpiece of multiculturalism and diversity. In that city, one need not speak or write English when doing official business.

Bilingualism, on a vast scale, is the law in New York, which has always catered to other languages. But recently it has stretched that anti-English to astounding proportions. In fact, New York City now has seven official languages in which they conduct business: English, Spanish, Russian, Chinese, Korean, French Creole, and Italian. "This executive order," said Mayor Bloomberg, "will make our city more accessible while helping us become the most inclusive municipal government in the nation."

Of course, he failed to mention that, like the federal government in education, New York has seen fit to use taxpayer funds to separate rather than unite the people, a further destruction of the American ethos.

How does one say "National Suicide" in New York's seven official languages?

B

BUREAUCRACY

In addition to continual policy errors that often make things worse, not better, the government suffers from an ineffective, overpaid bureaucracy. It is 1.9 million federal employees strong and costs us burgeoning, excessive billions in payroll.

That bureaucracy has been the subject of much contemplated but never achieved reform.

President Taft appointed the Committee on Economy and Efficiency in Government in 1910. President Herbert Hoover planned to reorganize the executive branch to eliminate waste and duplication. President Reagan appointed the Grace Commission, whose excellent suggestions were seldom acted upon. Then in the ultimate culmination of foolishly advertised plans, Vice President Al Gore planned a "reinventing government," which was once again a colossal failure.

The reason is quite simple. In addition to Congress's ineptitude, the federal workforce, from the top to bottom, has no incentive to improve the workings of the government.

The first hindrance to good government is that it is virtually impossible to fire a poor worker. Job security for life is taken for granted by federal employees, no matter how poorly they perform. As soon as they are hired, they can look forward to a healthy pension on retirement.

Former Senator Paul Douglas, who called the ineptitude of the bureaucracy a case of "elephantiasis," noted that not only did the agencies have no incentive for cost control—in fact quite the opposite—but that it is virtually impossible to fire deadwood employees. The procedure can take years and generally fails. According to the Office of Personnel Management, in the first 4 years of the current decade, only 136 workers of the 1.9 million were discharged for poor performance each year, less than 0.01%.

A federal job is a sinecure in uncertain times, a fact that destroys efficiency in government.

In the State Department, no model of efficiency, only seven employees have been fired in the last 20 years. This despite continual errors in visa procurement and the fact that Russian spies were allowed to bug a meeting room down the hall from the secretary of state's office during the Clinton administration. Because it takes 18 months or more to fire a worker, if at all, most managers instead just move the offenders to another department.

Federal employees are also immune to changes in the economy, unlike those in private industry. In early 2009, more than a half million private workers lost their jobs each month. But federal job security is so strong that in that same difficult economic period, the federal bureaucracy actually grew in size rather than implement temporary layoffs, which would have been sensible but was apparently unprecedented.

Once hired, a federal employee need not worry about his or her job as do other worried Americans.

Washington acknowledges having 1.9 million employees, which, in my opinion and that of several government watchdog groups, is at least 20% more than necessary. But in addition, there is a "shadow workforce" of millions more. According to the Brookings Institution, the total number of workers doing federal activities totals some 17 million. This includes 1.5 million uniformed personnel run by the Defense Department, 8 million in the U.S. Postal Service, 5.2 million federal contractors who are hired under arrangements that disguise the increase in the federal payroll, 2.9 million employees in federal grant-created jobs; and 4.7 million state and local workers doing federal business.

The total number of employees is unnerving, to say the least, and is a great—if hidden—contributor to the astronomical cost of government.

The bureaucracy is a very privileged one, receiving job benefits that far exceed those in private industry. Private employees are now lucky to have 2 weeks of paid vacation a year, while in Washington federal workers with seniority get more than 5 weeks paid vacation plus almost 3 weeks sick leave, which many manage to take illegally as vacation time, especially as 3-day weekends. The government also grants 10 paid holidays, more than most private companies. This gives workers some 8 weeks off a year, much like schoolteachers, but at generally higher pay.

In fact, federal pay scales, which match private employees, are well enhanced by an extreme benefit goodie that went into effect in 1994 and has been awarded each year since. What it does is raise the employee's pay considerably, based on the city in which he or she works. That increase is based on the cost of wages in a particular locality. This is no small benefit and of course is not available to workers in private industry.

In Houston, for example, say a person is hired at a G-12 pay grade, which would normally give him a salary of $65,405 a year. But because local wages in Houston are high, his salary is automatically adjusted to $83,320. In Dallas, the adjustment upward is about 19% and in Washington, DC, the center of American bureaucracy, it's about 21%.

This unprecedented, exaggerated benefit should not exist. It has shown its true light in parts of California, where federal workers receive an enormous bonus of 33% over their salary simply because they work in the San Jose–San Francisco area. The government stresses that this is not a cost-of-living bonus. It is merely extra pay to keep up with supposed salaries in the local economy, which at present is in big trouble.

Federal employee benefits are apparently endless. They include an excellent health insurance plan, savings plans, retirement, long paid leaves, unpaid leave for emergencies, life insurance, government paid Medicare premiums for workers over 65, and more and more.

These benefits are so great that, according to one reliable study, if we assume a federal employee with a starting salary equal to that of someone in private industry, then the value of the federal employee's compensation would exceed that of the comparable private employee by $586,000 during a full career. Another study showed that the excess cost of government employment is more than $40 billion a year over private employment.

The enormous growth of the cost of federal employee benefits started in 1980, when those benefits were equal to private employment. But in the intervening years up until only 1993 federal benefits increased by 105%, 3.5 times that of state and local government employees. By then, total federal compensation and pay benefits were 53% more than the average of private employees, reaching an average gain of $18,200 over private jobs and, of course, it is more today as private employee benefits recede.

The federal retirement plan is so superior to the typical private pension that there is nearly $1 trillion in unfunded federal civilian pension liabilities that taxpayers must eventually pay. That doesn't show up in the budget, but it must be paid. The Office of Personnel Management estimates that this would add another 20% to federal retirement costs.

One special goodie that destroys worker efficiency is a benefit called "flex time." Many American corporations provide this benefit to employees, but the federal government—as usual—carries it too far. Under this special, if novel and wasteful benefit, federal workers set their own work schedule. They can choose to work 10 hours a day but for only 4 days a week, with permanent 3-day weekends. They can opt to come in as early as 6:30 A.M. and leave as early as 2:30 in the afternoon.

I spoke with one such worker who told me that when he comes in early, he is the only one there and there is no work to do. He spends his time reading newspapers and doing crossword puzzles until others arrive. It is a rather idiotic system, like much in the federal capital.

What is the cost, in salary and benefits, of each and every bureaucrat in the federal government? There is no available official figure, but private studies indicate numbers north of $120,000 per employee and more, plus an uncalculated but enormous overhead that runs many thousands more.

How can we cut the federal employee roster by some 20%—a target that would automatically increase worker efficiency?

This can be accomplished without firing a single person. Each year, about 7% of all federal employees retire or leave voluntarily; a total of 135,000 individuals a year are lost through attrition. All that is necessary is to hire only an essential 2% and refuse to hire individuals to fill the remaining open positions. This reduces the bureaucracy approximately 100,000 people a year, for a savings of many billion, and a leaner, more effective government.

Federal elephantiasis is a grave ailment, especially when it infects Washington, DC.

C

CABINET MADNESS

As we have seen, the Department of Agriculture is a very aggressive cabinet agency, falsely believing that it is somehow the entire federal government. As a result, it has its hands into many of the far-flung functions of Washington that have nothing to do with agriculture. It is a grave mistake that is endemic to the entire government.

Agriculture's present functions are overexpanded. They include not only subsidizing farmers but running a juvenile delinquency agency, food welfare, a housing agency, a forest service, a utilities operation, and a bank. It also supports renewable fuels such as ethanol and operates a multitude of poorly designed subagencies that go far beyond agriculture and cost American taxpayers some $90 billion a year, much of it wasted.

Agriculture has almost 10,000 local offices, including one in Texas that handles only 15 farmers. There are 65,000 employees in the nonforest aspect of the agency, or 1 federal employee for every 15 full-time farmers, which is ludicrous. With the consolidation of farms into sizable agricorporations and with most farmers being "aggie" graduates who have rather complete knowledge of their profession, the cabinet agency is becoming vestigial. Instead it continues to grow in expenditures.

At one juncture, there was $9.7 billion in unpaid principal of direct loans to farmers, but 28% of the total was delinquent. The Department of Agriculture often forgives these delinquent loans, writes off the losses, and then grants new loans to those who have defaulted.

We likely do not need a full Department of Agriculture. Rather a noncabinet Office of Agriculture with a savings of some $50 billion a year would do. There are more people employed in the computer business but we do not, and should not, have a Department of Computers.

That poor cabinet model extends through the entire federal government.

The American cabinet system, which has grown to 15 agencies, is poorly designed, operating in the helter-skelter tradition in which Congress passes new and expensive legislation and then seeks a cabinet agency to carry it, whether it is appropriate or not.

Take the case of the Energy Department and its reach, which is excessive and duplicates that of several other agencies. Energy manufactures and stores nuclear weapons, researches solar-powered cars, and helps pay the heating bills for the indigent. It is heavily involved in climate change, environmental cleanup, and cutting-edge carbon capture and storage technologies.

The agency has trouble completing its projects, at great cost to the taxpayer. In a 16-year period, Energy worked on 31 projects costing over $100 million each, spent over $10 billion, then closed down half of them. They have worked on a permanent disposal site for nuclear waste at Yucca Mountain, Nevada, for 20 years, and have spent almost $10 billion. But they are still not sure it is a suitable project.

Strangely, that same cabinet agency has assumed the major role in science research in America, which goes far beyond energy. Through its American Competitiveness Initiative (ACI), it tries to lead in scientific research in general. It attempts to clean up our coal reserves and authorizes guaranteed loans of some $38 billion over a 3-year period. The Department of Energy also runs a $4.7 billion annual program that helps thousands of scientists and students.

Just as Agriculture handles corn ethanol production and subsidies, Energy does the other half, a $75 million program on cellulosic ethanol. It spends $368 million for supercomputers, although energy is not the main recipient of their output. It also spends another $146 million for climate change, competing with other agencies in this vague, controversial subject area.

Energy also competes, for example, with EPA. Their 2009 environmental management budget spends $5.5 billion to clear up legacy waste across the nation stemming from the Cold War.

The most egregious lack of definition and promise of a cabinet agency is, of course, the Department of Education. Despite the fact that it has cabinet distinction it has no real mission, and its promise is ephemeral and of little value. The fact is that, despite its title, it does not educate a single American, in K–12 or in higher education.

The Defense Department educates many of the children of service personnel and the Department of Interior educates the children of Native Americans. The states educate everyone else.

So ludicrous is its title in relation to its actual work that for years critics demanded that the Department of Education be closed and that it be turned into a simple agency with its budget reduced fourfold.

But just its title and promise titillated Americans, especially politicians, even though it supports only 7% of American K–12 education, and poorly at that. Instead of being closed for lack of mission, the agency grew under several presidents, especially George W. Bush, into a giant with a massive budget of $60 billion, yet we have to import math teachers from the Czech Republic.

One of its few concrete missions is student loans for higher education. In a single year, Education had to pay out $3.3 billion to make good on government-guaranteed and defaulted student loans.

The problem of confused and duplicative missions among cabinet agencies is epidemic. The Department of Commerce, for example, has multiple tasks and subagencies, not always appropriate to its mission. Commerce is involved in oceanography, the atmosphere, international trade, patents, minority business, telecommunications, imports and exports, economic development, all types of statistics, and even the census.

Its National Weather Service has spent a fortune modernizing, with great overruns and waste. The Advanced Weather Interactive Processing System, planned to cost $350 million came in at over $600 million.

At the nation's founding, the cabinet system was tighter and more directed.

We started out with three: State (then Foreign Affairs), War, and Treasury. In 1798, we added the Navy Department; then, in 1849 as people moved westward, the Home Department, which later became Interior, was added. In 1889, in recognition that we were then mainly an agricultural nation, the Department of Agriculture was created. The Department of Commerce and Labor was created in 1903, but a decade later it was split in two.

By the end of World War II, in 1945, we had seven cabinet agencies. There had been eight, but the postmaster general was dropped from cabinet status.

Today? Today, we have more than doubled the size of 1945 cabinet structure with 15 cabinet officers, making a roundtable discussion uncomfortable. And two more are whispered, the EPA and U.S. Trade Representative. As the budget grows, so too do the cabinet slots and their regularly increasing costs.

In 1947 we added the Department of Defense, which took the place of the War Department. In 1953, numerous agencies were coordinated under the name Health, Education, and Welfare (HEW), which has been converted to the present Health and Human Services (HHS).

In 1965, Washington added another cabinet agency, the Department of Housing and Urban Development (HUD), which has been a disaster, both in corruption and failed projects. One HUD budget included $517 million in items whose contracts had expired, had been terminated, or had never been executed.

In 1966, we created the Department of Transportation. That fateful year, the Office of Education of HHS was split off to become the Department of Education, undoubtedly the poster child of federal failure. The 14th was the Department of Veterans Affairs, created in 1989. The 15th was the Department of Homeland Security, created in 2003 as a result of the attacks on the World Trade Center and elsewhere.

The American cabinet system is excessive, overstaffed, and poorly designed. Several positions and departments should be eliminated and others redefined and consolidated, making the upper echelons of the federal government more efficient and understandable.

Follow me to the "Conclusion" (on p. 324), where I will save many billions while reorganizing the president's cabinet before your very eyes.

C

CHINA

U.S.-Sponsored Trade Scam

"China is eating America's lunch."

You hear this aphorism everywhere, a lament that the great industrial giant of America not only has a fierce competitor but one that is helping to destroy America's industrial might. Not only is China eating our lunch but, through connivance, deception, and political blackmail, they are probably forcing this nation into a number two position on the world's economic stage, resulting in a lower standard of living for Americans.

The tragic aspect of this rise of China and the decline of America is that it has been stage-managed by America's politicians in close coordination with our multinational corporate giants seeking cheap products to sell to easily conned American consumers.

"Free trade" is the advertised slogan that tempts Americans not to complain. But, of course, it has nothing to do with free trade. It is instead a matter of "false trade," a well-thought-out Chinese racket ignorantly supported by most of America's politicians.

Americans have lost as many as 5 million manufacturing jobs since China began its economic con job. It is only the beginning of the demise of American manufacturing, which is unable to compete with China in prices. I personally know of one small manufacturing shop in New Jersey that once employed 23 workers and is now down to 5. It will eventually have to close because of low Chinese competitive prices, created by trickery, lies, and illegal economic maneuvers.

The major success of China is based on subterfuges, including near-slave labor, lack of environmental concerns, Chinese government cash subsidies that falsely support their own industries, and a billion poor farmers who will happily move to the industrial cities of China and live in one-room apartments and work 50 hours a week at less than minimum wage. In some cases, those former farm workers live in barracks and are bused to factories, where they work for less than $1 an hour.

The result is the success of Walmart, whose lower prices for cheap Chinese goods will eventually only add to the impoverishment of Americans who have lost, and are losing, their jobs to China. What good is it to save 20% on goods if you have no job with which to pay for them?

The tragic aspect of all this is that it is being done with the help of American political leaders, who regularly complain to China but who eventually fall for the Chinese Machiavellian promises and continue to support their economic scam.

Not only do the Chinese cheat in their trade equation with America, but many of their goods are dangerously inferior. We should all remember the pet and baby food that was poisonous and the lead paint used for children's toys. The Chinese greed for money has turned a usually moral people into trade violators for whom we must be carefully watchful.

But possibly more important is their thirst for trade surpluses. The major leap in Chinese surpluses with America came after China was sponsored for the World Trade Organization (WTO) by President Clinton, a policy continued by George W. Bush. The WTO has given China, a rogue economic state, the legitimacy it seeks to continue its fraudulent operation, which also includes "dumping"—selling products for less than the cost of producing them—for which they were accused in the American steel trade.

A major core of the China racket is their open fraud in the price of their currency, which, unlike any other major nation, does not float freely in the open international currency market, as do the yen, the dollar, the pound, and the franc. Instead the yuan is basically fixed by the Chinese government and fluctuates in only a narrow band at a very low price against a few currencies.

Experts believe the Chinese yuan sells for some 40% less than its true value, which enables them to underbid Americans at every turn. In simple language, America pays for Chinese goods with real money, while the Chinese pay for American exports with Monopoly money, a surefire racket that our government strangely countenances.

A few years ago, the Chinese pledged to partially float their currency in a very narrow band against a few other currencies, but the positive effect since then has been virtually nothing.

The result is that China holds almost $1 trillion of American debt, which rises every year and increases our interest payments to them, raising the annual American deficit.

In 2008, America's trade deficit with China reached $261 billion, a system in which America imports $5 for every $1 of goods it sells to China.

The Chinese carefully keep that export–import ratio high in their favor by shunning American technology as much as they can and by developing their own, which is now accelerating as they enter the communications and heavy-industry market. China carefully limits what they buy from us, including financial services—which they generally exclude—while they increase production of goods that we want.

Equally important, they cheat American exporters of billions each year by counterfeiting products in publishing, fashion, and electronics, violating our copyright and patents laws.

In fact, with Western help, they are carefully bringing their auto industry up to modern standards and within a few years expect to be exporting a cheap vehicle selling for just over $10,000, which will find a market in depressed Western economies. And they have the trained manpower to accomplish it. The Chinese now turn out six engineers for every American engineer, while our young are more inclined toward the nonessential arts, especially video and film. Only one in seven young Americans is drawn to science, much to our loss.

Strangely, it is not that America's politicians are unaware of the fact that we are being economically raped by the Chinese. The American trade representative Susan Schwab cited "China's shortcomings in observing the basic obligation of WTO membership."

In simple language, she told Congress that China was not living up to its obligations under the WTO. The report of her trade agency noted that the Chinese government has violated the basic fundamentals of WTO principles: "At the root of many of these problems is China's continued pursuit of problematic industrial policies that rely on excessive Chinese government intervention in the market for an array of trade distorting measures."

Several American senators have been much more critical of Chinese currency manipulation and slippery trade practices, even threatening to place high protective tariffs on trade with China. Senator Chuck Schumer (D–NY) and Lindsey Graham (R–SC) offered a bill to slap a 27.5% tariff on all Chinese goods to make up for the false price of their yuan.

Even though that wouldn't fully compensate America for the manipulated price of the yuan and other trade tricks, it was a reasonable goal. But the senators were eventually talked out of that action by the White House.

Said Schumer in an address to the Senate: "Nearly all experts still agree that the Chinese yuan remains significantly undervalued; that this undervaluation is the result of deliberate intervention by the Chinese government in world currency markets; and that this policy gives Chinese products a tremendous advantage in the United States market."

Schumer added that "the Treasury Department has repeatedly used a technical and legalistic dodge to determine that China does not manipulate its currency. We all know that they intervene on the order of $200 billion a year to keep the yuan's value artificially low, yet our government can't call a spade a spade." He then stated that Fed Chairman Ben Bernanke agrees with him, arguing that the Chinese currency practices "amount to an export subsidy."

But the White House was so cowed by Chinese threats that,

in their mandated 2008 report to Congress on trade, they refused to say that the Chinese currency was being deliberately "manipulated." They did the same in April 2009 under the Obama administration. The new secretary of treasury claims that he will be much more aggressive on Chinese currency policy, but others before him have made that same claim, to no avail.

What are the last few presidents and Congress afraid of when failing to confront China? Some speculate that our loss of economic strength vis-à-vis China is due to our desire to keep friendly relations with a coming military superpower. Others feel that the trillion-dollar American debt that China holds could fracture our bond market if they decide to cash out.

That latter argument is no longer valid because a one-time trillion-dollar loss is meaningless when we are accumulating more than a trillion dollars in debt each fiscal year. What's the difference between 11 trillion, 12 trillion, or 13 trillion? Our debt is now near-fatal to begin with.

No, the true answer is that we have set on a policy of national suicide in many directions, and China is only one aspect of our unnatural drive toward extinction.

It is also a case of poor judgment, failing to realize that the more we yield to their clever blackmail and cooperate in sustaining their growth at our expense, the stronger they become—financially, militarily, and internationally—and the weaker America becomes. It is also a case of simple appeasement, of failing to reverse the blackmail and force the price of the yuan upward.

If China wants to continue to do business with America, they should be forced to stop their subterfuge, their lying, and their currency crookedness. Otherwise we should penalize them.

With large tariffs? No, that sounds "protectionist," which is a deadly word in international trade. Instead, we should put in place a "currency equalization program," which varies, going up as China lowers the present false value of the yuan and going down when China raises the value of their currency in the market.

Otherwise we will have to isolate them financially if we are to maintain our manufacturing base.

What does America gain from China? Very little at present. The numbers are five to one against us. But the American power brokers keep talking about the promise of business with China tomorrow, a promise that will never come if China continues its subterfuges.

With all the false talk of free trade and the evils of protectionism, we must admit that right now we have already adopted a protectionist policy. The only problem is that we are protecting China, not America.

If we crack down on this rogue economic state today, we have little to lose and much to gain. The only real victim will be Walmart. But of course, with the $250 billion a year trade balance that we will gain, and all the jobs we will recover, we can easily afford to bail them out.

C

COMMUNITY DEVELOPMENT BLOCK GRANTS

Money for Urban Poverty, or What?

This is a short but telling story about Washington and your money.

The federal government sponsors the Community Development Block Grant (CDBG) program with 42 field offices throughout the nation to administer grants to help low- and moderate-income cities and large towns. Their work is designed to mainly aid crowded urban areas; clean up slums; renovate bad housing; and provide water, sewers, and other desperately needed community improvements.

A recent government survey of their work, which costs taxpayers $4 billion a year, states: "The objective of the program is to develop viable urban communities by providing decent housing and a suitable living environment and expanding economic opportunities, principally for persons of low and moderate income."

It is an admirable pursuit for the federal government.

The study boasts examples of their good work, including $250,000 for a health clinic in Lafayette, Colorado, where 96% of patients were poor, at or below 200% of the federal poverty line. In Santa Monica, California, $242,422 was spent building a shelter with 110 beds for homeless adults. In Warner Robins, Georgia, $41,000 went to Gateway Cottage, a program that targets young homeless mothers recovering from substance abuse. In Beloit, Wisconsin, $7,068 went to a program that provides poorer senior citizens with screened qualified workers to do home maintenance at affordable prices.

But suddenly we located a recent and much less inspirational story from the Community Development Block Grant program. What happened was that the federal agency gave an unusually large grant of $1 million to a town of only 60,000 people, a disproportionate federal gift for such a small community.

What was so unusual? Was the town hard-pressed for funds to clear up a slum or to put in long-overdue sewers? Or refresh its sordid street image?

Hardly. It is surprising to discover that the gift was awarded to Greenwich, Connecticut, a leafy, wealthy suburb of New York City and one of the richest towns in America. Greenwich is the ancestral home of the Bush family and of scores of celebrities and is the hedge fund capital of America, where the average home price is $1.6 million.

It is the home of the families of Tom Watson of IBM and Leona Helmsley, the former real estate queen, who together paid for much of the town's new $250 million community hospital. With an allotment of over $15,000 for each child in local public schools, Greenwich hardly needs Uncle Sam's money.

More important, it is the antithesis of the poor or moderate urban environment targeted by the CDBG and a pure violation of Washington's goals.

What happened? Obviously, complaints and applications have come into Washington from regular or even wealthy—not poor—communities that they too pay taxes and would like some of it back from Uncle Sam, whether they need it or not and whatever the federal government says about its supposed noble goals, which of course we should never really take too seriously.

What will Greenwich do with the money? It will go to 21 local, already comfortable charities, including the Greenwich YMCA, which incidentally is in the midst of a multimillion-dollar renovation that's being paid for by the wealthy patrons of this very exclusive town. A town that boasts hundreds of mansions, including several of 30,000 square feet, with $25 million tabs.

Some in the town seem pleased with the federal largesse, but they should realize that the $1 million that came to Greenwich in Washington's cash will eventually cost them at least $2 million more in additional taxes.

What's next?

Surely a Community Development Block Grant of another $1 million to clean up the slums of Palm Beach, Florida.

C

CORRUPTION

WAS MARK TWAIN RIGHT?

Congress is often the butt of humor, especially because it is so large (535 members), so diffuse in the quality and character of its members, so cumbersome, and often so unpopular. For at least 100 years, it has been the target of those seeking to titillate the country's funny bone.

One of the best at this was American literary giant Mark Twain, who commented that "it could probably be shown by facts and figures that there is no distinctly native criminal class—except Congress."

Most Congressmen are of course honest. But Twain's allusion to facts and figures does indicate that they get into more trouble with the law than do ordinary Americans. This is the result of several factors: their general ego and audacity; their hubris and sense of self-importance; and their having the type of personality that seeks the limelight, which in many cases is what brought them to politics in the first place.

So while most members of Congress serve the nation honestly, if inefficiently, there are an inordinate number of legislators who stray, gaining them the condemnation of Americans who seek a more idealistic demeanor and conduct.

Twain seemed to have proved his case when about 100 years later, in 1980, the FBI initiated a sting designed to ensnare a passel of congressmen in its investigative maw. Called "Abscam," the sting involved FBI agents disguised as wealthy Arabs who rented a comfortable house in Washington, a yacht in Florida, and hotels in New Jersey and Pennsylvania as settings. They targeted 31 public officials, including several members of Congress, and invited them to meetings, at which they provided refreshments and offers of money to facilitate their investments in America. In essence, the disguised FBI agents solicited bribes.

Calling on convicted con man Melvin Weinberg for help, the FBI set up a sting. The supposed Arabs told the public officials that they had a great deal of money to invest in various American enterprises. Would the congressmen help?

They surely would. When the sting was over one senator and five members of the House of Representatives were convicted of bribery and conspiracy in separate trials in 1981. The most important conspirator was Senator Harrison Williams (D–NJ), who was convicted on nine counts of bribery and conspiracy to use his office to aid business ventures and become rich in the process.

Williams repeatedly met with the disguised FBI agents and agreed to a deal in which he would use his position in the Senate to get the federal government's help in starting up a titanium mining operation. In return he would get 18% of the company shares. Williams was sentenced to 3 years in prison and became the first senator to be expelled from the Senate since the Civil War. He passed away in 2001.

There was a great deal of controversy over whether the FBI used a sting or entrapment. Congress then held hearings on the bureau's crime-detecting technique. As a result the FBI was intimidated and has not used a sting against Congress since. However, one has to wonder what would happen if such stings of our politicians were regular occurrences.

The defense of entrapment resulted in reversing the conviction of one Abscam defendant, but that reversal was overturned, and the courts reaffirmed the conviction. He served 13 months in jail. One piece of evidence against him was a videotape showing him stuffing $25,000 into his pockets, after which he turned to the undercover FBI agent and asked "Does it show?"

One hero of the incident was Senator Larry Pressler (R–SD) who refused the bribe, saying: "Wait a minute. What you're suggesting may be illegal." He immediately reported the event to the FBI. On the evening news, Walter Cronkite called Pressler a "hero," to which the senator replied: "I do not consider myself a hero. What have we come to if turning down a bribe is 'heroic?' "

What we have come to is that too often we have become witness to both criminal and unethical behavior on the part of several Congressmen. The FBI recently came into direct conflict with Congress over the activities of William Jefferson (D–LA), who represents much of the greater New Orleans area.

In 2005, the FBI became suspicious of Jefferson when they received word from an investor that Jefferson was paid $400,000 in the name of a company owned by his wife and children. The money was to encourage Jefferson to perform several tasks: (1) persuade the U.S. Army to test a Louisville, Kentucky, firm's two-way broadband technology; (2) use his efforts to influence officials in Nigeria, Ghana, and Cameroon; and (3) meet with officials of the Export Import Bank of the United States to arrange financing for the company's business deals in those African nations.

Wearing a wire, a supposed investor working for the FBI met with Jefferson at the Ritz-Carlton Hotel in Arlington, Virginia, and gave him $100,000, in $100 bills, in a leather briefcase, all of which was videotaped by the FBI. A few days later, on August 3, 2005, the FBI raided Jefferson's home in Washington, the result of which has intrigued both Washington and the public.

At Jefferson's home, they found $90,000 of the cash in the freezer, in $10,000 increments wrapped in aluminum foil and stuffed inside frozen food containers. The serial numbers on the money in the freezer matched the serial numbers of the $100,000 the FBI had given to the informant.

Several months later, on May 20, 2006, the FBI executed search warrants and raided Jefferson's office in the Rayburn House Office Building, believed to be the first FBI raid ever of a congressional office. House leaders were outraged about the raid, stating that it could "set a dangerous precedent that could be used by future administrations to intimidate and harass the supposedly coequal branch of government."

Meanwhile, the FBI recovered several sensitive papers from Jefferson's office, which the FBI claims he had "surreptitiously tried to remove." From those documents, the FBI concluded that they discovered "at least seven other schemes in which Jefferson sought things of value in return for his official acts."

The fight between the FBI and the House of Representatives went on. Jefferson challenged the FBI in federal court and then-

House Speaker Dennis Hastert and then-House Minority leader Nancy Pelosi issued a joint statement demanding that the FBI return the documents and that Jefferson cooperate with the investigation.

The public, however, disagreed with the House. In an ABC poll on June 1, 2006, 86% of respondents supported the FBI's right to search a congressional office when they had a warrant, as the FBI did.

Former Attorney General Alberto Gonzalez is said to have threatened to quit if he had to return the documents that the FBI had taken. The House meanwhile subtly threatened to reduce the Justice Department's budget. On May 24, 2006, President Bush intervened and directed Justice to seal all the materials taken from Jefferson's office.

Finally, the House came around and demanded that Jefferson resign from the Ways and Means Committee. He refused, but the full House voted to remove him. On June 4, 2007, a federal grand jury indicted Jefferson on 16 charges of corruption, to which he pled not guilty. At the hearing, he stated that the $90,000 was the FBI's money. "The FBI gave it to me as part of its plan—part of their plan—that I should give it to the Nigerian vice president, but I did not do that. When all the facts are understood, I trust I will be vindicated." Meanwhile, two of his associates have pled guilty and have been sentenced to 1 to 8 years in jail.

Jefferson sought reelection against seven Democrats seeking his seat, but he was defeated.

Simple bribery is among the common crimes errant congressmen commit. (Most congresswomen seem immune to charges of bribery, at least thus far.) The temptation is enormous because the legislation they are passing often commits hundreds of millions in taxpayer funds. They possibly feel that they are stealing only small amounts, relatively speaking.

This lapse of the public trust happened again when, tragically, Congressman Randy "Duke" Cunningham, a Vietnam war hero and a former navy commander and ace pilot, was convicted of bribery and sentenced to 8 years in jail, which he is still serving.

Cunningham was a larger-than-life hero, having shot down five MiGs in Vietnam and later reportedly becoming the model for the film *Top Gun*. A burly fellow, who to some was reminiscent of John "Duke" Wayne, Cunningham was invited to run for Congress in 1990 by the Republican Party after he became locally famous for his wartime exploits and his speeches about the war.

In Vietnam, he was decorated several times, receiving the Navy Cross, the Silver Star twice, the Air Medal 15 times, and the Purple Heart for wounds he received in combat. He retired from the navy in 1987 as a commander and settled in Del Mar, California. In 1990, Cunningham ran for Congress against an incumbent Democrat and won, serving on the House Intelligence Committee and becoming a recognized expert on national defense.

He also gained a seat on the House Defense Appropriations Committee, which ended up being his undoing. Cunningham became friendly with defense contractor Mitchell Wade and directed large defense contracts to him in return for bribes and favors. In one case, Wade bought Cunningham's house for $1,675,000, and a month later placed it back on the market, finally receiving only $975,000 for the house, indicating that it was an indirect piece of bribery on behalf of Cunningham. Wade plied Cunningham with gifts and favors in exchange for still more defense contracts. The FBI started an investigation and on July 1, 2005, raided Wade's home.

In still another incident, defense contractor Brent Wilkes tempted Cunningham into pushing the Pentagon to buy a $20 million document digitalization system created by Wilkes's firm. It was later claimed that Wilkes reportedly gave Cunningham more than $630,000 in cash and favors. Finally, on November 28, 2005, Cunningham pled guilty to tax evasion and conspiracy to commit bribery, mail fraud, and wire fraud in federal court in San Diego.

Among the bribes Cunningham admitted receiving was the house sale at an inflated price, the use of a yacht, a used Rolls-Royce, antique furniture, Persian rugs, and jewelry, plus $2,000 for his daughter's college graduation party. Cunningham submitted his official resignation from Congress and shortly after was sentenced to 8 years and 4 months in prison—a tragic ending to a once-bright life story.

Congressional bribery is not uncommon. Among the more recent offenders are James Traficant (D–OH) who was convicted in 2002 and who is now serving 8 years in prison for bribery racketeering and tax evasion. Another is Carol Hubbard (D–KY), convicted of fraud in 1994. A recent conviction involved Bob Ney (R–OH), who pled guilty to charges that involved him in the Jack Abramoff lobbyist scandal. Ney was sentenced in 2007 to 2.5 years in prison for trading political favors for gifts and campaign donations.

In 1980, Representative Daniel Flood of Pennsylvania was charged with the "use of official implements on behalf of private parties and foreign governments in return for unlawful payments." He resigned and pled guilty. In 1984, House member George V. Hansen of Idaho was convicted of making false statements to the government for his violation of the Ethics in Government Act. He failed to report $200,000 in loans and income and was sentenced to 5 months in prison.

In 1987, Representative Mario Biaggi of New York was convicted of accepting illegal gratuities, conspiracy, and obstruction of justice and was sentenced to jail. And again in 1988 he was convicted of bribery involving a Bronx, New York, defense contractor and sentenced to 8 years in jail. In 1991, he was released from jail because of failing health.

In 1989, Representative Albert G. Clemente of Texas was convicted of accepting $35,000 for trying to get a lucrative air force concession and was punished with 3.5 years in jail. In 1988 Representative Patrick L. Swindall of Georgia was convicted of nine counts of perjury in lying to a grand jury about trying to negotiate a loan from a drug money launderer and was sentenced to a year in jail and disbarred.

In 1979, Representative Frederick W. Richmond of New York pled guilty to tax evasion and resigned from Congress. In 1979, Representative Charles C. Diggs admitted inflating the salaries of his staff so that they could get kickback money to pay his personal expenses.

One of the most colorful of congressional violators of our trust was Representative Dan Rostenkowski, Democrat of Chicago, who was the longtime all-powerful chairman of the House Ways and Means Committee, which handles taxation. He was so powerful that he virtually single-handedly wrote and rewrote the IRS tax code. He was almost a caricature of power as he walked the halls of the Capitol.

But according to the government, he was also the epitome of

political corruption. A burly man who could play himself in a movie of his life, he spoke in Chicago shorthand. "Rosty" is what he was known as by those who both loved and feared him. Chicago politics incarnate, he was elected 18 times by his working-class neighborhood.

He operated in the tradition made famous by the late Mayor Richard Daley, but he took his power one step too far. According to the U.S. Attorney General Eric Holder, he dipped into the public trough to the tune of hundreds of thousands of dollars.

Rosty had his comeuppance in 1994 when he was defeated in his district by a political amateur after a federal grand jury indicted him on numerous charges, including excessive interest in the House Post Office where he allegedly converted $21,000 in government stamps into cash for himself and falsely reported the transaction. He was also charged with taking $28,000 in checks from his campaign donations.

The federal charges against Rostenkowski covered 17 points, including one that he had allegedly hired 14 workers and put them on the federal payroll even though they did little or no work for the government. This amounted to $500,000 in federal funds over 21 years. Actually, much of that work was for his family, including cutting the grass at his summer home in Wisconsin.

In March 1996 a federal district court threw out four of the six counts, including one involving lying to Congress. However, in April 1996 Rosty pled guilty to two counts of mail fraud and was sentenced to 17 months in jail.

The public has regularly been entertained by the sexual peccadilloes of several legislators. Although homosexuality is quite legal—and in fact there are two openly homosexual members of Congress—suspected homosexual behavior that is not considered ethical sporadically comes up in the Washington legislature.

In one recent case, Congressman Mark Foley of Florida was forced to resign when it was charged that he had flirted with a 16-year-old former page through indiscreet e-mails. However, in September 2008, Foley was exonerated after an investigation by the House. In another case, Senator Larry Craig (R–ID) was allegedly caught in a sting in a public bathroom in the Minneapolis airport. He initially pled guilty to disorderly conduct but now claims his innocence and is attempting to have that plea removed in court.

On the heterosexual side, former senator from North Carolina and former vice presidential candidate John Edwards recently admitted that he had an affair with a campaign worker, who subsequently gave birth to a child. Both the woman and Edwards deny that the baby is his love child. In another case, Representative Vito Fossella (R–NY) was arrested on a drunk driving charge. The investigation led to the revelation that he was on his way to his mistress's home. Fossella acknowledged that he had had an affair with the woman, which resulted in the birth of a child.

The volume of recent cases of unethical behavior has led to a debate in Congress about whether perpetrators should lose their congressional pensions. Finally, in January 2007, the Senate approved a measure that would cancel the pensions of members of Congress who had committed such serious crimes as bribery, perjury, and fraud. The law, however, includes only certain crimes and does not take away the pension of those charged with making false statements to Congress, nor does it penalize those convicted of income tax evasion.

In any case, the law will not penalize those already convicted. The statute cannot be retroactive, as the bill's sponsor, Senator John Kerry (D–MA), pointed out, reminding members that that would be unconstitutional.

It is not only Congress that has ethical and criminal problems. Corruption has reached into such places as the executive branch, including the vice presidency of the United States.

Spiro T. Agnew, former governor of Maryland, became vice president on the Nixon ticket in 1968 and again in 1972. Allegedly he was on the take while a county executive in Maryland, when he regularly received $1,000 a week in kickbacks from contractors. It is startling that Agnew's bribes allegedly continued when he was vice president. When called before a federal grand jury, Agnew quickly pled nolo contendre (no contest) to the charge of not paying income tax on the tainted money.

He resigned from office in October 1973, just 2 months before the Watergate break-in. Had Agnew not been caught in time, he would have ascended to become the 38th president of the United States, when Nixon resigned in August 1974.

Corruption has also involved major federal agencies. In September 2008, during a debate in Congress over extending the drilling of oil to the offshore continental shelf, it was revealed that several members of the Department of Interior who handled such leases were involved in a massive scandal. An investigation by the department's inspector general (IG) found a "culture of substance abuse and promiscuity" by agency workers.

The 2-year, $5.3 million probe found workers at the Minerals Management Service in Denver, which handles royalty collection on drilling leases, having sex, using drugs, taking ski trips, and going on golf outings with and accepting gifts from energy company personnel with whom they did over $4 billion in government business.

The IG report stated: "Employees frequently consumed alcohol at industry functions, had used cocaine and marijuana and had sexual relationships with oil and natural gas company representatives, who ostensibly referred to some female government workers as 'MMS chicks.'"

A more massive financial scandal took place at the Housing and Urban Development Department (HUD) in the 1980s. HUD was investigated by the House Committee on Government Operations, which issued a report in November 1990 stating: "During much of the 1980s HUD was enveloped by influence peddling, favoritism, abuse, greed, fraud, embezzlement and theft in many housing programs." The committee added that a housing rehabilitation program designed for the poor "became a cash cow" that was milked by "former HUD officials and the politically well-connected."

One HUD accountant reportedly stole $1 million by electronically transferring HUD funds to his personal account. In all, there were 16 convictions of HUD officials and others along with $2 million in criminal fines and the recovery of $10 million in extorted federal funds. (See "Housing, Public" on p. 171.)

America likes to think of itself as a nation steeped in Anglo-Saxon law and jurisprudence, where corruption is only an occasional smear. In reality, in an international study of corruption, Finland came out cleanest as number one, whereas America scored 17th, close to the bottom of the most developed countries.

There is actually a tally of corruption committed by all public officials, a report issued regularly by the Department of Justice.

The department has established the Public Integrity Section, which tries to keep tabs on crimes prosecuted by federal authorities. Its latest *Report to Congress*, available to all citizens, is a wakeup call.

The most recent annual toll of corrupt public officials—both elected and appointed and either convicted, indicted, or awaiting trial for crimes involving bribery, extortion, or conflict of interest—is shocking. The number of possibly corrupt officials comes to approximately 2,600 a year, a sad reflection on the body politic. Since 1987, when the figures started to be compiled, the total tally is over 50,000 politicians.

When will it end? When can we expect that public officials will be at least as honest as ordinary citizens? The answer is when the political establishment itself is cleansed. The villain, of course, is the system in which politicians make the rules that encourage corruption, both in their laxity of oversight and the reality that campaign contributions are as suspect as behind-the-screen bribes.

As we shall see in "Lobbyists" (p. 198), the connection between campaign contributions and corrupt political behavior is very close. Reforming the political landscape will require disentangling this sort of subtle corruption, including much closer oversight and tighter ethical rules.

And although most citizens will disagree with me, I believe that congressmen are underpaid. In the Abscam sting, one perpetrator told the FBI undercover people that they had no idea how "poor" he was. The present $165,000 salary seems quite sufficient, but to reduce the temptation to steal, we should pay our House representatives $250,000, and our senators $300,000.

In any case, we have too much corruption, so much that it has become part of the political culture, a danger that regularly strikes at the heart of our democracy.

Yes, unfortunately, Mark Twain was not only clever, but also absolutely right.

C

CREDIT CARD RACKET

WHY DOES WASHINGTON ENCOURAGE BANK USURY?

In May 2009, to great Hosannas, the federal government issued new regulations designed to help beleaguered credit card holders, many of whom are paying small fortunes in order to carry a balance on their cards.

But once the public relations fog has cleared, credit cards will still be the greatest banking racket in recorded history, charging as high as 30% interest and rolling up fortunes in late fees from busy citizens.

Beginning in June 2010, the government will alleviate the pain of some of the peripheral rackets involved by giving credit card holders a 45-day notice before raising their rates—as if they could do anything about it anyway—and by not making those raises retroactive, which seemed illegal to begin with. Furthermore, the companies will be able to raise rates only after the first year.

All to the good, but as we shall see, these "reforms" avoid the two biggest problems with credit cards: that their interest rates are usuriously high and illegal according to state-by-state standards, and that they just don't give citizens enough time to pay their bills before hitting them with penalties and, in some cases, large rate hikes.

As for the federal government's involvement in the usurious rates, which are as high as 30% and akin to those charged by loan sharks: In America, the usury laws are controlled by each state. I checked and learned that the legal limit for interest on loans in my state was 8%, similar to the usury laws in most states, which range from 6 to 14%.

Then how can the credit card company charge 30% to some cardholders?

I checked further and found that the federal government was, once again, the villain in this fiscal horror show, continuing to take power away from the states and divvying it up in a madhat Washington.

The banking industry had lobbied Washington and managed to get a law passed by Congress that lifts all state usury laws, allowing any "national" bank—those that issue virtually all credit cards—to charge whatever it wants. Thus usury, once illegal and a smear on the character of a bank or corporation, not only became legal, but was encouraged by our politicians in Congress.

Specifically, the lifting of state usury laws was the work of the House and Senate Banking committees and the presidents who signed those abusive banking laws.

If a borrower is using the credit card to the limit of his or her income and savings, and the balance is large, as many are, the borrower cannot pay it off immediately and is stuck with the usurious figure—what would be a criminal interest rate if the state laws were still intact.

But haven't the new regulations helped the credit card holders in such cases?

No. Thirty percent interest is still perfectly OK with Uncle Sam. The only protection consumers now have on new purchases is that their interest rate cannot be raised retroactively, and not at all during their first year. But again there is a catch: this does not apply if the cardholder is late on his payment.

According to the Survey of Consumer Finances conducted by the Federal Reserve, three out of four families have credit cards, and the average balance is approximately $6,000. The bigger problem is that the cards not only charge excessive interest, which now averages 18%—more than any state usury law—but that the card issuers have a whole series of fees and abuses that make credit cards the most profitable part of America's banking system.

The banking abuses are legion. One of the most common is "late payment" fees. These are arranged by the credit card companies to ensnare people who are used to paying in a reasonable time frame. Credit grace periods from most other companies are generally 30 days, after which the payee is late. A few days here or there are generally overlooked by most businesses. But not by credit card companies, which have the late-fee racket down to a science.

The new law supposedly extends the grace period for payments before you are hit with a late payment fee. But this is not the case. The government has just set it at 21 days, which is about the same as before, or even less than most credit cards now permit. My card, issued by Chase, allows me 25 days, but even that is a false figure.

This is how my credit card company does it, cleverly. That 25 days' grace includes the mail time for delivery of their statement to me, plus the usually slow postal time for the delivery of my check to them, plus the time for the credit card company to process my check—all a clever time-eating set of rules for the greedy bank.

The closing date on my account is the fifteenth of each month, when statements are sent out. Generally I receive the bill on the nineteenth, which uses up four days of the grace period. When I mail my payment back to them, it takes another four days for the credit card people to receive my check. But I am told by them that it also takes three days more for them to process my check, which eats up another seven days.

So, magically, the 25-day grace has suddenly been reduced to 14 days, less than half the usual 30-day grace. If I take 15 days to pay, I receive a late payment fee of $39. Averaging, for example, a $3,000 balance at 10%, that late fee is greater than the entire interest payment on the account.

But that is only half the problem. In the new 21-day rule, take off four more days from my more generous grace period, which usually gives the payee a mere 11 days to make good before he gets hit with a huge penalty.

Does it pay off for the credit card companies? I would say it does, big time. Last year they took in $18 billion in fees, mostly late fees, with no cost to them whatsoever. This incidental made up 40% of their revenue, and increased the cost to cardholders some 41% since 2003.

Not only is the late-payment racket still intact, but it allows the credit card company to raise your interest rate when you are late, the icing on their fiscal cake.

Law enforcement officials and regulators have accused companies of deceptive practices such as fake late-payment fees. The US Office of the Comptroller of the Currency and the San Francisco District Attorney's Office ordered one credit card company to pay $300 million in restitution after customers complained that the company didn't credit late payments on time and then hit them with late fees.

Up until the 1980s, credit card companies charged the same interest to all cardholders. Today, it is a sliding scale called "risk-based pricing," which the sets the rate based on income and credit worthiness. This adds some 6% in interest for the poorest clients, making their typical card interest at least 18%, and often more.

This rate discrimination only increases the amount of defaults, as the poorer clients find themselves in a cycle of debt, paying only the minimum payment, which makes it virtually impossible to ever pay off their debt.

Paying the minimum amount, as many people unfortunately do, keeps the balance going forever, which is the intent of the credit card company. What do the new "reforms" do to help those suckered cardholders? Nothing except rhetoric. Now, the rules require only that the card companies "disclose" that it will take longer to pay off the debt—which, of course, customers already know!

The deceptive nature of credit card companies when default is involved is shown by a case in Cleveland, Ohio, where the borrower was sued. The judge threw the case out when he discovered that on the original debt of $1,963, the borrower had already paid $3,492 over a period of six years. Yet, with late fees and finance charges, she still owed $5,564. In all, she had accumulated a $9,000 debt on a credit card loan of less than $2,000.

"Most of the credit cards that end up in bankruptcy proceed-ings have already made a profit for the companies that issued them," said Robert R. Weed, a Virginia bankruptcy lawyer. "That's because people are paying so many fees that they have already paid more than was originally borrowed."

What did the new "reforms" accomplish for cardholders? Something around the edges, but the big racket—up to the usurious 30% interest and fake late fees—is still the result of the friendly collaboration between the banks and Uncle Sam against the interest of citizens.

What should be done to protect the cardholders from vicious usury? Obviously, a maximum interest rate of 18% should be put in place, and the usual 30-day grace period for payment due should be reinstated.

Anything else is a violation of Uncle Sam's fiduciary trust.

So what else is new?

C

CREDIT CARDS: FEDERAL EMPLOYEES

A Pure Pleasure Plastic Paradise

When a young woman's breast-enlargement surgery became involved in a lawsuit, it was discovered that her boyfriend had paid over $3,000 for the operation—on his government employee credit card, designed for small purchases for Uncle Sam.

Someone in Washington back in the 1980s came up with the idea that it would save $92 per transaction in paperwork if federal employees were able to buy supplies for the government by using credit cards.

But the government did not consider that in the loose Washington environment, where discipline is lax, that employee honesty would be challenged. The result is that federal employees illegally used the convenient card to charge items for themselves, to the tune of many millions of dollars.

The program, under the umbrella of the General Services Administration, is called "SmartPay," one of the great oxymorons of our time.

The government made it easy for employee criminals. The federal bureaucrats were never billed personally for the purchases they made with these cards, ostensibly for the government. The bills go to a bank contractor hired by the government, which then bills Washington. Employees supposedly require approval from a superior for purchases, but that control too often proved to be in name only.

The whole idea seemed ludicrous to outsiders because Washington is not noted for a culture of discipline that would curtail thievery.

Nevertheless, the program was put in place, and soon 500,000 plastic money wands were in the hands of federal employees, bosses and minions alike. The only restraint was that "control officers" were supposed to oversee the program, and no one could supposedly spend more than $2,500 on a single purchase. This was handled by clever, dishonest employees by simply splitting purchases in half. The program grew so rapidly that it soon reached the cost of $16 billion a year.

The ease of using the card to steal from the government spread like wildfire through the ranks of Washington bureaucracy. So rampant was the theft—using the card for personal goodies—that Congress asked the Government Accountability Office (GAO) to investigate several agencies for the extent of the looting. In addition, the inspectors general of various victimized agencies chimed in.

At the Department of Education, 37% of the charges were approved by the wrong official. At the Department of Agriculture (USDA), a spot check of only a small sample of credit cards turned up $7.7 million in unauthorized charges in only a 6-month period. In one horrendous theft, 45 employees of that department used their credit cards illegally to run up personal bills of $5.8 million. Purchases included Ozzy Osbourne concert tickets, tattoos, lingerie, bartender school tuition, car payments, and cash advances.

The USDA promised an investigation, but they have 55,000 credit cards to check, including 1,549 cards held by people who no longer work there.

At Housing and Urban Development (HUD), GAO discovered that the program was being abused big time. Of a $1.8 million sample they found that 77% of purchases were debatable, may not have been truly authorized, and may not have been for a legitimate government need. They found, incidentally, that the HUD employees in that small sample spent $27,000 in department stores for their own personal items and $9,000 more in restaurants.

At Interior, some employees used their cards to get cash advances at a gambling casino. At another agency, $12,000 was charged by one employee for personal-use computers, gift certificates to friends, and groceries. The investigation also revealed that $439,000 was charged by employees after their credit cards were canceled. One ingenious Department of Defense (DOD) employee used 13 different government credit cards for his personal purchases and had to pay $282,840 in restitution.

One check of civilian DOD employees at two naval bases turned up the following mad scenario: When a group of employees decided to buy briefcases, many chose Coach and Vuitton luxury brands, paying up to $500 for each. When asked why, they uniformly stated brazenly that it was "their preference." No disciplinary action was taken.

The DOD also found that one employee bought two cars and

a motorcycle for himself on government plastic. The navy reported 25 fraudulent credit card transactions for a loss of $1,342,000.90. In one 18-month period, air force and navy personnel used government credit cards for such very personal purchases as $102,000 for admission to entertainment events, $48,000 for gambling, $39,000 for cruises, and $74,000 for exotic dance strip clubs and prostitutes.

The Defense Department had 214,999 cardholders, almost one for every two defense personnel, a lapse of common sense that is increasingly typical of our federal government.

Perhaps the record for credit card misuse was held by a Pentagon supervisor who used her credit card to embezzle $1.7 million over a period of 3 years.

Though amply warned about the program, Congress did the expected. Rather than cancel the cards as a result of abuse, they raised the limit on credit cards purchases tenfold, from $2,500 to $25,000. And with that strange move, the amount of thievery escalated.

Faced with still more abuse, the GAO investigated again. They found that internal controls were still as bad, or worse. Audits, they stated, "identified ineffective management oversight and weak internal controls, leaving agencies vulnerable to fraudulent, improper and abusive purchase card activity."

Employees used their government credit cards to purchase jewelry, designer leather goods, clothing, stereo equipment, and entertainment. There were even some creative choices such as charging Uncle Sam for a 7-day Alaska cruise.

There is an absence of documentation for personal purchases, and the supposed authorizing officials were mere rubber stamps used to support the buying, whether for the government or for themselves, says the report. Because of the lack of documentation, many of the items supposedly bought for Uncle Sam could not be found. At the Department of Education, 241 computers bought with credit cards and valued at $261,500 had simply disappeared.

The cheating involves virtually every government agency, over 300 of which issue these cards. Army personnel used the cards to get $38,000 in cash to buy lap dancing at strip clubs near military bases. One employee even used his card to pay $7,373 in closing costs on his home. In the U.S. attorney general's office in Los Angeles, a worker charged nearly $500,000 in personal expenses before she was caught. At Education, some employees used their cards to buy pornography on the Internet.

There are several ways to cheat taxpayers with government credit cards. To hide $14,000 in personal use, one worker used the names of legitimate companies doing business with his agency to submit false invoices. Others used small, discreet stores to cover their thievery, especially pawn and antique shops. At one pawn shop, a federal worker used his credit card to bill taxpayers for $2,443, a down payment on an expensive sapphire ring, ostensibly for a female loved one.

Another casualty of the credit card program is the loss of valuable discounts. Almost all the purchases are retail, in such establishments as Best Buy, for example. This negates the procurement policy of obtaining large discounts from many suppliers, which had previously been established by the government. The credit card program has lost the great majority of these discounts.

The price to taxpayers?

One official estimate is that the card program loses some $300 million a year in wholesale discounts in just 6 of the nation's 15 cabinet agencies. When added to the high cost of thievery, which has been well documented, this makes the program one of the worst planned and worst executed in American history.

Despite the problems encountered with thousands of federal employees, the program was extended to employees of contractors who worked for the government, an increasing phenomenon used to make the number on the bloated Washington payroll look smaller than it truly is.

A report from the inspector general of the Department of Energy showed that a contract program manager used his card to buy $85,000 of personal items, while his subordinate's card was used to pilfer another $13,000. The IG also found that in 11 other cases, the government lost $1.5 million in fraudulent card use, making contractors just as dangerous as regular federal employees have proven to be.

There have been various attempts at reform of the card program, but they have all failed. The number of credit cards has been cut down from 500,000 to slightly more than 300,000, but in the third GAO report, in 2006, the credit card policy looks just as distorted. Checking their use in the aftermath of Katrina, the investigation found continued abuse, including using a card to buy a 61-inch, $8,000 plasma television, which was later found unopened in its box.

Calls for reform continue. In 2007, Senator Chuck Grassley (R–IA) introduced the Government Credit Card Abuse Prevention Act, stating—more than a decade after the flawed program began—that "it is time we put a stop to wasteful, abusive and fraudulent use of government credit cards." That bill is now sitting in committee with an uncertain future.

We wish him luck with an impossible task, one he expects to solve with greater documentation and policing, especially by agency inspectors general.

But the reality is that in an ethically loose Washington environment where theft is made as easy as slipping a credit card through a monitor, Uncle Sam, in all his ignorance, has gone several levels over the top.

The only obvious solution is to close the program down, save a half billion dollars a year, and stop the giddy temptation of a plastic heaven for our too-often dishonest civil servants.

D

DUPLICATION

THE SAME EXPENSIVE PROGRAMS, OVER AND OVER AND OVER AGAIN

Americans are justifiably concerned about drug abuse among our youth. Does the federal government have a program, or even two, to address this urgent problem?

Yes, they do, and with more programs than you could possibly imagine. In fact, there are actually 70 different programs in 13 different federal agencies, all working on the same problem: drug abuse among young people. This far-reaching duplication has even worried federal auditors, who "raised questions about the efficiency and effectiveness of this overlapping system."

As we have seen, there are 160 job-training programs, at a cost of $20 billion a year, scattered throughout the federal government. It is all part of an epidemic of duplication, of every agency doing much the same thing without any coordination or even without the knowledge that somewhere in the federal maze their work is being repeated, over and over again.

It is part of a Washington syndrome—that everyone does

the same thing, a foolish practice that is crippling the federal operation.

Since I began researching the excesses of the federal government, I have been struck by that peculiar phenomenon. I've always been intrigued by the fact that Congress continually passes legislation establishing the same or similar programs without the public, or the president, or anyone else, being aware of that duplication.

Congress is not interested in following up on legislation they have passed, even as recently as a month ago. As we shall see, it proves the maxim that no one really knows what is happening in our bloated government, not Congress or the president—no one. And the greatest sin is that no one in Washington truly cares.

This duplication is particularly unique to the U.S. government. In the parliamentary system in England and on the Continent, a specific minister is in charge of both legislation and execution, and knows that similar programs exist and generally refuses to duplicate them. He correctly sees that such behavior is not only a waste of money but a threat to his reputation as a legislator and as a government executive.

But in our system, legislators feel they gain reputation and publicity by developing a new seemingly popular program, whether or not it already exists, either exactly or in a similar form. The American separation of powers—once the beneficent hallmark of our system—stimulates duplication. Congress acts independently of the executive branch, with less than ideal motivations. It passes obviously duplicate legislation to gain notoriety, appease a certain segment of voters, and satisfy the ideology of their party.

Meanwhile Congress is ignorant of, or not concerned about, the mountain of legislation in the same field that is buried in the archives. Not only are programs passed without any "sunset" provisions but they are still operating even decades later, getting their yearly allotment of federal money, including the usual increases.

The result, of course, is absolute and total chaos, the best description of the federal government invented by modern Washington.

Fortunately, the poor results have been codified by the investigative arm of the Congress, the Government Accountability Office (GAO), which regularly examines government operations, but whose findings are generally ignored by the politicians who pass these peculiar repetitive laws.

Over the years, GAO has issued scores of reports showing the duplication of laws and missions, horrifying any intelligent taxpayer.

Says the GAO: "Most federal missions were assigned to multiple departments and agencies. In fact, for example, most agencies made obligations to three or more budget functions, and six of the budget functions were addressed by six or more executive departments and major agencies."

The same is true of the numerous programs of the Economic Development Administration. The GAO also reports that "at least 12 federal departments and agencies were responsible for hundreds of community development programs that assist distressed urban communities and their residents. Historically, there is but little coordination among the agencies, posing an unnecessary burden on urban communities seeking assistance."

Exactly how many of these economic development programs doing much the same job are we paying for? Unbelievably, the number is 342.

In the field of promoting exports from the United States to foreign nations, the government is active—actually overactive. There are 10 different federal agencies doing the same job, spending $2.7 billion a year. "The agencies offer export promotion services in an often inefficient and sometimes confusing manner," says another report.

Let's look briefly at federal drug control agencies. How many agencies are involved? Actually, 50.

The federal government, as we shall see, owns a large slice of America (see "Land Grab" on p. 192) and is heavily involved in land management. How? There are six different land management agencies, with "little commonality existing among the 31 different mission-related activities."

The federal government is responsible for much investigation and prosecution of crimes. We all know of the Department of Justice and the FBI. But is much of that work duplicated elsewhere? In fact, there are 13 federal agencies that employ more than 700 law-enforcement investigative personnel. There also 32 other federal agencies that employ between 25 and 700 investigative and legal personnel. It seems that some coordination, or a lot of coordination and consolidation, with a great savings, is called for in this vital task.

What about a simple job like checking for water quality? Surely the federal government is involved in that endeavor. Actually, it is more than involved. It turns out that there are 72 different programs in 8 different cabinet departments and agencies that work on that problem, advising the states, cities, and individuals on water quality. Of course, that same work is once again duplicated by the states, cities, counties, and towns.

Regularly, on television and in the press, we are exposed to various government statistics on health, wages, inflation, et cetera. Are there one or two central federal statistical agencies? How about 72 of them? That's the number of federal agencies that spend at least $500,000 a year on statistics. Most important, there are 11 different agencies whose primary work is statistics and who collectively spend well over $1 billion a year.

And how about delinquent or at-risk youth? They too have many adherents in the federal bureaucracy. Perhaps too many. It seems that there are 131 federal programs serving delinquent youth, costing at least $4 billion a year. One report notes: "Many programs provided multiple services and had multiple target groups, raising questions about the overall efficiency of federal efforts." Amen.

How about international cultural and educational programs?

This sounds like a noteworthy objective. But how many different ones are we supporting? Apparently 75 programs in 16 different federal agencies. This seems like the ideal effort to be consolidated into one program in one relatively small agency, perhaps called "U.S. International Cultural and Educational Agency."

How about HUD and housing? The beneficiaries are tenants in public housing or assisted housing for low- and moderate-income people. This is big business, made much more expensive by the fact that there are 23 different HUD programs doing much the same job.

The federal government is highly involved in laboratories of all sorts, for a total of 515 research and development (R&D) labs, including 185 in the Department of Agriculture alone.

Washington is concerned about Americans with disabilities, and shows it with numerous, uncoordinated, overlapping programs. To be exact, there are 130 disability programs in 19 different federal agencies, a helter-skelter approach about which auditors say: "Often services are not coordinated between programs, and people with disabilities may receive duplicate services or face service gaps." They add that these "federal programs could work together more efficiently to promote employment."

Investigators see the same discouraging operation in the 86 different teacher-training programs in 9 different federal agencies.

As we know, the federal government places its often destructive hand into every aspect of American life, inefficiently replacing work traditionally done by the states themselves. This is especially true in rural areas.

One rural concern is water and sewage, for which Uncle Sam gets bad grades, as usual. Says one report: "The patchwork of water and sewage programs is difficult to use." It then adds that "the complexity and number of programs hampered the ability of rural areas to utilize them."

Over the years, audits have cataloged the horror of duplication and inefficiency in the federal government, but the somnolent Congress has stubbornly refused to do anything about it, preferring to maintain the public relations fantasy that Washington truly loves its citizens, even if they have a most peculiar way of showing it.

For those who are interested in even more of these failed opportunities to deliver services simply and directly, here is a quick survey of still more waste in duplicative programs that were supposed to help but are daily injuring both the service and pocketbooks of the American people:

- Telecommunications projects in rural areas: 28 programs in 15 federal agencies.

- International environmental programs: 5 agencies spend $1 billion supporting 12 different agreements.

- Homeless assistance: 50 programs.

- Teenage pregnancy: 27 programs.

- Trade agencies: 17 programs monitoring 400 international agreements.

- Food safety: 12 agencies.

- Early childhood development: 90 programs.

It is not too difficult to find and catalog these long-forgotten and costly duplicative programs and either eliminate or consolidate them. All that is missing is the will of Congress and the White House to stop doing the same job perpetually in various venues.

The process continues, not to get it right, but to get it wrong, over and over and over again.

E

EARMARKS

PORK FOR THE PEOPLE BACK HOME, SUPPOSEDLY

How about $107,000 to study the sex life of the Japanese quail?

This was one of the memorable pieces of "pork" that I exposed on a fateful day years ago when I appeared on national television to discuss my first book on the failings, including foolishness, of the federal government.

It was titillating, but as time has shown, my research on congressional goodies for the folks back home proved to be quite important. Last year, pork cost taxpayers some $17 billion in 11,610 special appropriations for the voters in the districts of the members of Congress using this legislative gimmick to help them campaign for reelection.

In the $410 billion Omnibus Appropriations Bill voted on in March 2009, covering only 6 months of partial spending, there were 8,500 earmarks, totaling some $7.7 billion—just for that short period. Though President Obama promised during his 2008 presidential campaign that he would eliminate earmarks, he seemed to forget and nevertheless signed the bill.

As we will see, when it comes to pork, America's members of Congress are highly imaginative, more so than they are in protecting the people's money.

Going back to my early reporting on pork, the other pieces of unneeded legislation buried in that federal budget included such expensive esoterica as:

- $3.1 million to convert a ferry boat into a crab restaurant in Baltimore.

- $43 million for Steamtrain, USA in Scranton, Pennsylvania, to re-create a railroad yard of old.

- $6.4 million for a Bavarian ski resort in Idaho.

- $150,000 to study the Hatfield–McCoy feud.

- $320,000 to purchase President McKinley's mother-in-law's house.

- $84,000 to study how people fall in love.

- $19 million to examine gas emissions from cow flatulence.

Measuring and fighting pork is the specialty of Citizens Against Government Waste (CAGW), the nonprofit watchdog group that tries to keep wasteful spending, the specialty of the federal government, under some kind of reasonable control.

Each year they put out the *Pig Book*, a blow-by-blow recita-
tion of the madcap spending of members of Congress, items
generally inserted somewhat furtively at the last moment
into the federal budget at the House–Senate conference. The
pork is not designed to help America but to make members
popular with the most foolish of the folks at home. Pork has
even been awarded a technical governmental moniker—namely,
earmarks.

The *2008 Congressional Pig Book* put out by CAGW features
much the same federally useless, but locally popular, items that
raise the ever-increasing federal deficit. To be eligible to make
the pork list, the item must fit one of these criteria: be requested
by only one member of Congress, not be specifically authorized,
not be competitively awarded, not be requested by the president,
not be the subject of congressional hearings, and serve only a
local or special interest.

It is not petty cash. The total pork found by CAGW since
1991 now adds up to $271 billion, testimony to the costly imagina-
tion of Congress.

Some of the 2008 pork items that raise questions, even eye-
brows, are as follows:

- $3 million for First Tee, a social work program for young
  people based on learning to play golf.

- $211,509 for fruit fly research—in Paris, France.

- $11,808,756 by the "chief porker," Senate Appropriations
  Chairman Senator Robert Byrd (D–WV), including $1,529,220
  for the Appalachian Fruit Lab.

- $845,043 for agritourism where people go to watch cider being pressed or to pick their own apples on a farm.

- $1,843,008 (notice the specifics, down to the last dollar) for the University of Wisconsin Geographic Information System.

- $1,117,125 for the study of Mormon crickets in Nevada.

- $460,752 for research on hops for beer.

- $329,000 for the American Village Citizenship Trust in Alabama, where lovers can rent out the chapel and barn to get married for $2,650.

- $846,000 for the Father's Day Rally in Philadelphia.

- $590,400 for the Atomic Testing Museum in Las Vegas.

- $787,200 for the advanced green design at the Museum of Natural History in Minneapolis.

- $492,000 for the Rocky Flats Cold War Museum in Colorado.

- $2,400,000 for the renovation of the Haddad Riverfront Park in Charleston, West Virginia.

- $625,000 for the Congressional Cemetery in Washington, DC.

- $123,050 for a Mother's Day Shrine in Grafton, West Virginia, population 5,489.

- $984,400 for managing noxious weeds in Idaho.

- $196,880 for restoring the Wilson Theatre in Rupert, Idaho.

- $295,320 for Knox College in Galesburg, Illinois (where I went to school in the army), the home of the Lincoln–Douglass debates. (The school, incidentally, charges $30,000-a-year tuition.)

- $393,760 for the City National Bank Building in Iowa, designed by Frank Lloyd Wright and being renovated into a private hotel.

- $221,490 for the Brown Mansion in Coffeyville, Kansas, believed to be the site of paranormal activity and popular with ghost hunters.

- $246,100 to renovate the Grand Opera House in Dell Rapids, South Dakota, which is planned to become a privately owned bar and restaurant.

- $98,440 for the Philadelphia Art Museum, which has net assets of over $300 million.

- $146,000 for the Italian American Cultural Center in Des Moines, Iowa.

- $1,500,000 for the AFL-CIO Working for America Institute.

- $316,000 for the best remedy for lower back pain at the Palmer College of Chiropractic.

- $126,000 for the First Ladies Museum in Canton, Ohio.

- $125,000 for the University of Mississippi music archives.

- $14,878,000 for the International Fund for Ireland, which has received $250 million since 1995, though no one knows why except that former Speaker Tip O'Neill was of Irish heritage.

The 2009 Omnibus Bill registered over 8,500 examples of pork including this brief selection of the best—or is it the worst?—of them:

- $200,000 for tattoo removal.

- $1.7 million for a honeybee laboratory.

- $162,000 to control rodents in Hawaii.

- $40 million additional funds for three presidential libraries.

- $208,000 to control the cogongrass weed.

And, of course,

- $1.8 million to study pig odor and manure management.

The Democratic majority controlled the agenda, but Republican members sponsored some 40% of the pork. Senate Republican Minority Leader Mitch McConnell refused to vote for a ban on earmarks, making that aberration a solid bipartisan operation.

If only our legislators would match their porky imagination with sensible hard work and patriotism on the everyday activity of the federal government instead of conjuring up ways to pander to their local constituents, their approval rating might rise above 19% and America would be in a more sanguine and prosperous condition.

Meanwhile, one last punch line: "$105,163 for research on the 'Evolution of Monogamy in a Biparental Rodent.'" This is obviously a follow-up on the sex life of the Japanese quail, which is now in competition with almost $2 million for research on pig odor, a fragrance that is surely now enveloping the austere halls of Congress.

E

EDUCATION

We are in the midst of an extensive debate over the effectiveness of No Child Left Behind, the creation of Senator Edward Kennedy and former President George W. Bush, a $24 billion-a-year program intended to raise standards in the K–12 fiasco of public schools.

I use the word *fiasco* because, as should be well known by now (see my book *The Conspiracy of Ignorance: The Failure of American Public Schools*), American elementary and secondary education is the worst in the developed world.

In all international academic competitions, American youngsters score strangely and negatively. On 4th-grade exams, our children do well. But by the 8th grade they are only average. But most significant, by the 11th and 12th grades, as they are about to enter college, our kids trail all other developed nations by a large margin.

This statistically expresses the truth: Teachers and the entire educational establishment are academically inferior, are geared mainly to very young children, and have no place in the tutoring of anyone past the 4th grade.

In one telling anecdote, American children are shown to be highly deficient, the product of our backward educational establishment. In the Third International Mathematics and Science study, a worldwide competition among 21 nations, the American students scored 19th out of 21. They outperformed teenagers from only 2 underdeveloped countries, Cyprus and South Africa.

Dishearteningly, their scores were 20% lower than those of students in The Netherlands, a nation that must live mainly on its brainpower—as America increasingly is being forced to do.

In another discouraging competition, 24,000 13-year-olds from the United States, South Korea, the United Kingdom, Spain, Ireland, and Canada, chosen at random, were given the same 63-question math examination in their native language.

How did Americans do? Shockingly, they came in last. The South Koreans came in first, which demonstrated an interesting educational paradox. The math scores were in inverse ratio to the self-esteem responses. The Americans lost badly in math but they vanquished their opponents in self-confidence, a product of the American idea of promoting self-esteem rather than academics. The South Koreans, on the other hand, lost in the self-esteem contest, but won the coveted math prize.

This bears an uncanny relationship to the American education establishment, those in charge of teaching our children. They are confident, even arrogant, about their methods even though our children continue to fail.

Who is the primary villain in this scenario?

First, and surprising, it is the 50 states of the Union. Usually in the contest between the federal government and the states, it is the states that prove more stable and more reliable. For example, most states are required to balance their budgets while Washington runs amok in near-fatal debt. The states are also usually in the forefront of positive change as in new health plans that run more effectively than Medicaid for the poor.

However, in this case, the states are constitutionally responsible for elementary and secondary public education, which makes them the primary villains, although Washington is not far behind. The states are the villains because they have permitted, even openly aided, the educational establishment—the teacher unions, the education professors, the education colleges and education departments of universities, and the educational personnel from teachers to principals to superintendents—to operate as it sees fit, which is almost always at a very low academic level.

The basic problem is that unlike Europe and much of Asia, American teachers are chosen right out of high school at age 18, rather than out of a liberal arts college with a B.A. degree at age 22, as they generally are abroad. Most of our teachers do not have a degree from a legitimate liberal arts college. Instead, they are products of teachers colleges, now often disguised as regular colleges or universities, but with the same "education" curriculum, which is generally lower than that of a community college.

Only 15% of American teachers have graduated from a true liberal arts college. The rest come from an undergraduate college with an education major, even though some schools cleverly disguise the degree by falsely enrolling these students as sociology or psychology majors. But the basic curriculum is still "education," which is surely a nonexistent subject.

We know that definitively because Alternate Certification teachers, who have graduated from a real liberal arts college with no education training whatsoever, are graded by their peers as being better teachers than current Ed grads.

This, of course, is the basic reason for the poor performance of our children. Our youngsters develop well through the 4th grade, which appears to be the intellectual limit of the present teaching community.

The exact correlation between poor student performance and poor academic background of our teachers is no accident. The reason is that most teacher candidates occupy the academic basement of our high schools, generally graduating in the bottom third of the class, while the better students go on to liberal arts colleges and study everything from medicine to finance. Those in the high school class who intend to become teachers shockingly score lower on their SATs than their own future suburban students.

Young schoolteacher trainees just out of high school, however, are very happy to advance themselves from what would typically be a menial job to that of a "professional" career, teaching school.

Their academic ignorance is exploited by the leaders of the establishment, who are equally low in academic prowess. We know that exactly because the Graduate Record Exam (GRE), which tests eight different professions for admission to graduate school, shows that education graduates score in the bottom, or eighth, position—perhaps not surprising.

Among educators who rank at the absolute bottom of the GRE scale are elementary school teachers and school district superintendents and principals. Those administrators take a non-academic course of training, which leads to a false degree, doctor of education (Ed.D.), a much inferior diploma to that of a Ph.D., which was once considered necessary to become a principal or superintendent of schools.

Instead, these false doctoral graduates, who mainly study budgeting and public relations rather than liberal arts, become our principals and superintendents and still carry the honorific title of doctor, which confuses the American public who falsely believe they are scholars.

In academic accomplishment, the states are locked into this conspiracy of educational bureaucracy with the schools of education, the teachers union, and the state legislatures. They seem to have no way out. The only hope would be the intervention of the federal government, which although it does not educate a single child, does spend some $40 billion a year on K–12 education, all of which now seems to be wasted.

Why? The reason is the federal government, in the form of the obsolete Department of Education, is equally guilty with the states in our educational failure. Instead of forcing changes in the system through the use of its money, the federal government helps subsidize and maintain the present system of failure.

An example is some $16 billion in direct aid to K–12 plus $24 billion for No Child Left Behind. The latter program is under attack on two fronts: First, it hasn't been truly valuable in raising the test scores of students, and second, it has too large a price tag.

Critics in the educational establishment believe that No Child Left Behind concentrates too much on testing youngsters. From an objective viewpoint, that's probably the best aspect of the failed federal program. The teaching establishment would prefer to not teach our children properly, but wouldn't want anyone to know about it. So there is at least some value in the expensive testing, which our students mainly fail.

This is more than just proof of the ignorance of our students, our teachers, our administrators, and the entire educational establishment; it is also an indictment of the Department of Education, which, I repeat, does not, and never has, educated a single American child. Therefore, there is no mission for the department, and as critics once proposed, the department should be closed, with a savings of at least $40 billion a year.

But the dire story now gets even more horrific.

President Obama has made education one of his prime priorities and is spending $81 billion more from his giant stimulus package on federal programs to help educate our children. It is, of course, good money wasted after bad. Washington doesn't have a clue how to educate our children. But that fortune could, if Washington were more knowledgeable, do wonders to erase American student ignorance.

That is, if the president were willing to make a revolution in our failed public school system, which, so far, he hasn't.

What should actually be done to improve education in America? The answer, as the Europeans learned, is not to deal with the prospective universe of very low to mediocre 18-year-old high school graduates as the universe of future teachers.

Rather, we should close all undergraduate schools of education and all undergraduate departments of education, as most of the civilized world has already done. We should seek our teachers from a totally different group: 22-year-old graduates of true liberal arts universities, all of whom majored in anything other than education.

Once they have graduated with a true bachelor's degree, the better college graduates should take 1 year of teacher training, not the psychobabble now at the core of education colleges.

Having learned basic methodology married to academic excellence, they will be ready to teach a much higher curriculum and with higher standards than the present corps of undertrained, intellectually inferior teachers and principals. If such a revolution is accomplished, we will surely be able to compete internationally, perhaps even best most civilized nations, something we are not now able to accomplish.

Whether these new teachers study biology, math, history, or English, they should, like Europeans, be allowed to take up teaching only in graduate school. Europeans have discovered that system not only works but enables small nations like the Czech Republic to send math teachers to instruct New York City's undereducated kids in mathematics.

By doing the same here, the new teacher trainees will have established a well of knowledge to draw on and will learn to fashion a wholesome view of learning and scholarship that will make them competent teachers. This is unlike the near-children who now train in narrow, anti-intellectual schools of education controlled by the not-overly-bright education establishment.

What then is the role of the federal government in creating a good teacher corps, one far superior to the present obviously inferior group?

What can President Obama do with his $81 billion to achieve his goal of improving American education?

First, he has to truly enforce his Change slogan, and with enormous force. He has to get into the political trenches and fight the educational establishment in the Department of Education and in the Commissioner of Education offices in all 50 states, which are all part of, and wedded to, our present inferior system.

He needs to use the money to give many thousands of tuition scholarships to only superior liberal arts college graduates to attend graduate schools of teaching—students who have never seen or smelled an inferior education course, known in the trade as the "Mickey Mouse curriculum." He has to use the bully pulpit and the persuasion of money to close down the nation's inferior undergraduate schools of education, where knowledge is now dishonored.

He has to transform Change from a mere political slogan into a fighting one.

Having seen Washington spend federal billions on education to no avail, he has to learn the basics of good education in the trenches and fight the enemy, the anti-knowledge, ignorant educators who are persecuting our children with a process of dumbing down, of psychology instead of intellect, of condescension instead of truly earned confidence.

Is he up to it? Since he is a politician, probably not.

E

EMINENT DOMAIN

Has the Supreme Court Gone Senile?

My home is my castle.

This saying has long been an accepted part of common law and the essence of private property. No one can seize your home, except government, and then only in case of "eminent domain," a strong public need such as a highway or flood basin, and always with adequate compensation.

However, today that constitutional federal protection is only history. Your home is the government's, when they want it for any reason.

A recent Supreme Court ruling has made the title to your home a mere trifle in a local government's desire to supposedly improve its economy. Apparently, they can take your land not just for a public need but for a private moneymaking enterprise in which you will not only lose your home but receive none of the gain.

Americans are increasingly critical of both the legislative and executive branches of the federal government as they spend our hard-earned tax money without logic or concern. But the Supreme Court, which is the head of the third branch of government, the judiciary, has retained public trust—until now.

It was in the case of *Kelo v. The City of New London,* by a 5–4 decision, that the Court negated the once-supreme power of private property. It was part of that Connecticut city's intention to seize certain homes for private, not public, moneymaking economic development by others.

The plaintiff in the Supreme Court case, Suzette Kelo, opposed the New London, Connecticut, redevelopment plan, which intended to turn 90 acres of waterfront land into a private, for profit, development of office buildings, upscale housing, and a marina. The city planned to use eminent domain to seize the homes on the land, including that of Kelo, who had just remodeled her home and wanted to stay, especially because of the water view. She was joined by 14 other homeowners, such as Wilhelmina Dery, who was born in her house in 1918 and wanted to live out her life there.

Banking on the 5th Amendment to the Constitution, Kelo sued the city of New London, but the Connecticut Supreme Court upheld the city. The homeowners then appealed to the Supreme Court in Washington, which also ruled against them.

The 5th Amendment of the Constitution, part of the Bill of Rights, prohibits the taking of property by the government except in the case of needed public use. But Justice John Paul Stevens, who wrote the majority decision, arbitrarily stretched *public use* beyond such traditional public projects as highways and granted cities the right of home condemnation for private economic gain.

The excuse for that seizure was for such ephemeral activities as creating jobs and raising the city's tax income in the name of progress.

This, Justice Stevens stated, satisfied the restraints of the 5th Amendment to the Constitution, the handiwork of James Madison and other Founders. Of course, this is judicial nonsense. Close to 90% of Americans polled were appalled by the decision. Distrust in the federal government, which had already reached the stage of contagion, has now escalated into an epidemic.

In her dissent, Justice Sandra Day O'Connor noted that the most powerful people in society are benefited by such a decision, and small property owners may lose their homes with little recourse. "The specter of condemnation now hangs over all property," she warned. "Nothing is to prevent the states from replacing any Motel 6 with a Ritz-Carlton and any home with a shopping mall, and any farm with a factory."

Justice Rehnquist joined with Justice O'Connor and wrote that the majority had favored those with "disproportionate influence and power in the political process, including large corporations and development firms."

Perhaps the most scathing attack on the Court came from Professor Jonathan Turley of the George Washington University School of Law.

Speaking of the court's decision during congressional testimony, Turley stated: "Over 90 percent of Americans oppose the court's decision, the plain meaning of this amendment [the 5th], which was so lost on the court, is well understood by citizens." He added: "You might debate what public use means, but it is clear what it doesn't mean. It does not mean private use."

This tragic deficiency in judgment by the Supreme Court, which has now repealed the Bill of Rights, has become obvious.

One more agent of government has yielded to the fashionable temptations and prejudices of "modern" society. In doing so, they are violating proven American tradition and have presented us with a shifting relative scale of jurisprudence and public morality, a dismal swamp in which we may all drown.

No longer is our home our castle—thanks to the confused, too often irrational federal government, this time in the form of the once-sacrosanct Supreme Court.

Now, sad to say, they are just nine more government bureaucrats, masquerading as jurists in black robes.

F

FARMER SUBSIDIES

It's Time to Call It Quits

There was a time during the Great Depression when America's farmers faced desperately hard times. The New Deal passed the Agricultural Adjustment Act (AAA) in 1933 to help these distressed Americans.

The triple A used simple economics and reduced the supply of food to raise prices. Farmers were required to destroy 6 million piglets and 220,000 pregnant cows and to cut the cotton crop by plowing under 25% of their plants. In return, they received a subsidy check from the Department of Agriculture.

It worked somewhat. Food prices rose, but not as much as farmers' incomes, which increased 50% in the first 3 years. The AAA was then declared unconstitutional by the Supreme Court but was replaced by a similar piece of legislation routed around the court's objections.

Today, the American farmer is in a totally different position. The typical farmer, who tills some 2,000 acres of corn, for example, earns much more than the average American, yet regularly receives checks from Washington. Meanwhile, the typical middle-class family just sends checks to Washington. The farmer no longer has need of government help because he or she is farmer to the world, exporting efficiently raised food throughout the globe.

And equally important, today there are only 2 million farmers—less than 1 million full time—so that the subsidy pool, now some $20 billion a year, is a too-large sum for those farmers who receive government funds.

The prime rationale for the subsidies is supposedly the protection of the small, struggling family farm. But that group has virtually disappeared. Instead the subsidies mainly go to large farmers and agribusinesses plus "gentleman" farmers, corporations, and even celebrities who dabble in farming, shamelessly taking the government's money. But these multimillionaires seldom wear overalls.

The program favors the richest farms, with the largest 10% receiving 65% of the giant sums from Washington. In 2002, based on that farm bill, some 78 farms received $1 million each in subsidies, while 13 took in $2 million each from Uncle Sam. Some welfare. At the bottom, 80% of the recipients took in only 19% of the subsidies.

But the entire farm community is doing better than ever and is in no need of government welfare, which is basically what it is, although it is never called that.

"On average, farm households have higher incomes, greater wealth, and lower consumption expenditures than all U.S. households," says the U.S. Department of Agriculture. The average farm household earned $86,798 in 2008, about 27% more than the average American household. Incomes were even higher among the 136,000 farms with annual sales of $250,000, which also received the largest subsidies. Of those farmers, the average income of $180,000 is triple that of the national nonfarm family.

Farm income varies by states. California is the highest, with an average of $133,419 in 2007.

Traditionally, subsidies went only to growers of the five basic crops—corn, wheat, cotton, soybeans, and rice. But in the new 2008 farm bill, touted as a reform, the government has added subsidies for those who didn't need it, like California growers of vegetables and fruits. (As always, *reform* means more taxes for the average American who must pay, dearly, for these unneeded subsidies.)

The subsidy money goes everywhere, even to a number of Fortune 500 companies. In fact, 12 major corporations took in farm welfare, including $2.3 million for John Hancock Mutual Life Insurance, according to Brian Riedl of the Heritage Foundation. And nine members of Congress—including five who once sat on the Agriculture Committee—took in farm subsidies 46 times greater than those received by the median farmer.

Business celebs who drank at the agricultural trough include David Rockefeller and Ted Turner, whose subsidies, by normal standards, were rather large and obviously unneeded.

But because we are dealing with an irrational government, Washington insists on continuing to send checks to farmers who don't need it and who are now the recipients of the largest subsidies in our history, some two thirds of the $309 billion over the next 10 years.

This farm bill, passed in June 2008, was so extravagant, bordering on the corrupt, that it even aroused the opposition of

President George W. Bush, who had long been a political friend of the politically powerful farmer. In fact, in May 2008, he vetoed that farm bill, only to find Republicans and Democrats—almost all fans of the affluent farmer—joining together to override his veto and passing the bill triumphantly by a vote of 317–109.

The political rationale, as we have seen, is simple. A citizen of sparsely populated South Dakota, a major farm state, has 25 times the power of a citizen of New York, each of which has two senators. In the electoral college, voters in farm states have about double the power of a citizen of California.

Undaunted, farmers are proud of their political power and stick together, ever gaining more, and more.

George Bush tried to buck the farm lobby and eliminate direct government payments to all farmers whose gross income was more than $200,000, but Congress defeated him. Now, President Obama wants to cut direct payment to all farmers who take in more than $500,000 in sales, and already the farm belt, and its Washington politicians, are screaming foul.

Neither president tried going far enough. Why not instead subsidize the computer business, which is just as important? There is only one reasonable, fair solution to farm welfare. Repeal the farm bill of 2008 and close down all subsidies—now.

In that case, for humane purposes and to replace their lost farm welfare, we may just have to put David Rockefeller and Ted Turner on New York City home relief instead.

Fair enough?

F

FOREIGN AID

CAN'T WE GIVE AWAY $25 BILLION SMARTER?

In December 2004, an earthquake in southeast Asia caused a tsunami that devastated Indonesia and Sri Lanka. Congress rushed to aid, appropriating $908 million, most of it through the U.S. Agency for International Development (AID).

How well did this foreign aid project do? How did it compare with the usual inefficiency of Washington in domestic affairs?

Unfortunately, about the same if not worse. Most of the money was dedicated to two signature projects: the construction of a major road in Indonesia and the construction of a bridge and other infrastructure in Sri Lanka. In Indonesia, AID estimated construction cost per mile at $1.6 million. However, as the work progressed, they suddenly increased the cost by 75%, up to $2.7 million a mile.

This was a familiar event to those who follow federal contracting and its common cause, low balling designed to make the program look attractive—only to later face reality.

In addition, AID, by then strapped for contract cash, reduced the length of the road to be built from 150 miles to only 91 miles. Then the agency extended the completion date to February 2010, 5 months later than they had planned. As of January 2007, construction crews had begun to build only 26 miles of the road, and AID had not even awarded a contract for the construction of the remainder.

Simultaneously, the government of Indonesia had obtained less than one quarter of the nearly 3,700 right of ways needed to build the road.

In Sri Lanka, the activity was also failing. AID increased the estimated cost for this project by nearly 40%, from $35 million to $48 million. A report on these two projects showed that AID "lacked disaster recovery guidance, including the lessons learned from prior disaster reconstruction efforts."

America is heavily involved in foreign aid, some $25 billion a year. About $2 billion of that goes to support basic education for children in the poorest nations. A GAO report on that effort shows an incredible lack of coordination between five agencies doing much the same work: AID; the State Department; the Department of Defense; the Department of Labor; and the Millenium Challenge Corporation, the newest federal agency to help poor nations, one curiously designed to eliminate the lack of coordination in foreign aid.

This basic education program to eliminate illiteracy among children has increased considerably in cost. In 2001, it was $163 million. In 2006 it had risen to $506 million, or $2,228 billion in 5 years. Says the critical report: "In the eight countries we visited, we noted several instances where project implementers in the country did not collaborate or take advantage of opportunities to maximize U.S. resources in areas in which they had similar objectives of improving the quality of education."

The title of the report says it all: "Enhanced Coordination and Better Methods to Assess the Results of U.S. International Basic Education Efforts Are Needed."

A critical study of American food aid is even harsher.

The United States is the largest global food aid donor in the world, accounting for half of all food aid to alleviate hunger. But despite a $2 billion annual allotment from Congress, the federal agencies involved, AID and the Department of Agriculture, have apparently been doing a very bad job over the last 5 years. During that period, in which starvation, especially in Africa, has increased, our government has overseen an enormous decline—some 52%—in the average tonnage delivered to the hungry.

These two agencies were singled out for (1) poor planning that increased delivery costs and lengthened delivery time, (2) ocean transportation contracts that increased risk and thus raised costs, (3) awarding of contracts to more expensive service providers, and (4) the old bugaboo, the lack of coordination between the U.S. agencies and food stakeholders.

Summing up, the report states: "As a result, these programs are vulnerable to not getting the right food to the right people at the right time."

Oops.

By world standards, the United States is not a large contributor to foreign aid, considering its gross national product. That honor goes to Denmark and other developed smaller countries, which proportionately give four times the amount provided by Uncle Sam. In fact, the American contribution to foreign aid is heavily skewed in favor of our world political needs, which is perhaps the way it should be.

Israel, for example, gets almost $3 billion a year, whereas Egypt receives almost $2 billion. Both grants are connected to the Camp David accords shaped by President Jimmy Carter, which won him the Nobel Prize and which are the basis of the peace between the two previously antagonistic nations.

A substantial portion of the remaining American foreign aid goes to nations related to the present conflicts—namely Pakistan, Iraq, and Afghanistan. A sizable amount goes to what is referred to as the Middle East Partnership (MEPI), which is made up of Morocco, Algeria, Tunisia, and Jordan, Saudi Arabia, Yemen, Oman, Lebanon, Gaza, the West Bank, and the United Arab Emirates.

Several billion of the remainder goes to Africa for work with hunger and disease. including malaria and especially AIDS.

Americans are, of course, of two minds about foreign aid. As strong believers in the Judeo-Christian concept of charity and large contributors to private funds that help the poor overseas even more than does the American government, they are pleased to help others who are less fortunate than they are. But as skeptics on government spending, many Americans are wary about how foreign aid is spent, as well they should be.

Another federal audit shows that part of America's poor reputation overseas is due to the failure of the State Department and other agencies to publicize just how much we are helping other nations. One report reads: "Little reliable work has been done to assess the impact of U.S. assistance on foreign citizens' awareness of the source of U.S.-provided assistance." In simpler words, we're keeping our charitable image in the dark, and feeding into anti-Americanism.

The foreign aid programs of the United States are heavily criticized, with justification. But Washington is trying to fix the problem, especially the fact that so many agencies are involved and seldom talk to each other.

The government has tried to make two large changes to correct what the Brookings Institution has called the failure of American foreign aid. First, the State Department has named a director of foreign assistance to attempt a nationwide system of coordination and stop the duplication of work among the five agencies now involved.

Whether this will work out is problematic, for the virus of "the buck starts here" syndrome is endemic in Washington, with everyone trying to do everything, exemplified by the wide ambitions of the Department of Agriculture.

A congressional research report on the move says that the "current effort is the first step in a more thorough overhaul of U.S. foreign assistance," which most agree has been mainly a failure.

The second move was the creation of still another foreign aid agency, the Millenium Challenge Corporation (MCC), which is supposed to be different but that so far has managed only to add $3 billion a year to the budget, with no known benefit.

The MCC is supposed to deliver foreign aid in a novel way—designed to avoid the black hole of corruption in many poor countries and to coordinate the various programs and avoid duplication. The MCC was considered "brilliant" when it was introduced in 2004 because it supposedly would change the system by rewarding nations that were eliminating corruption and creating capitalist prosperity along with better democratic rule.

But experts now state that the program has achieved very

little, if anything, to date. Meanwhile, the taxpayers not only are supporting MCC but are still paying for all the old foreign aid programs, which continue their inefficiencies and their failure to work together.

As time goes on, there is only one constant, which has been obvious for some time. Foreign aid is much like our domestic aid programs, very Washington and very wasteful and inefficient.

What is the new administration's view of foreign aid?

During the campaign, President Obama pledged that during his first term of 4 years, he would double our investment in foreign aid to $50 billion. But can America afford such a program? And, second, shouldn't we fix the creaky present system before we expand it astronomically?

This may be a good public relations concept for the world, but it isn't realistic. We surely can't afford it. And what is going to make a troubled, inefficient program suddenly blossom into a working miracle just by doubling it?

Did you expect anything better just because we are spending our money overseas instead of wasting it right here in Washington?

G

GOVERNMENT FOOLISHNESS

CAN YOU BELIEVE WHAT'S GOING ON IN WASHINGTON?

We hear occasional snippets about Washington performing in eccentric, even foolish, ways.

I thought it might be edifying to try to compile a random list of miscellaneous items that collectively explain much about the Washington operation that bedevils the American public. Here then is a very partial compendium, from various sources, of government follies, which will, I hope, entertain and exasperate you.

- Investigators examining various federal programs found that in 38% of cases, programs failed to show any positive impact on the public they served. Still, Congress appropriated $154 billion to these programs in one recent year.

- Lawmakers took $13 million from Hurricane Katrina relief funds to build a museum celebrating the Army Corps of

Engineers, the federal group that built the levees that proved inadequate against the storm.

- Congress spends more on corporate welfare than on homeland security.

- In testing the Department of Education, investigators performed a sting and received $55,000 in student loans for fictitious students to attend a college that never existed.

- The Department of Agriculture paid farmers $2 billion not to farm their land.

- The inspector general of the Department of Health and Human Services reported that Medicare foolishly paid each of 203,377 ambulance claims, not once, but twice, at an extra cost of $21 million.

- The inspector general of the Health and Human Services Department sampled payments made by Medicaid and found that $27.3 million in benefits were paid to individuals who were already dead.

- Amtrak, the federal railroad operation, costs taxpayers some $1.3 billion a year. Worse yet, it seems those who run it are amateur businessmen, losing $245 million in selling meals and drinks on the train, hardly a difficult job considering they have a captive audience of customers.

- Much of an $8 billion federal program for 9/11, designed to repair damaged New York offices near Ground Zero, ended up going to build luxury condos and other buildings not in lower Manhattan.

- Of 80 in-house thefts of money at the IRS, 12 of the employee crooks had previous arrests before they were hired.

- A check of the Coast Guard Academy found that $107,000 of purchased laptop computers and printers weren't inventoried and were suddenly missing. A broker was paid $228,000 to procure 11 flat-bottom boats, but only 9 arrived in the government's hands.

- Government employees who use trains and buses instead of cars to commute qualify for a benefit of $105 a month. But many of them still sought out free subway Metrochecks, and 58 of them auctioned the "check" off on the Internet to the highest bidder. One married couple in the Defense Department took in $6,000 for benefits they didn't consume.

- A recent Defense Appropriation bill included $13.2 million for several military-themed museums throughout the country, from Hawaii to New York.

When I say this is only a partial list of ludicrous Washington operations, all I can add is that by multiplying these by 100, or perhaps 1,000, you'll just be approaching the total, heart-shattering truth about our dysfunctional government.

G

GOVERNMENTS, GOVERNMENTS, GOVERNMENTS

86,000 of Them Is Just Too Much for Taxpayers

If you live in Westchester County, New York, a relatively affluent suburb of New York City, you are quite familiar with the tax man. Local taxes there are among the highest in America, as are New York State income and sales taxes.

That high taxation is understandable, for Westchester, like many counties in America, is overstuffed with governments. In that one county alone, the people have to put up with 43 different formal governments, including six cities, 14 townships, 23 villages, and scores of special tax districts, all with their hands in the taxpayer's pockets. It is too much for the taxpayer to bear or even contemplate.

At the core of this tax punishment is the American county, a political subdivision between the local government and the state, one that was here before the states, based on the old English system. It's an expensive piece of history because the 3,043 counties cost the taxpayers $225 billion a year, supporting, among other things, 2.5 million county employees.

The county is a strange political animal. Sometimes it is small and insignificant as Loving, Texas, with a population of 107 people. Other times it is a massive and wasteful organization such as Los Angeles County, California, with a population of 9 million people, more than 44 of our states. It is indecipherable in that it covers the entire city of Los Angeles and 88 additional cities, including Pasadena, Long Beach, and Beverly Hills, duplicating much of the cities' functions.

Chicago is another massive case in point. Cook County includes all of Chicago and several suburbs, all doing much the same work, twice over. In an inverse case, New York City is made up of five counties called "boroughs," long considered useless political units.

When the country was first founded, based upon the English system, counties were indispensable because they provided the first internal boundaries within the colonies. Later, they were included in the new states and western territories. But today, the county is an unneeded intermediary between the states and localities, duplicating, very expensively, virtually every function of government with the cities, towns, villages, and states.

In the hamlet of Armonk, Westchester County, New York, the waste and duplication can be seen right on its Main Street, when a car from the Westchester police department pulls up alongside another police car, this one from the local North Castle police department, both there to do the very same job.

Within the counties, there is another massive form of pseudo-government, the so-called special districts, covering everything from school districts to swimming pool districts, all with the same taxing power of the county. In total, there are 33,000 of these special districts, a large part of the 86,000 governments, which also includes another form of government, the "unincorporated areas" of the townships.

It is, in common parlance, a bureaucratic mess.

But why complain? Isn't the county, the center of this bureaucracy, a necessary unit? Apparently not.

Just a few yards away from little Armonk, New York, is the state line that separates New York State from Connecticut. But that small distance equals many millions in cost to taxpayers. If a house in Armonk, part of Westchester County, New York, costs the homeowner $20,000 a year in local property taxes, walking across the street to a similar house in Connecticut, in nearby Fairfield County, is likely to run only half in property taxes, saving the homeowner $10,000.

How is that possible? Because, in fact there is no longer a Fairfield County, Connecticut, to tax the people. It is now only an extinct name on an uncorrected map. In fact, there are no longer *any* counties in Connecticut. In 1960, then-Governor Abe Ribicoff, with one stroke of the pen, revolutionized the state by eliminating all counties, breaking up the state into 169 municipalities, making them the only existing governments in the state, closing down all tax-collecting counties and hundreds of local bureaucracies.

If America were to contemplate doing the same nationally, the first step would show a savings of at least $100 billion a year from the cost of county governments. That would also eliminate the 33,000 special districts, which would be incorporated into the new municipalities in the county-less setup, as they are in Connecticut. That one step would not only close the 3,053 counties and the special districts but the 16,666 townships as well.

If the 48 other state legislatures (Rhode Island never had counties) were to learn from Connecticut, that one stroke would cut the size of government in America down from 86,000 units to 40,000 clearly defined, nonduplicative, independent municipalities—with a savings of at least $300 billion a year.

It's easily doable, as Connecticut has shown. But it has one obstacle: the politicians who live off bureaucracy, duplication, and outright bad government. They would rather you spend twice or more for your local government as long as they can get elected, and reelected, forever.

H

HOUSING, PUBLIC

ABUSE UNDER THE FEDERAL ROOF

Beginning in the 1930s, America became aware that the poor needed better housing and at an affordable cost to them. So began the massive, generally redbrick multistory public housing "projects" under the New Deal.

Today, almost 3 million people live in federally supported public housing, which puts a roof over their heads at a cost of about $300 a month to the tenants, and some $9 billion a year to taxpayers.

In addition, several million more people live in mostly private housing in which, under a program called Section 8, they are subsidized by the federal government at a cost of over $20 billion. In all, we spend more than $30 billion a year providing housing for the poor.

Some of the housing is simple and basic, but other units are rather luxurious, such as $1,300-a-month apartments in Stamford, Connecticut, where one would not expect the poor, who average $12,000 a year income, to live.

Philosophically, it is up to the taxpayer. Either he or she credits the government for taking care of the poor or resents the tax burden, which is becoming increasingly onerous.

But perhaps the larger problem is that all this housing is administered by the Department of Housing and Urban Development (HUD), by far the most corrupt and inefficient department of the federal government, which itself is not noted for its efficiency.

In the last few decades, there have been three HUD cabinet-level politicians who have resigned or been forced to resign, mostly as a result of improprieties and worse. In the Reagan administration, a full-scale scandal involved the agency and its relations with developers who used the government illegally to gain riches.

In the 1980s, HUD Secretary Samuel Pierce took the 5th Amendment and resigned after the government had appointed a special prosecutor to look into the agency's corrupt connection with developers. When the inquiry was completed, 16 HUD officials were convicted or resigned. Pierce himself was not charged with a crime. The special prosecutor said he decided not to prosecute Pierce because of his age and because he had not personally profited from the misdeeds of those under him.

One official, a former deputy assistant housing secretary, served an 18-month prison sentence for taking illegal gratuities from contractors. Former Congressman Tom Lantos exposed what he believed was the worst outrage of the scandal—the transfer of a career employee to keep him from reporting the wheeling and dealing at HUD to the inspector general.

Another HUD official, the former executive assistant to the

housing secretary, was convicted of 12 felony counts of defrauding the government, taking a bribe, and lying to Congress. Three other criminal convictions of former assistant secretaries of HUD confirmed how widespread the corruption was in the department.

HUD can play rough with its enemies. At the time of the scandal, David Burns, a senior staffer in the New York office, asked permission to talk to the press. It was surprising that it was granted, and HUD was later sorry. He told of political pressure put on department bureaucrats in the New York office, which made national headlines. Burns immediately paid a price for his whistle-blowing. The week after he went public he was excluded from senior staff meetings he had attended for a decade and was never invited back. "I've been isolated at HUD," he said.

Later, under President Clinton, Secretary of HUD Henry Cisneros, former popular mayor of San Antonio, resigned when he became involved in a lesser, more titillating scandal. Cisneros was accused of lying to the FBI regarding payments to his mistress. It all came out when his mistress of many years sued Cisneros for support. She taped their conversations and sold them to a tabloid, which brought it all to the attention of the FBI. Cisneros told the bureau that he had given the woman $60,000 over the years. But it turned out the true sum was actually over $200,000. Though supported by the Clinton administration, Cisneros resigned and became chief officer of a Hispanic television network.

Under George W. Bush, Alfonso Jackson became secretary of HUD in 2004. His undoing was not a matter of personal corruption but basically a comedy of errors that revealed the truth about the agency—that HUD has always been, and still is, a strictly political entity that rewards only its own with its large housing contracts.

His undoing was in revealing to the public what insiders have always known. On April 28, 2006, Jackson spoke at a meeting in Dallas on the subject of government contracting. He said a contractor gave him a "heck of a proposal" and ostensibly had the contract. But later, the contractor, the head of a minority advertising firm, said he didn't like President Bush. As a result, Jackson reportedly said that he did not give the developer the contract. This, of course, violated federal law, which supposedly has made federal contracts nonpolitical.

But of course, HUD has always been a political animal in handing out its billions to its friends, as the prior scandals showed. Senator Frank Lautenberg asked for Jackson's resignation, and the secretary obliged.

Providing housing for America's poor is a touchy and expensive proposition, and the agency has gone through a number of shifts in emphasis. For decades, they built large high-rise projects that invited crowding and crime, including narcotics and violent youth gangs. Lately, some 100,000 of these units have been demolished and the emphasis has switched to lower-density mixed-income developments.

In addition, there is now more emphasis on vouchers, in which tenants pay 30% of their income toward the rent, and HUD picks up the balance—the Section 8 program. This is very popular with tenants, but it has its drawbacks. It is quite expensive for the government, and it tends to reduce the desire of people to increase their incomes. And, of course, it invites fraud—of people purposely underestimating their incomes so that they can pay less rent.

In New York, the U.S. attorney general indicted 30 tenants for theft of government funds for collecting money from HUD not due to them because they lied about their income. In all, a $1,150,897 loss was charged, including money from a stock exchange employee who concealed her $96,000 salary, several Section 8 landlords who secretly lived with their tenants while collecting rent subsidies for their apartments, and a tenant who concealed her $70,000 income while buying a home elsewhere.

Although New York, which has some 100,000 Section 8 tenants, is more aggressive in prosecuting offenders, the fraud is perpetrated throughout the nation.

The Section 8 rental subsidies are based on the local price for apartments, the fair market rent (FMR). Unfortunately, the agency finds it hard to get the FMR right, at great extra cost to taxpayers. At two Section 8 projects in Rhode Island, rents were approved that were five times more than similar apartments. In one apartment complex, HUD increased the rents to 311% of the FMR, costing taxpayers an extra $17.5 million.

It is not just tenants that defraud the government under Section 8, but HUD officials as well. In Chicago, a former Section 8 manager was indicted for misusing federal funds. She invented fictitious "ghost tenants" and received $100 a month in subsidized rent for each one. On Long Island, New York, the chairman of the local housing authority (there are close to 3,000 of them nationwide) used landlords to cover his ownership of a property rented to a Section 8 tenant. He continued to collect $30,000 in rent payments for 2 years after the tenant moved out.

Other aspects of HUD are regularly abused. A $2.5 million HUD grant intended for low-income housing was used instead to build luxury homes, including a 5,300-square-foot house for the executive director of the local public housing authority.

Housing the poor is expensive—much too expensive at present—and obviously necessary. The question is how best to do it.

But one thing is certain: HUD is not the agency to rely on for this vital mission.

I

IMPROPER PAYMENTS

Gone with the Wind

How much money is Uncle Sam giving away, willy-nilly, to people, corporations, and others who are not entitled to the cash?

How much financial mayhem in improper payments could our government accomplish each year? What could be the extent of mistakes, and worse, resulting in improper payments that are depleting the beleaguered federal treasury?

Could it be as much as $1 billion a year? Heaven forbid.

It is sad to discover that our money, painfully earned and painfully paid to Uncle Sam, has been disbursed as if those in fiduciary responsibility were inebriated, or in the vernacular, dead drunk.

Cut to the chase. A recent study of Uncle Sam's finances shows the startling size of improper payments. In another recent study, covering 2006, it was admittedly $42 billion! Was that a 1-year freak? Hardly. It was $38 billion in 2005 and even higher, $45 billion, in 2004.

Yes, in just 3 years, Uncle Sam—you should excuse the vile street expression—pissed away $125 billion. In a decade, we're talking about a minimum $420 billion down the fiscal drain and into the sewer of federal financing. Improper payments are perhaps the fastest-rising of all federal costs. In 1999, the cost of improper payments was estimated at $19.1 billion, less than half of what it is today.

But that is hardly the full story.

"Some agencies have not yet reported for all risk-susceptible programs," says the report. "For example, in fiscal year 2006, total improper payment estimate of about $42 billion did not include any amounts of 13 risk-susceptible programs that had fiscal year 2006 outlays totaling about $329 billion."

One of these nonreporters is the Medicaid program, which spent $183 billion in federal funds that year and that, like Medicare, probably has over a 10% improper payments rate plus, of course, massive fraud. That adds another estimated $20 billion, which all by itself brings the loss rate up to $62 billion a year. A truly reasonable estimate, as we shall see, is closer to $100 billion or more down the financial drain each year.

But surely, the agencies that have reported the $42 billion a year loss have managed to recover the money once they learned it was sent out in error.

Hardly.

A total of $256 million, some 0.5%—a ludicrously small amount—was recovered, leaving $41.7 billion still irrevocably gone. When queried about the amount they had recovered, several agencies confessed that they didn't even try.

That was true of the Department of Housing and Urban Development (HUD), the Department of Education (one of the great improper payers), and the Department of Labor, which reported that it was not "cost beneficial" to try to get the money back.

Many agencies and cabinet divisions did not bother to report any improper payments at all, as if they were somehow free of that error. Those include the Export-Import Bank, the Federal Communications Commission, the FDIC, the Federal Trade Commission, the General Services Administration, the Medicare Prescription Drug program, the State Children's Insurance program, the entire Department of Commerce, and NASA, plus many other diffident, or worse, agencies.

These agencies are, of course, lying to both the government and the American public.

Improper payments are probably considerably higher—perhaps double or triple what the agencies, which are responsible for reporting these amounts themselves, actually state. That is, they simply lie. For example, the Government Accountability Office (GAO) checked up on improper payments in the cost of travel at the Department of Defense (DOD).

They found that the department's estimates were mostly fiction. The DOD told the government investigators that of the $8.5 billion spent on travel, only 0.1%, or $8 million, was improper. The GAO found that their claim was nonsense, that they were hiding millions more in losses.

First, only 10% of the $8.5 billion in travel expenditures was studied, which immediately raises the amount lost to $80 million. Then, sadly, the DOD excluded the improper travel payments of the entire U.S. Army, which would raise the risk by some 50%. "Finally," states the GAO, "the statistical sampling methodology and process used by DOD . . . had several weaknesses and did not result in statistically valid estimates of travel improper payments."

So much for self-reporting by federal agencies of money they facilely dispatched down the drain.

The Department of Agriculture is one of the worst offenders in every category of federal missteps. In 2005, it stated that its Marketing Assistance Loan program (loans for commodity purchase) had only $45 million in improper payments, or less than 1%. Then suddenly, in 2006, they decided to confess. The result is that $1 in every $5 (20.3%) they spent was an improper payment.

The loss to the government—eventually the people—was $1.6 billion, almost as much as the improper payments in the food stamp program, which reached $1.645 billion.

Agriculture also confessed in 2006 that their Noninsured Assistance program, which supposedly showed a loss of "zero" in 2005, had suddenly developed a large loss. In 2006, they admitted it was $25 million. Worse yet, that proved to be a catastrophic improper payment rate of 23%, almost $1 in every $4 spent by the relatively small agency.

Some agencies had similar high rates of missing monies. The U.S. Speaker and Specialist Program, part of the State Department, lost $1 in every $4 to improper payments. The numbers were, of course, higher in large-dollar agencies like HUD, whose Section 8 Tenant-Based program had improperly sent out a fortune—some $723 million.

Similar large amounts were permanently gone at the Department of Education, whose Pell Grants mistakenly gave recipients and others $422 million in misapplied funds and an additional

$401 million in Federal Family Education loan disbursements.
Even Head Start finds that $210 million is effectively missing.

The exact cost to taxpayers in this frivolous waste of big
money will probably never be known. But we know of at least $62
billion a year, which does not include improper payments from
some $200 billion in other expenditures. Plus, and perhaps equally
important, we know that the agencies have a tendency to lie.

How much we may never know. But the cost of $100 billion
a year in improper, fiscally catastrophic payments gone from the
treasury is most realistic, perhaps even understated.

What can be done?

What can and must be done is to totally reorganize and
cleanse the entire federal government, a task that is far beyond
the grasp of the present group of American politicians.

While we await a political messiah, I will make a futile stab
at it in "Conclusion: Instructions for the President" (p. 324).

J

JOB TRAINING

Can 160 Programs Really Work?

There are several things wrong with the federal job-training programs that have existed for two generations, costing the taxpayers up to $20 billion a year.

Surely these programs are better than nothing, especially in times of high unemployment, but they are very duplicitous and provide few jobs, and those they do provide come at great expense.

"The history of federally funded job-training programs strongly suggests that WIA (Workforce Investment Act) will not substantially raise participants' incomes. Similar programs funded under the Job Training Partnership Act (JTPA) were found to be largely ineffective," says David Muhlhausen, Ph.D., senior policy adviser at the Center for Data Analysis.

The government itself is skeptical of its many job-training programs. The Government Accountability Office (GAO) shocked

Congress when it reported that half the federal job programs failed to track the results of their work—that is they never checked whether their job training actually produced any jobs.

The first problem is that there are too many programs trying to do the same job and falling over each other's feet. At last count, and this is rather unbelievable, Washington supports 163 different job-training programs in some 14 different federal agencies, all uncoordinated and generally unevaluated, or falsely so.

Only 11% of the job-training agencies actually conducted studies to find out if they were effective. The GAO also found extensive duplication and inefficiencies that frustrates job seekers and even employers looking for workers.

"Despite spending billions each year, most federal agencies do not know if their programs are really helping people find jobs," said a GAO official covering employment issues.

One of the greatest frustrations comes from the chance to help disadvantaged youth, often from the inner city, who are high-school dropouts and most of whom have never held a regular full-time job. The government's answer to that quandary is a complex and expensive program called the Job Corps, which handles about 65,000 workers aged 16 to 24 in over 100 centers, where they often live together and train for up to a year. The costs are high, about $1.5 billion a year, or some $23,000 per participant, a cost that has outraged critics.

The problem is that the training is mostly in the classroom, where the government tries to make up for the deficiency of K–12 education by providing remedial education, along with some vocational training, again mainly in the classroom.

In many ways it is a social work program as well as job training, hoping to make the student employable. The students get health and academic education, learn to drive, and learn how to live with others. They receive medical examinations, tests for drug use and pregnancy, and dental exams and treatment— basically a wide-ranging attempt to make up for a deprived childhood.

A major goal of the program is the GED, the high school equivalency certificate, which many of the participants, if they stay in the program, do receive. Unfortunately, there are dropouts there as well, and the average stay at a Job Corps center is only 7 months.

Controversy surrounds the results of this program, with some believing that it is of value, and others convinced that it is just another government boondoggle, and an expensive one at that. Critics also point out that the program takes care of only 65,000 youngsters when millions of high school dropouts are in need of practical training and a job with a future.

Somewhat discouraging is that a government audit of the program refuted the Job Corps's own estimate that it was generally successful in training these youngsters. The Department of Labor, which runs the Job Corps, reported that 62% of its graduates were placed in jobs in the private sector. But the audit challenged that, casting doubt on 41% of those purported job placements. Often, youngsters trained in healthcare or masonry were found instead to have been placed in a job flipping hamburgers, which requires no training at taxpayers' expense.

But either way, the Job Corps misses the point in the training of young men and women. That point is made every day by the successful apprentice work program in Germany, which starts off millions of young people in good industrial jobs. The American Job Corps is basically a theoretical social work policy "wonk" idea, like many federal programs, that has little basis in practical reality.

Meanwhile, the German apprentice program uses most of the country's industry to employ millions of its young, whether they are college material or not, an idea generally ignored in America.

The apprentice program began hundreds of years ago in the form of the craft guilds of the Middle Ages. Today, that program has been expanded so greatly that two thirds of Germany's young (aged 16 to 19) participate in apprentice programs, working toward certification in some 380 different occupations, from electronics to computers to bricklaying and plumbing and heating.

The program is considered the core of Germany's amazing industrial might, which has long made that country the world's most successful exporter, a title it will probably relinquish to China in 2010.

Instead of being saddled with nonproductive high school dropouts, as we are, Germany combines high school studies with work beginning at age 16. If students were to drop out of high school, they would also lose their valuable apprenticeship, which actually pays them $500 a month while they attend school and work.

They generally work 3 days a week on the job and 2 days a week in technical school. After 3 years, if the trainee meets the standards set by the employer and the trade union, the apprentice takes a national exam and receives a certificate recognized throughout the country.

The German states fund the technical schools and the companies spend 2% of their payroll on the apprentice program. Because they have experience with the young trainee, more than half the companies employ them after they finish their apprenticeship.

After working for a few years, the former apprentices can take additional training and pass other exams to become a *meister*, or "master," often setting up their own businesses and training other apprentices.

The American system in training youth for jobs is a failure, yet such an apprentice program could salvage millions of wasted young lives. But the federal government, which now only dabbles in apprentice programs, is not only ill-equipped to run such a program but stubbornly resists adopting the German system, opting to try to make every dropout a college aspirant, an impossible and not necessarily desirable goal.

Many youngsters who fail in conventional schools would thrive in a work-oriented apprentice program, which can build dignity and a strong work ethic in teenagers who are bored and even disruptive in a conventional book-learning school.

The same technique might be applied to adults instead of the present job-training programs. As part of the GI bill, I got my first reporting job because the government paid the newspaper half my salary as a hiring bonus for the first year. If we take the $20 billion now spent on job training and gave employers a $20,000 bonus for each adult hire, it would mean almost a million new jobs every year.

Washington doesn't need more of the same, which they insist on. Success in job training, as in other government programs, requires a closer connection to the real world instead of the insulated theoretical Washington nonsense.

Whenever you see a classroom training project you're staring at defeat. Whenever you see a trainee on the work floor at the job, success is surely in the air.

Can Washington itself ever be trained to do its job?

K

KATRINA

A FLOOD OF FRAUD

Much has been written about this massive hurricane of 2005, one of the worst in American history. One result was a flood that nearly destroyed New Orleans and that has been the subject of anger and frustration ever since.

The head of FEMA, the agency responsible for alleviating the hell of the storm, resigned after tardy and sloppy action in the aftermath that displaced several hundred thousand citizens of the city and neighboring Gulf Coast communities.

The best description of the failure of government was, of course, done by the opposing party, in this case the Democrats, after the Republican administration failed miserably. Not that the Democrats would have done any better, but being in opposition, they had the most to gain from describing the bureaucratic mayhem that accompanied the storm.

In August 2006, the minority Democratic staff of the House of Representatives' Committee on Government Reform, through its Special Investigative Division, issued its report, aptly titled "Waste, Fraud, and Abuse in Hurricane Katrina Contracts."

A summary of that report indicates the basic inability of the federal bureaucracy—Republican or Democrat—to solve the simplest emergency problem, let alone a catastrophe like Katrina.

A digest of the bureaucratic mayhem follows:

- In its introduction, the report identifies 19 Katrina contracts, worth $8.75 billion (only a small part of the total federal cost) that have experienced "significant overcharges, wasteful spending, or mismanagement."

- Of the $10.6 billion awarded to private companies in 1,237 contracts, only 30% were awarded in full, open competition.

- The never-learn syndrome: In August 2006, FEMA awarded another $1 billion in contracts to companies already implicated in wasteful Katrina spending.

- Over 550 reports from the Defense Contract Audit Agency, the Government Accountability Office, and several inspectors general showed waste, fraud, and abuse in the Katrina relief programs.

- FEMA spent $3 million for 4,000 camp beds that were never used.

- About $10 million was spent to renovate military barracks that were used by only 6 occupants, or more than $1.5 million per person.

- The "Blue Roof Deal": The government contracted with

three main suppliers to put temporary roofs on wind-damaged homes using blue tarps, at a cost of $300 million. However, in many instances, these contractors subcontracted the work to others, becoming highly paid middlemen at the government's expense. Then many of the subcontractors subcontracted the work, creating another level of contractors. According to one published account, says the House study, a tiered contract was 1,700% higher than the job's actual cost. A second account reported that the taxpayers paid an average of $2,480 per roof for a job that should have cost under $300.

· Corruption: According to the inspector general of Homeland Security, there were 1,395 cases of criminal activity then under investigation in the work done to alleviate Hurricane Katrina. In one case, two FEMA officials pled guilty to accepting bribes from a food service contractor. They demanded a $20,000 payment plus $2,500 a week for inflating the number of meals provided by the contractor.

· The Army Corps of Engineers awarded four contracts worth $500 million each, or $2 billion, to remove and dispose of debris created by Katrina. But lax government oversight allowed the contractors to double the bill for the same debris, overstate mileage, and inflate prices by mixing low-cost debris with high-cost construction and demolition debris. One favorite trick was to mark up the prices by not fully unloading the trucks, thus getting paid twice. Say the auditors: "This provides the opportunity for truck drivers to leave debris in the bed of the truck while receiving full credit for each load."

- In the aftermath of Katrina, the government bought 24,967 manufactured homes and 1,755 modular homes for $915 million to provide housing and temporary office space for victims and relief workers. But by January 2006 only 4,600 manufactured homes had been used. Why? Because not one house could be sent to the most ravaged areas. Government regulations prohibit the use of homes in floodplains—where the most damage was done! More than 2,360 manufactured homes could not be used at all because they exceeded FEMA's size specifications, the ultimate federal bureaucratic nightmare. Just 6 months after Katrina, 11,000 homes worth over $3.9 billion were still sitting on the runway at an Arkansas airport.

So much for Washington, yesterday, today, and tomorrow.

L

LAND GRAB

HOW THE WEST WAS LOST—
TO WASHINGTON

There is a new real estate boom in the U.S. Southwest, especially in the deserts of Arizona, Nevada, and California.

In the desert? And why now, when real estate is generally in a downward trend?

The answer is the new boom in solar energy. Spurred on by a substantial federal subsidy, hundreds of small solar plants, some only experimental, are filling the desert where the sun is strongest.

In Arizona, for example, it is a thriving new industry that has an enormous future. In fact, the world's largest solar plant is coming to Arizona in 2011 and will create enough electricity from Old Sol to power 70,000 homes.

For that area of America, the future lies in solar power, capable of transforming the desert into a busy factory for electricity. It will mean jobs, hundreds of millions, perhaps billions, of dollars—if only new solar operations are allowed to progress at an entrepreneurial pace.

The desert has been humming in the past few years, until July 2008 when the U.S. federal government abruptly, and foolishly, called a halt to all solar activity in such sunbaked desert states as Arizona. The work was put on a 2-year moratorium by the Bureau of Land Management (BLM) in Washington so that the agency could conduct an environmental study before America could proceed with making the solar power it needs.

The energy industry viewed that edict as catastrophic for the burgeoning solar technology and contradictory to Washington's generous subsidy for solar development.

"It doesn't make any sense," said an executive of Asura, a solar thermal energy company. "The Bureau of Land Management has some of the best solar resources in the world. This could completely stunt the growth of the industry."

The spokesperson for the BLM pointed out that the environmental 2-year study was necessary to determine various factors, including the effect on water supply and, of course, on such endangered species as the desert tortoise and the Mohave ground squirrel.

But how could Washington tell the state of Arizona what to do with its commerce and its desert? Isn't Arizona a sovereign state in charge of its own business?

Not really. It turns out that since the federal government owns only 0.04% of the land in Connecticut, that state can do what it wants with electricity, solar, or anything else. But Arizona cannot.

The reason is a result of history. Connecticut was here before the United States, so that it didn't have to cede any land to Washington when the federal government was formed in 1789. In fact, there are 10 states in which the federal government owns less than 2% of the land, stretching from New York to Maine.

But when Arizona was allowed to become a state in 1912, a virtually unilateral deal was conducted by Washington, which decided on its own to appropriate (seize) almost half of all the state's land—exactly 48.1%—for itself, which it has held since that date. It was as if Washington had won the land in a war against a weaker enemy, which in a figurative sense it had.

It is not just Arizona that has Washington as an arbitrary landlord. Unlike the eastern states, 12 western states are virtually dominated by the federal government and controlled by the Bureau of Land Management and several other agencies, such as the Forest Service and the Fish and Wildlife Service.

In Nevada, Alaska, Utah, Oregon, and Idaho, the federal government owns a majority of the state's land. Washington also owns almost half of the land in Arizona, California (45%), Wyoming (42.3%), New Mexico (41.8%), and Colorado (38.6%). When Nevada entered the union in 1864, Uncle Sam expropriated 84.5% of its land, leaving only a sliver for the citizens of the state to use and develop as they wish. Washington holds on to that enormous land grab to this day.

The extent of the land owned by Washington is shockingly large. In all, the U.S. government has direct ownership of almost 650 million acres of land, nearly 30% of all of the territory in the United States, an area larger than all of the United Kingdom, France, Germany, Italy, and Japan combined.

The national parks, which are a legitimate holding of the federal government, are only a small part, some 15%, of the federal lands and less than 5% of all America, a perfectly reasonable ownership.

Not only does Washington own its land in the West and elsewhere outright, but it controls the land in a rather imperious manner, as was witnessed by that recent Bureau of Land Management edict to stop all research and activity for solar energy.

The arbitrary anti-development history of federal lands within state borders is epidemic today. The government-owned lands of the Rocky Mountain area hold a world-record amount of oil in the Bartlett Shale formation. It exists in the form of rock shale, mainly in Colorado, Utah, and Wyoming.

The oil is now easily recoverable by high technology. In fact, a recent report by the Department of Energy's Argonne National Laboratory states: "Even a moderate estimate of 800 billion barrels of recoverable oil from oil shale in the Green River Formation in those three states is three times greater than the proven oil reserves of Saudi Arabia."

Oil shale contains a chemical called kerogen, oil that never made it to the liquid stage. But with modern technology, including heating it to 700°F, the oil just oozes out. In addition, these same Rocky Mountain basins hold a record reserve of natural gas, ready for use in its natural state.

But, unfortunately, Washington owns some 70% of the Rocky Mountain shale land and has steadfastly refused to allow the states and private interests to develop these much-needed resources. As recently as 2008, the U.S. House of Representatives voted against allowing the issuance of leases to develop these vital oil and gas deposits.

But in Texas, things are different. That prosperous state, filled with oil and gas development, is mining the Barnett Shale area in their state for natural gas, including tapping it right in downtown Fort Worth.

But why can Texas benefit from these deposits while Colorado is stuck with an obstinate, unsympathetic federal government? The answer is straightforward. While Washington has reduced Colorado's land ownership to only 38%, and Utah owns less than 50% of its land, Texas escaped the long hand of Washington.

Why and how? Simple.

When Texas entered the Union, it did so with a strong bargaining chip. In 1845, when Texas applied for statehood, it was already a sovereign nation, the Republic of Texas, not ready to submit to Washington's excessive demands. That was quite unlike the other Western territories, which had no bargaining power and were quite willing to hand over much, or most, of the most valuable mining lands in the world to Washington to gain statehood.

The result is that only 2% of Texas is owned by the federal government, which accounts for the success of its vibrant oil and gas industry, developed on state-controlled land for the general prosperity of Texas. Texas and Connecticut are case histories of what a state can do when it is not parceled in two by the federal government and its imperious Bureau of Land Management.

But there is a positive lesson in this unfortunate land grab. When the citizens of Arizona and neighboring Western states learned about the halt of the solar power industry in their deserts, they howled so loudly that Washington and its bureaucrats eventually backed down and allowed Old Sol to continue making electricity for the state and the nation.

What's next? Because Washington has shown that it cannot manage these lands in the best interests of either the states or the nation, citizens should demand the return of all mineral rights, including oil and gas, back from Washington to the states. They can then develop them properly by calling on commercial lease-holds, which will bring the states enormous royalties.

This is only fair because the rights were taken away from the former territories years ago, when they were too weak to fight Washington.

As a result of such arrogant federal mismanagement, debate should start on the final objective. We should return all federal land—except for national parks—to the states so that they, and the American people, can reap the harvest of our own good earth.

Washington succeeded in its initial land grab. Now it's time for the American people to regain their birthright.

L

LOBBYISTS

What Can We Do with These People?

Article I of the Constitution, the first item in the Bill of Rights, spells out clearly that Congress should pass no law that would impede the people's right to free speech, free exercise of religion and press, "or the right of the people peaceably to assemble, and to petition the government for a redress of grievances."

That right to petition, which the framers innocently inserted in the Bill of Rights, has now grown into a massive industry called "lobbying," with more ingenious and devious operations than the Founders could ever have imagined.

No laws have been passed to limit our freedom of speech, except in the case of slander or in the event that it triggers chaos, as in yelling "fire" in a crowded auditorium. But in the case of lobbying, the government has constantly felt pressed, correctly, to regulate that enormous and growing industry, including forcing lobbyists in Washington to register and even, in some cases, to register as "foreign agents" when they represent other countries.

What started as a decent civil right has now morphed into a highly paid, too often corrupt civilian army of such proportions that the phenomenon seems to backfire on the American democracy. What some still call the right to "petition the government for redress of grievances" is now more likely highly paid, often corrupt, influence peddling.

The cost to petitioners is enormous, a cost naturally passed on to the American taxpayer through higher prices from corporations or fees from service organizations and associations. In 2007, figures show that the lobbying business spent $2.8 billion trying to influence politicians and the federal government. That is double the price of 7 years ago, with one third more lobbyists on the job, a dimension of influence over government never envisioned by the Founding Fathers.

Today there are 17,000 registered lobbyists, typically earning a lot more than the 535 members of the House and Senate, who are regularly in their gun sights. In 2008, the winner in lobbying outlay belonged to the pharmaceutical industry, which spent $227 million. Educators added $88 million to our school costs in lobbying fees, while our health professionals, including doctors and hospitals, paid out $70 million to protect their economic interests from potentially damaging federal regulations.

What makes lobbying such a generally disliked, perhaps pervasively negative industry is that the best and most effective lobbyists are the same people who only a few years before were making or executing our laws. No one is more effective as a lobbyist than a former representative who only a year before was holding subcommittee hearings on the same legislation he or she is now trying to influence on behalf of some corporation or industry.

In fact, the lobbyist often knows more about the situation than the member of Congress, who is sometimes quite willing to have the expert lobbyist aid in the drafting of legislation.

We have already seen the extent of the revolving door, the phenomenon of former members of Congress and former federal officials now serving as lobbyists pressing the government to do things their way, while the average American has little political power to seek a "redress of grievances."

In all, there are now 68 former members of the House who, from 1998 to 2005, moved just a mile away to K Street in Washington as lobbyists, with a raise in pay from $165,000 to upwards of $500,000, or even $1 million a year. A study by Public Citizen of the swift movement from Congress to Lobby-land shows that 43% of the eligible Congressmen who left Congress have become registered lobbyists. The percentage in the Senate was even higher, some 50%, or 18 out of 36 senators, a statistic that should shock sleepy citizens.

Former party officials are also in great demand as lobbyists. Former Republican Party chief Marc F. Racicot, who had also been governor of Montana, was granted a $1 million-a-year salary as president of the American Insurance Association, a potent lobbying group whose industry spent $136 million in 2007 trying to influence the government.

Another fertile pool of lobbyist candidates is former executive branch executives, who have moved from 1600 Pennsylvania Avenue to a K Street address with an enormous raise in income.

That includes former Attorney General John Ashcroft, now a successful lobbyist; Charles Black, a former official in the Reagan administration; Jim Blanchard, former governor of Michigan; Linda Daschle, former Federal Aviation Administration head who is now a leading airline lobbyist; Kenneth Duberstein, former chief of staff to a Republican president; Rich Gold, a former Clinton administration official; Jack Quinn, a former White House official also under President Clinton; and Jonathan Yarowsky, once a senior attorney for President Clinton.

Some lobbying firms are quite bipartisan, because unlike straight politics, money trumps ideology. For instance, Ann Wexler, a former aide to President Clinton, has a Republican partner, former Congressman Bob Walker.

The revolving door from government officialdom to lobbying, and often back again to government, can sometimes seem crude in its strong swings. In 2007, some 90 officials of the Department of Homeland Security and the White House Office of Homeland Security left government employ to take jobs as lobbyists and executives in companies that sell security products, many directly to the federal agencies they once ran.

"People have a right to make a living," said Clark Kent Ervin, the former inspector general of the Homeland Security Department, "but working virtually immediately for a company that is bidding to work in an area where you were just setting the policy—that is too close. It is almost incestuous."

Another source of talent to peddle influence is former staff members to both the legislative and executive branches and to the presidential campaigns of both parties. Lobbyist Dan Tate Jr. is a former congressional and White House aide. Other staffer-lobbyists include Alan Roth, former chief counsel to the House Energy and Commerce Committee; Melissa Schulman, a former aide to House Majority Leader Steny Hoyer; Jarvis Stewart, chief of staff to Representative Harold Ford Jr.; and Daniel

Mattoon, former top aide to former Republican House Speaker Dennis Hastert.

Most lobbyists are quite honest and straightforward about their jobs, but the apparent innocence is clouded by the fact that many are former members of Congress or executive branch officials or staff members. They not only are close to government but are wise in the arcane ways of Washington, which gives their clients great advantage over the American citizens, who have no effective way to "redress grievances."

Their only outlet is their vote for either party, organizations that are themselves at the core of the lobbying industry.

One massive source of conflict, one that philosophically taints the entire industry, is that lobbyists are permitted to give money to the campaigns of elected politicians, or their PACs. In some circumstances, that money might be seen as subtle, or not so subtle, legal bribes. In fact, contributions of campaign cash to members of Congress from lobbyists are enormous. In 2008, they were an estimated total of $140 million, a flood of cash that can hardly be overlooked by citizens seeking cleaner government.

Congress periodically passes new reform bills aimed at cleaning up the relationship between lobbyists and legislators. But most prove to be useless because they are easily twisted to benefit the lawmakers.

In 2008 Congress passed a new "ethics" law that prohibits lobbyists from treating lawmakers to meals, free vacations, discounted use of private jets, and other traditional goodies. But the new regulations are smoothly avoided by both members of Congress and lobbyists. The trick is quite simple. Instead of the lobbyists giving them the goodies directly, the gifts of trips and other benefits are funneled through campaign fund-raising committees.

Included in this "legal" subterfuge are such fund-raising outings as lavish birthday parties, high-priced meals at posh Washington restaurants, hunting and fishing trips, and weekends at
Disney World. The campaign finance committees arrange all the
goodies for the lawmakers and are apparently exempt from the
new ethics laws. Mellifluously labeled the Honest Government
and Open Leadership Act, the new ethics regulation is an obvious sham.

Meredith McGehee, policy director of the Campaign Legal
Center, says that organizing a fund-raising trip does not have the
onus of accepting a free vacation, "but that at the end the day it
is the same thing. Members of Congress are becoming more and
more creative in finding ways to engage lobbyists to help pay for
their campaigns."

Previously, the lobbyists directly picked up the tab for all
goodies, but under the new ethics act, it is very much the same
except that now the congressman's or the party's campaign finance committee pays for the very same outings and parties.

The influence of money and gifts combined with influence
peddling can jointly create deep and grievous corruption. That
was shown in the case of lobbyist Jack Abramoff, now serving
time in a federal penitentiary.

The Abramoff case came to a head in January 2007 when
Congressman Robert W. Ney was sentenced to 30 months in
prison followed by 2 years of supervised release. He was also
ordered to serve 100 hours of community service for each year.
Ney pled guilty to two counts of conspiracy to commit multiple
offenses, including honest services fraud and making false statements.

Ney admitted that he corruptly solicited and accepted items

of value from Abramoff and his employee lobbyists, including international and domestic trips, meals and drinks, concert and sporting tickets, and tens of thousands of dollars of campaign contributions plus in-kind contributions such as free fund-raisers with the intent to be influenced to take official actions on behalf of the lobbyists.

His free trips included a golfing voyage to Scotland. Another prime goodie was use of a luxury box at Camden Yards, the Baltimore Orioles' baseball stadium.

Ney admitted that he agreed to work on behalf of the lobbyists' clients, including opposing legislation they did not want passed. He also agreed to insert certain statements in the *Congressional Record*, and as chairman of the House Administration Committee—better known as the "Mayor of Capitol Hill"—he helped propel an application for a contract to install wireless telephone infrastructure in the House of Representatives.

The disgraced congressman had also accepted thousands of dollars' worth of gambling chips from a foreign businessman, who was hoping to send U.S.-made airplanes and airplane parts to a foreign country, and agreed to help the businessman obtain exemptions from U.S. laws prohibiting the sale of these goods to the foreign country.

That conviction and the guilty pleas of Jack Abramoff and his four lobbying associates are collectively known as the Jack Abramoff Case, a series of events that revolved around this very accomplished and corrupt lobbyist, who was the one who induced Congressman Ney and possibly others to break their civil oath.

Abramoff, a former Hollywood producer, carried out his work as if it were a script for a film. He was a colorful and accomplished lobbyist who diverted millions of dollars from various Indian tribes into the hands of several members of Congress. He and his aide, Michael Scanlon, a former press secretary to a congressman, ostensibly received $82 million from wealthy Native American tribes, who operated gambling casinos, to secure favorable legislation.

On January 3, 2006, Abramoff pled guilty to a series of charges involving fraud, tax evasion, and conspiracy to bribe public officials. In a deal with federal authorities, Abramoff pledged to provide evidence against other members of Congress, as well as congressional staffers, Interior Department workers, other executive branch officials, and fellow lobbyists.

Abramoff admitted to defrauding four wealthy Indian tribal clients out of millions of dollars and also pled guilty to inducing former Capitol Hill staffers to violate the 1-year ban on lobbying their former bosses when they changed status from staffers to lobbyists. Abramoff received a sentence of 9.5 to 11 years and must make restitution of $26.7 million to the IRS and to the Indian tribes he defrauded. Standing before a U.S. District Judge, Abramoff said, "I only hope that I can merit forgiveness from the Almighty and from those I have wronged or caused to suffer."

One charge is quite illuminating. Abramoff had arranged payments of $50,000 to the wife of an unnamed congressional staffer. In return the staffer agreed to help him defeat an Internet gambling measure that would harm one of his clients.

Scanlon, who also pled guilty to similar charges, lived a life even more colorful than that of Abramoff. In fact, his high-flying lifestyle helped trigger the investigation. Scanlon had a beachfront house in Rehoboth Beach, a home in St. Bart's, and an apartment at the Ritz-Carlton Washington. He was required to make restitution to the Indian tribes he defrauded and was sentenced to prison.

There are two pressing problems that stimulate bribery and corruption among legislators and their staff members and executive officials, problems that need to be corrected if we are to have a working democracy not tainted by illegal lobbying.

The first is the revolving door in which legislators and executive department officials cash in on their experience when they leave their public jobs and become paid lobbyists. For most of our history, that was an immediate situation. A legislator left Congress and the same day could take a taxicab to K Street, where he became a paid lobbyist, generally at two to three times his public salary.

But Congress eventually realized that there had to be a cooling-off period between public employment and private lobbying activity. The Ethics Reform Act of 1989 required a 1-year hiatus before a legislator could become a lobbyist. This proved a false restriction because former members of Congress were still hired immediately by lobbying firms and assigned to "supervise" young lobbyists until the year was completed.

Then in 2008, Congress again took up the question of the revolving door and tried to extend the cooling-off period to 2 years. The House of Representatives refused, but the Senate did extend the 1 year to 2 years in the grandiosely titled Honest Government and Open Leadership Act of 2008.

This, of course, will also prove inadequate. To shut down the revolving door, the cooling-off period has to be extended to 5 years. That is a long enough time for K Street to lose interest in a once-famous legislator, who might now be forced to truly retire or return home and take up a totally different occupation. This would be a great boon to our democracy and its citizens.

The second problem with the present situation is that lobbyists directly give vast amounts of money to House and Senate members' campaign funds or their PACS, which casts a great shadow over this money and whether it is actually a simple contribution or a disguised bribe.

The answer is direct and simple. Not only should lobbyists not be permitted to give gifts to legislators, but that prohibition must be extended to campaign funds. A new, true ethics law would prohibit the passing of any money to the legislators or to their campaigns.

Only these two measures, and not the thin, transparently false ethics reforms that have thus far been enacted, will bring some decency back to the halls of Congress and to the executive suites of any administration.

Every administration becomes involved in the lobbying dilemma. These people often know more about government than even our elected officials and the temptation to use them seems to be genetic in Washington.

President Bush had lobbyists in his administration and President Obama campaigned on the promise that he would not employ any lobbyists. But it seems that when it comes to lobbyists, there are always exceptions. Obama has made a few, including the number two man in the Defense Department, who had been a well-paid lobbyist for Raytheon, a large Defense supplier.

So much for true reform.

Good government requires tighter controls on the activities of lobbyists and their too-often tainted contacts between themselves and lawmakers.

The Founding Fathers wrote of the right to "petition the government for a redress of grievances" but did not imagine or condone the shenanigans of contemporary lobbyists now spending billions to seek enormous gains for themselves and their clients—too often at the public's expense.

L

LOW BALLING

So They Lie about Costs. A Lot.

The system is simple. It doubles and triples the cost of federally supported construction projects, from highways and bridges to spectacular civic monuments in Washington. It wastes billions and billions. And it is used all the time.

It's a simple psychological trick called "low balling," a method that pretends that things will cost a lot less than they really do. All it requires is for the public to be gullible, which it always is, and for politicians to lie, something that is endemic to their trade, perhaps even a genetic requirement of that peculiar profession.

The purpose, of course, is to get a massive project started, one that can cost a great deal of money. Supposedly it will also eventually cast honor onto the member of Congress, or the president—whoever is the mastermind behind some excessive spending of borrowed money, the brilliant fiscal strategy of the U.S. government.

One of these grandiose projects was just opened late in 2008—the Capitol Visitor Center in Washington.

For many years, millions of Americans have participated in authentic visits to the halls of Congress. They sat in the gallery and listened to debates, walked through its historic corridors and peeked into Congressional offices, ogled the hundreds of marble statues of the deceased famous, from Daniel Webster to George Washington, eaten in the House or Senate restaurants, walked up and down the majestic outdoor staircases, even taken the electric subways that shuttle Senators to and from different parts of the Capitol.

So famous are these truly realistic visits that they became the mainstay of senior-year high school trips, including that of former President Bill Clinton who, at age 16, met then-Senator John Kennedy in such a visit and decided he wanted to become president—a dream he achieved. But this authentic tradition was too much for Congress. Perhaps they feared too much curious citizen traffic in their hallowed halls. So they decided to shunt the crowds elsewhere, to a virtual activity, an underground museum and facility that would herald their accomplishments, such as they are. It was called the Capitol Visitor Center.

Besides, it was going to be enormous—three quarters the size of the Capitol itself and cheap, a mere $265 million. Construction started in 2002, and it was to be completed in 2005. But Washington being Washington, it was low balled both in cost and in time. It was finally completed at the end of 2008, for $615 million, some 2.5 times the original estimate.

The champion of federal low balling is the Big Dig, the Boston traffic interchange that was designed to improve highway traffic through the city. In 1985, the government predicted it would cost $2.6 billion and would be completed in 1998. It kept being delayed, and contractors were rewarded for their inefficiency, with added cash and profits. When it was finally finished in 2005, it ended up costing a record $14.6 billion ($8.5 billion federal money), including repairing a series of leaks in the ceiling.

A simple parking lot for the Kennedy Center, begun in 1998, was estimated to cost $28 million, but when completed in 2003, the price had mushroomed to $88 million, more than 3 times as much.

The Denver International Airport, heavily built with federal funds, eventually cost $4.8 billion when completed in 1995. But its original low-ball estimate was only $1.7 billion.

Another Big Dig–type fiasco was the Springfield, Virginia, highway interchange, which was originally estimated at $241 million. But when completed in 2005 the cost had risen to an astonishing $676 million.

The disparity in highway costs between the estimate and the true figure is partially due to the problem of meshing the federal interest with that of the states in which the road is being built. The states have little interest in keeping the costs down because Uncle Sam is paying some 80% of the total. When the figures run out of control, as usually happens, Washington points a finger at the states, which in turn, blame the contractors. In effect, no one is truly in charge.

The cost of federal construction in outer space is just as unreliable as on earth. The International Space Station, estimated to cost $17 billion when begun, actually ran some $30 billion when completed in 2002.

Low balling is not restricted to construction. It is a technique used by every branch of the federal government, especially by advocates of obviously expensive projects, which they hope to get through Congress—and have the president sign— by the simple expedient of low balling the cost.

This seems to have been the case with the relatively new Medicare R_x plan, an entitlement for all Medicare members that covers a good part of their prescription cost regardless of income.

Soon after the bill was signed in 2003, the administration informed the public that a mistake had been made. Instead of the cost being $400 billion over a decade the estimate was immediately raised to $534 billion, one third more. An investigation showed that Medicare's cost analyst knew about the higher cost but held back revealing it.

Why? Because he was threatened with being fired if the public learned of the intentional low balling.

It is surprising that the best overall study of government low balling was done by a foreign nation, Denmark, which studied 258 government transportation projects in the United States and elsewhere. They learned that in 9 out of 10 cases, there were overruns, averaging some 28% of the total cost.

Most important, Danish researchers concluded that the overruns were mostly intentional, prompted by outright deception by public officials or, more simply stated, by lies. Says the report: "Project promoters routinely ignore, hide, or otherwise leave out important project costs and risks in order to make total costs appear low."

The overrun epidemic runs throughout the government. In 2005, a review of the Federal Aviation Administration projects designed to improve the nation's air control system learned that the cost of 16 projects had somehow increased from $8.9 billion to $14.6 billion. A computer system called STARS rose in cost from an estimated $940 million to $2.8 billion. The inspector general noted that the project is "facing obsolescence" even before it is finished.

Even the new Washington baseball stadium, financed with government tax-free bonds, ended up costing $614 million, even though the enthusiastic mayor was selling it as a $435 million deal.

What's the answer to the double-dealing, low-balling, hustling estimates of federal taxpayer paying projects?

First, the public and members of Congress who must approve these extravagant deals should understand that the numbers are all figments of someone's perhaps self-serving imagination and are not to be taken seriously. What is needed is a mandatory audit, before legislation, of contracts by an outside appraisal firm knowledgeable in the field. Then the true numbers might possibly be brought to bear before the fiscal accident takes place.

Second, each project should be audited annually in its progress, with public disclosure, and the swift termination of any lowballing, swift, lying bureaucrat who is costing us those extra billions.

Honesty in government begins with the personal honesty of our federal employees and major bureaucrats, a public trait that requires a great deal of improvement if we are to face the remainder of this challenging century with a sense of fiscal security.

But how can we budget anything if the original estimate is a corrupt, devious, low-balling, purposeful distortion of the financial truth by dishonest government bureaucrats?

M

MEDICARE FRAUD

Whatever Happened to the
Hippocratic Oath?

Primum non nocere.

"First do no harm" is the motto of the medical profession, a symbol of integrity that is disappearing daily as doctors, hospitals, and all those involved in America's healthcare system increasingly take advantage of the giant pot of government money available in Medicare insurance.

Willie Sutton, the bank robber, when asked why he robbed banks, said simply, "That's where the money is." Today for thieves, the money is more apt to be in the health care industry, which pays out almost $2 trillion a year to keep us healthy.

Estimates of Medicare fraud by doctors, hospitals, and medical suppliers of every shape started out with an official statement a decade ago that it probably had reached $20 billion a year. The reality today is that just the overpayment of bills submitted by providers to Medicare comes to some $40 billion a year. When added to fraud, the number is astronomically higher.

A decade ago, a lecturer at the Harvard Kennedy School of Government believed that Medicare fraud could be as large as $63 billion. Today, a conservative estimate is that Medicare false claims, cheating, and fraud is probably closer to one quarter the cost of the entire program, or some $100 billion a year.

Former FBI Director Louis Freeh testified to Congress that in American medicine "the crime problem is so big and so diverse that we are making only a small dent in addressing the fraud." The inspector general of HHS added that the Medicare program is "inherently at high risk" for fraud.

We regularly read about individual doctors stealing money from government insurance. A Philadelphia cardiologist, for instance, was convicted of defrauding the government of a half million dollars by making false claims to both Medicare and private insurance systems.

Testifying before a U.S. Senate committee, he said he was surprised that his claims were actually paid. "The problem is that nobody is watching," he told the legislators. "The system is extremely easy to evade. The forms I sent in were absolutely outrageous."

Are we dealing here with just individual unscrupulous doctors hiding from government scrutiny? Absolutely not. Most doctors are honest with the government, but a large minority abuse the system. In fact, the most prestigious hospitals in America regularly violate the Medicare trust, sponging illegally off the government for their own egos and pocketbooks.

Today Washington has become the main support of hospitals'

ever-expanding operation in their quest to make the U.S. media's "best" lists. Financial chicanery is the end result.

The Massachusetts General Hospital, one of the finest institutions in America, connected to Harvard Medical School, was fined $418,000 for submitting false claims to the government for work done by physicians, edging out similar chicanery by the Boston University Medical Center. A common scam among prestigious teaching hospitals is double billing, in which the hospitals receive Medicare money for the teaching of the medical residents—as much as $100,000 a year for each postgraduate student.

But they still often double bill Medicare for work ostensibly done by faculty members when the actual medical care was performed by these federally subsidized residents in training. This Medicare scheme was run by the University of Pennsylvania at a cost of $30 million to Washington, while Thomas Jefferson University paid $12 million to settle similar false claims.

Medical university hospitals have been involved in this and other subterfuges aimed at cheating Medicare and the aged. At one Boston institution, Medicare received a $177,000 reimbursement when the hospital tried to twist the rules. Uncle Sam says that a cardiologist cannot bill Medicare for interpretation of coronary angiograms but that a radiologist can. Simple. The radiology department of the hospital billed Medicare, then paid kickbacks to the cardiology group.

The university hospital of Yale, the Yale-New Haven Hospital, has also been involved in Medicare fraud. In a $3.75 million settlement with the Department of Justice, the hospital admitted to overbilling Medicare for infusion therapy, chemotherapy administration, and blood transfusion services performed on patients. Federal prosecutors alleged that the hospital's oncology infusion service dispensed medication and conducted laboratory studies without the order of a physician.

The Beth Israel Medical Center in New York had to pay a much larger fine, a total of $72 million, to resolve civil charges of cheating, another prestigious institution to join the growing Medicare racket.

Cheating Medicare seems to be routine among the best hospitals and medical centers in America. The University of Medicine and Dentistry of New Jersey, one of the largest health-care universities in the country, has been accused of serious Medicare fraud and mismanagement.

Senator Chuck Grassley, chairman of the Senate Finance Committee, stated, "the scope of the wrongdoing at that institution is staggering. More than $700 million in no-bid contracts were awarded over five years, often to politically connected recipients, some of whom did little or no work for the money. Jobs were filled by patronage. . . . Lavish perquisites and bonuses were given to administrators. The board was riddled with conflicts of interest. The most egregious fraud was double billing."

Medical racketeering against Medicare in hospitals is epidemic, turning American hospitals into centers of deception, obfuscation, and fraud. Beginning with the Hill-Burton Act of the 1950s, we have created too many hospitals with an enormous number of empty beds. That coupled with increased competition for patients has forced honesty to virtually disappear from the scene. Federal investigators have found that of the nation's 6,200 hospitals, some 4,600 have submitted "improper" bills for outpatient services, for instance, helping deplete Medicare's ever scarcer funds.

One simple scam involves the inpatient–outpatient racket in which Medicare is billed twice. The scam is particularly popular because Medicare is openly more generous with outpatient than with more expensive inpatient hospital work, in the hope that it will cut down hospitalization. But the plan partially backfires because it increases Medicare fraud. The hospital nonphysician outpatient work is billed once, separately. Then the same work is too often billed a second time as part of the inpatient invoice.

Thus far, a thousand hospitals have confessed to this practice. Four hospitals, two in Pennsylvania and two in South Dakota, operated a similar scam—double billing Medicare for lab tests, which were also billed on the regular patient invoice. One hospital in Colorado had to reimburse the government because of a unique double-billing trick—charging both Medicare and the VA for the same patient.

Three proprietary hospitals in Los Angeles allegedly went even further in unethical behavior. They sent out ambulances to Skid Row and gathered the homeless off the streets, then put them through expensive screening and medical procedures, billing the government millions of dollars in the process.

The extent of the unethical hospital deals with Medicare is blatant, confirmed by a report from the U.S. attorney general's office in Massachusetts, which revealed that 83 hospitals had filed false Medicare claims. Nationwide, settlements of over $1 billion have been made with over 1,000 hospitals to date, and there are more to come.

National Medical Enterprises Inc., the nation's largest psychiatric hospital chain, paid the U.S. government the largest settlement ever—$362.7 million—for running a kickback and bribery scam to get patient referrals, a conspiracy that included more than 50 doctors.

The abuse of psychiatric care is commonplace. The inspector general of HHS conducted a 10-state review of outpatient psychiatric services and found that almost 60% of the $382 million spent one year did not meet Medicare reimbursement requirements, including services not authorized or supervised by a physician and alterations of medical records after they were selected for review.

Another racket in the psychiatric business is that Medicare is forced to pay for expensive partial inpatient hospital services for beneficiaries who had no history of mental illness. Their so-called therapy sessions consisted mainly of recreation such as watching television, dancing, and playing games. The inspector general found that over 90% of the services, or $229 million in Medicare payments, were unallowable or highly questionable.

The largest general hospital fraud case involves Columbia/HCA Healthcare Corporation, a $20 billion conglomerate that controlled 300 hospitals and numerous HMOs. Columbia, whose name was changed to HCA, was a for-profit institution, surely the fastest-growing and most controversial part of the American hospital system. Agents of the FBI, the Department of Defense criminal investigation service, the Department of Health and Human Services, and the U.S. attorney general's office raided the company's offices in El Paso, Texas, seeking confirmation of their suspicions.

One was that the health giant overbilled the government and required doctors affiliated with them to send blood and other samples to labs in which the owners of Columbia/HCA had a financial interest. The government seized documents from more than 35 Columbia hospitals in seven states seeking proof of suspected fraud. Richard Scott, the firm's CEO, resigned and three mid-level executives were indicted for conspiracy to inflate the amount of money they were to be reimbursed by both Medicare and Champus, the military health insurance plan.

When the investigation was completed, Columbia/HCA agreed to pay the United States $631 million in civil penalties and damages arising from false claims that they had submitted to Medicare and other federal health programs. The Justice Department announced that before that, their subsidiaries pled guilty to substantial criminal conduct and paid more than $840 million in criminal fines. When all fines are collected, the government will have recovered $1.7 billion, by far the largest ever reached in a health care fraud investigation.

"We are grateful for the assistance given by the whistleblowers of the cost of the past nine years of investigation litigation," the government stated.

Medicare whistle-blowing has become a giant industry, since the successful insertion of capitalism into a government program. In this case, the reward was astronomical. Whistleblowers received $152 million, the highest combined award ever paid.

The HCA fraud highlights the dastardly practices adopted by

many hospitals in the hope of remaining solvent by misappropriating federal Medicare funds. In fact, these practices are penalizing the aged who are both the patients and the premium payers of the Medicare program the doctors swore to help. It has become obvious that Medicare is permissive with the hospitals. Even when they recapture money, as with Massachusetts General and others, they do not place any charges against the hospital management or the doctors involved.

Clever hospital administrators take advantage of the government's naïveté. "Cost reporting," as it is called, is an easy opportunity for hospitals to cheat. If they are caught, all they risk is having to pay back the money, creating a unique interest-free loan. "It's a bizarre world," says James Plonsey, a cost-reporting specialist. "There is an incentive to abuse the system and wait for Medicare to catch you. And there has been no penalty for doing it."

This permissiveness can result in a funny kind of capitalism, one operated at taxpayers' expense. A favorite trick of privately owned hospitals, for example, has been to "recapture" money from the government. This happens when there is a takeover of a hospital, which was Columbia's main method of growth. The acquisition of a Miami Beach hospital was so structured that they didn't pay a cent for the hospital yet received $24.7 million of recaptured money from Washington. An investigation by Medicare revealed that the practice was so widespread that in one recent year, hospitals received $150 million in government funds using the technique.

Little wonder Medicare is constantly short of cash.

In this sea of fraud, the government is normally negligent

when it comes to reclaiming money on its own. But as we have seen, it has developed a working reward system based on whistle-blowers in which Uncle Sam shares the recouped money from fraud with the whistle-blower.

Justice Department fined the Olsten Corporation and its subsidiary, Kimberly Home Health Care, $61 million as part of the settlement for fraud committed in Florida, Georgia, and New York. Under the settlement, Kimberly pled guilty to conspiracy and mail fraud for violating the Medicare Antikickback Statute.

In this case, the whistle-blower (officially known as a Relator) who brought the case, former Olsten Vice President Donald McClendon, personally received an enormous reward, $9.8 million of the settlement, some 15% of all the monies collected—a victory of reward over fraud.

That program is ongoing and is quite successful, as opposed to Medicare's lenient, forgiving attitude toward nonprofit hospital cheaters. Anyone can participate and will be protected by the government. If you have any suspicions about Medicare (or Medicaid) fraud, just call the hotline of HHS, at 1-800-HHS-TIPS and seek a reward.

Pharmaceutical companies are also heavily involved in Medicare fraud, which often brings them to the attention of whistle-blowers. TAP Pharmaceuticals had to pay an enormous fine, $875 million, to settle claims that it paid kickbacks to doctors to promote Lupron, the company's prostate cancer drug, then cheated Medicare by filing false claims.

In this racket, the company gave doctors free samples of Lupron and coached them to profit from the gifts by billing

Medicare $500 per dose for each sample. Two whistle-blowers were involved in bringing this case to government attention. One was Douglas Durand, a former vice president of sales, and the other Joseph Gerstein, a physician.

Gerstein told prosecutors that when he had switched from Lupron to another drug, a TAP salesman offered him a $25,000 "grant" if he agreed to switch back to Lupron. The final reward given to the two whistle-blowers in the Lupron case was more than $94 million.

Medical equipment fraud also threatens Medicare to the tune of several billion a year. Medtronic Spine, formerly Kyphon, has agreed to pay the government $75 million to settle a whistle-blower lawsuit that exposed the racket.

Kyphon was a spinal medical device company that created a minimally invasive procedure of inserting bone cement into the spine, a procedure that can be performed safely in about 1 hour on an outpatient basis. But they persuaded doctors and hospitals to keep the patients overnight, which allowed hospitals to charge Medicare up to $10,000 per procedure, even though the patients typically had fully recovered within a few hours. The two whistle-blowers, Craig Patrick and Chuck Bates, were, respectively, the reimbursement manager and a regional sales manager for Kyphon. Patrick left when the complaints he made went unheeded. Each whistle-blower received a several-million-dollar reward.

Medical equipment fraudulent claims are fairly common, and strangely enough the entrepreneurs who do business with Medicare need not hold a medical license or be doctors or nurses. Because anyone can supply medical equipment, even sophisticated equipment, to the aged, little wonder that this part of the health world is rife with fraud.

The most common fraud activity is in south Florida, an area with a high percentage of elderly. One south Florida couple pled guilty to making millions by filing $410 million in false claims for medical equipment. That category includes oxygen equipment, standard wheelchairs, motorized wheelchairs, semi-electric beds, cervical collars, electric lamps, and other durable products. A total of 42 claims for orthotic body jackets were for more expensive items than those that were actually provided. Nearly 25% of certificates of medical necessity for home oxygen use were inaccurate.

The government investigated 32 new durable medical equipment companies in the Miami area and reported back that 32 of the 36 were not bona fide businesses. A study in several states found that one out of nine new applicants didn't even have a required physical address, and many did not have an inventory of supplies.

In a New York study, three companies billing for ear implants received checks from Medicare totaling $1 million in less than a month. Later it was learned that these companies had previously submitted fraudulent claims. In another case, the inspector general uncovered a Russian organized crime syndicate, which had submitted faulty claims for durable medical equipment that was not prescribed or delivered. The loss to Medicare from the scheme was $1.7 million.

In another New York scheme two individuals visited senior citizen high-rises and conducted supposed health fairs in which they coaxed beneficiaries into giving them their Medicare numbers. The two then furnished these seniors with certificates of medical necessity and connected them to two durable medical equipment companies. They then billed Medicare $750,000 for equipment, much of which was never supplied. The two con artists were sentenced to prison terms of 2 years and 9 months.

Another prime area of Medicare fraud for durable medical equipment is Los Angeles. "We have found Los Angeles is permeated with fraudulent health care operations including laboratories, clinics, and DME," said an inspector general report to Congress.

The inspector general's office found that Medicare paid an estimated $2.6 million for services that started after beneficiaries had died. Almost half of this was durable medical equipment. In another case, the Government Accountability Office (GAO) learned that Medicare had paid out $2 million to various medical equipment companies for braces for limbs that had already been amputated.

Another area that accosts the Medicare program with fraudulent activity is the home health care industry, the fastest growing portion of medical care in America. In that program, Medicare pays to have medical and nursing services in the home for very sick patients.

At the St. John's Home Health Agency, one of the 6,000 licensed home health care agencies in the nation, the inspector general found that they had billed Medicare for nonrendered home health services, that nurses and aides permitted subcontracting groups to use their names, and that they created fraudulent documents to support nonrendered services. Some of their nursing visits were actually provided by unlicensed personnel.

In addition, some subcontractors paid kickbacks to St. John's employees to do business with them. Finally, 26 people were indicted for racketeering, conspiring to launder money, and conspiring to submit false claims. Of the 26, 24 received guilty verdicts.

In one case, a married couple, neither of whom had medical certification, portrayed themselves as physical therapists and contracted with several home health agencies to provide services. One of the subjects began her own HHA using ghost employees, assuming the identities of six licensed therapists, and walked away with $400,000. Both husband and wife were found guilty of fraud and sentenced to jail.

One witness testifying before a Senate panel described how she acquired $7 million by charging $5 for gauze surgical dressings that cost a penny each. A former nightclub owner revealed that he made millions after he obtained a Medicare license and proceeded to open a crooked home health agency charging Medicare $86 for each home visit while paying a nurse $16 to $22.

Much Medicare fraud involves not corporations or pharmaceutical companies or major hospitals but is perpetrated by doctors in private practice who have decided to violate their Hippocratic oath. Although the dollar amounts of these frauds cannot match those of corporations, the number of errant physicians is, unfortunately, much too large.

Some of the doctor scams are quite ingenious.

Medicare paid one physician $871 for 40 hospital visits. However, it turned out that on checking, they learned that he made only 18 visits.

One common false physician claim is for "nail abridgment,"

or routine foot care. Medicare seems to pay it regularly even though the inspector general has stated several times that it is not covered by Medicare unless the patient is diabetic, which is not usually the case.

One California ophthalmologist pulled off a medical tsunami when he billed Medicare the unbelievable amount of $46 million over 3 to 4 years. According to the government, he created a "surgery mill" that falsified patients' records to justify numerous unnecessary cataract and eyelid operations.

One Pennsylvania obstetrician-gynecologist had to pay $980,000 to Medicare for twisting the truth. He billed Medicare for Pap smears never performed and toyed with the codes by marking routine office visits with pregnant women as emergencies.

The Medicare coding system is the doctor's explanation for the work he or she has done, and of course it's on the honor system. Doctors who want to take in more cash than they should can easily manipulate the code by "upgrading" it. If a patient comes in with a headache, for example, the doctor can charge Medicare for procedures that didn't take place, can mark off more time than was actually spent on the patient, or can check a more complex treatment than was actually performed. It's almost impossible for Medicare to know the truth.

On Long Island, a physician practiced minor cosmetic surgery by injecting patients with collagen to smooth out wrinkles and to pop up deflated lips. He knew that the procedures were not covered by Medicare, but to collect he claimed he had performed such procedures as bronchoscopy, an examination of the windpipe leading to the lungs.

In Boston a psychiatrist filed hundreds of false claims, some for more therapy sessions than he actually conducted, and on patients he had never even seen. But the billing fiasco is only the beginning of his mad escapade. Once he became aware of the investigation by Medicare he called the patients involved and sought to get them to lie for him. The psychiatrist's last option took place when he pled insanity, claiming he suffered from a psychosis that caused him to overbill Medicare.

In Colorado, one surgeon stretched his imagination and invented heart bypass operations he never performed.

An Illinois physician was sentenced to 2 years in jail for using fraud trying to rescue a failing multimillion-dollar diagnostic clinic he had built. When he couldn't get enough referrals from doctors to make it pay, he billed patients in the clinic between $4,000 and $6,000 in unnecessary tests. To make matters worse, he tried to justify the billing by entering false symptoms on the patients' records.

What can be done to curb the resounding and ever-growing Medicare fraud? The government tries to save a great deal of money by using computers rather than personal examination of most doctor claims. It does save some money but results in a great loss by paying for more fraudulent and mistaken claims.

Another aspect of the situation is that the continuing fraud is based on the negligence of the medical societies to discipline its member doctors. For example, when major hospitals put in false claims and then have to make restitution to the government, little or nothing is done to the offending doctors.

The medical profession should not wait for a criminal conviction to exercise some discipline on its errant physicians. On rare occasions, Medicare does expel doctors from privileges because of false statements, but it is more uncommon than common. Tighter discipline here would also be of great value.

But overall, it appears that the medical profession—whether the single practitioner, a member of a group practice, or the university hospital professor—needs to change its ethical view of society. Doctors do receive some short education in ethics, but the entire culture of the profession has to change considerably, with greater emphasis on serving society rather than exploiting the commonwealth by cheating the government through the massive taxpayer-supported Medicare system.

Medicare itself, which has been growing in cost at least double that of inflation for the past decade—in 2005, it went up 9.3%—is in trouble without the added onus of fraud. It is now supported by several payment methods: patient premiums, which were $96 a month per person in 2008; plus a 2.9% payroll tax on everyone, old and young alike; plus 40% of its total cost paid by the federal treasury.

Legislation that went into effect in 2007 raises premiums for couples earning more than $160,000 a year. In addition, hospital patients pay a deductible of $992, while nonhospital patients pay a deductible of $135 a year. And since 2007, Medicare Part D pharmaceutical coverage recipients pay a premium of approximately $26 a month.

All actuarial studies, however, show that this is not sufficient as medical costs soar.

Part of the escalating costs, which will exhaust the Medicare trust fund in 10 years, is due to the greed and subterfuge of doctors and hospitals. To make ends meet, the trustees of Medicare have often tried to put in reductions in disbursements to

America's richest class—its physicians. But pressure from the medical profession forces Congress each year not only to rescind those reductions but generally to raise doctor allotments from Medicare.

America's hospitals are a major flaw in the fiscal strength of Medicare, which is much more (or less) than a hospital insurance policy for the aged.

Medicare funds are also drained, without public awareness, in that they support the training of doctors at hospitals to the tune of some $100,000 a year per resident. Even more important is that hospitals secretly look to Medicare to keep them alive. This despite the fact that we have too many hospitals and that they are totally unregulated in terms of increased growth, all greatly paid for by Medicare.

Meanwhile Medicare has absolutely no say in the hospital's expenditures or its competitive growth, building expansion, or new technology and must fight a daily war against astronomical, often fictitious, hospital bills presented to it for payment.

The problem is vast, and the medical profession, including hospitals and physicians, is often careless about the dire situation of growing Medicare insolvency, especially when it interferes, as it does daily, with the medical profession's own greed and growth.

America needs and deserves a complete overhaul of Medicare—and Medicaid for the poor as well—with new talent, new ideas, and a rigorous look at and repair of the fraud and error that permeates and threatens valued medical care for the aged.

The excessive rise in medical costs is helping force America more rapidly onto the path of economic national suicide. Bringing health costs down by curbing fraud is an essential part of our urgent need.

And it wouldn't hurt to remind doctors that they once vowed to uphold, not defy, the sacred Hippocratic oath.

M

MONETARY MAYHEM

One of the gravest problems in the federal government is not only its apparent inability to be prudent about money but its failure to properly record the taxpayers' assets and liabilities.

Basically, it appears that large portions of the federal establishment have trouble with arithmetic, especially when it comes to government expenditures.

From various sources, we have compiled some startling revelations about how poorly Uncle Sam keeps our books:

- In one recent year, the federal government could not account for $24.5 billion it spent. Buried in the Treasury Department's "Unreconciled Transactions Affecting the Change in Net Position," is the fact that the enormous sum is unreconciled—that is, it is missing. It was spent by some people, somewhere in Washington, but that information is unknown. The Treasury finds it a "priority," if only because the missing amount is large enough to fund the entire Department of Justice for a year.

- In a study of 26 federal departments and major agencies, 18 received the lowest possible score for financial management. Auditors felt they could not even express an opinion on the financial status of those agencies.

- According to the GAO, the IRS could not verify $3 billion of its expenses, adding that the agency "had not kept its own books and records with the same degree of accuracy it expects of taxpayers." Refunds of $233 billion "could not be verified or reconciled."

- In one recent year, the Department of Agriculture could not account for $5 billion in receipts and expenditures.

- In Medicaid, a federal program executed by states, several states used accounting tricks to secure extra federal funds.

- About $3 billion is still owed to the Department of Veterans Affairs.

- Around $7 billion is owed to Uncle Sam by Medicare contractors.

- Until recently, there were 22 different payroll systems handling federal payments.

- The U.S. Navy underestimated the value of its property by almost $11 billion.

- In reviewing the "Consolidated Financial Statements of the United States Government," the GAO's chief accountant

scolded the government for "having problems with funda-
mental bookkeeping" that "prevent the government from
accurately reporting a large portion of its assets, liabilities,
and costs." The GAO said that, unfortunately, it could not
certify the accuracy of the books of the U.S. government.

· The Federal Aviation Administration's records of property
included $195 million in supposed assets that no longer
existed, while $245 million in spare parts were missing from
its books.

· The Department of Education lacked "a reasonable methodology and system" that could ascertain its large losses on
defaulted student loans, which ran $3.3 billion in one year.

· Money managers at the Department of Defense did not
retrieve $100 million in refunds on unused air tickets even
though they were fully refundable.

· At the Department of Housing and Urban Development, a
recent budget included $517 million in items, even though
the contracts had expired, been terminated, or had never
been executed.

· The Department of Energy, over a 15-year period, closed
down 31 unsuccessful major projects after having spent $10
billion on them.

Waste in government is one thing. But when the agencies
can't even calculate the dollars and cents involved in their operations, that's another, more tragic, problem—one that apparently
will never be resolved.

N

NONPROFITS

THEY DO WHAT THEY PLEASE
WITH UNCLE SAM'S MONEY

In the olden days, you had private organizations, government organizations, and nonprofit organizations, with a simple separation of duties.

Increasingly though, the federal government is becoming all-encompassing, spending our money not just on government programs, but generously subsidizing a multitude of nonprofits, even including such organizations as the United Way.

It is all part of the federalization of American life, a most disturbing and expensive philosophy, as we are beginning to learn to our infinite distress.

This is not just petty cash but reportedly $46 billion other than hospital health support, which is well over $200 billion. That $46 billion (almost $100 billion when state and local government are included) is given mainly to social service nonprofits, who at one time supported themselves with charity from individuals and foundations.

But today, that enormous amount of charity for nonprofits comes from Washington through taxpayer money—without taxpayer permission or generally even without taxpayer knowledge.

The problem is not only excessive federal spending but a total lack of control. Washington is unable, or even unwilling, to know what actually happens to its grant money to nonprofits. It has enough trouble trying to control the wild spending of its own bureaucrats.

In 2008, we learned at least some of that hidden truth. The U.S. Senate, led by Senators John F. Kerry and Olympia J. Snowe, investigated a nonprofit organization, the National Veterans Business Development Corporation, and found that the nonprofit had spent most of the federal grant on itself instead of on its mission, which was to operate walk-in business centers for veterans.

In 2007, the nonprofit received $17 million from Washington, but only 15% on average was spent running the centers. That percentage dropped to 9% in 2008. The Senate report took the nonprofit to task for its spending on itself. Besides receiving high salaries, top executives sometimes dined in ultra-expensive restaurants on the government's nickel. According to the Senate committee's findings, more than $5,000 was spent on two meals without a business justification. In fiscal year 2007, the group spent $240,000 on fund-raising but collected only $64,000 from donors.

More often, the nonprofits do not spend excessively on themselves. But in dollars spent, they are almost federal agencies, without federal controls. For example, one reputable organization, the Urban Institute, receives 62% of its total income, or $42 million, from the federal government. But its activities are strictly its own business. The taxpayer is only a silent contributor.

It's not a very complicated problem. The federal government can't afford to be a vehicle supporting either profit-making organizations or worthy nonprofit organizations and still remain solvent. In addition, critics point out that federal support of nonprofits discourages private donations and volunteerism in general, something that once made American charity noteworthy throughout the world.

The federal contribution to nonprofits is even larger than recorded. The reason is simple. Congressional earmarks—which bypass traditional grant and contract competition—often spend their pork on nonprofits. For example, in one recent year, charity earmarks included $2 million for Helen Keller Services for the Blind; $2 million for the Native American Cultural Center; $1.5 million for the Missouri Historical Society, $100,000 for the Arab Community Center, and $100,000 for the Boys and Girls Harbor in Harlem, all nonprofit organizations.

Today, federal charity to nonprofits has stimulated the growth of its main vehicle, the tax exempt 501(c)(3) organizations, which from 1982 to 1992 grew in number from 322,000 to 546,000, and today has mushroomed to 1.4 million nonprofit organizations, challenging Uncle Sam's charity budget even further.

I believe it's time to take a drastic step. We should stop all federal charity to nonprofits and let them rise or fall on the generosity of their own donors—just like it used to be when the federal government made some sense.

This will be very important as President Obama's new charity tax rules are put into effect. In the new 2010 federal budget, those earning over $250,000—the main supporters of the nonprofits, from United Way to the Red Cross—will get less of a tax break from those donations. This will put more pressure on the nonprofits to try to get more money from Washington, forcing us to lose out twice.

There is a simple solution to the problem of the nonprofits, organizations we can't seem to control.

We must once again distinguish between government and private charity. All we need do is to cut out all federal money for private charities and force them to tap into the enormous generosity of the American public, instead of continuing to use the almost bankrupt federal treasury for their survival.

O

OVERSIGHT

BY THE WAY, HERE'S A FEW
BILLION MORE WE CAN SAVE

The federal government is so massive and so intellectually unreasoning that one can throw a dart at the federal budget and cumulatively save billions without even trying. I have stressed this throughout this book, and I offer still more ways to save in the "Conclusion" (p. 324).

However, an additional study compiled from the work of the Congressional Budget Office (CBO) and the Government Accountability Office (GAO) adds to the cumulative information ignored by our politicians.

Not too long ago, in a 300-page report to the Committee on the Budget of the U.S. Congress, called *Opportunities for Oversight and Improved Use of Taxpayer Funds,* these agencies offered so many cost-saving ideas that I decided to give a few examples to show how much was being overlooked by Congress and the president.

The problem is that I read the entire report, while I'm sure that almost all members of Congress did not. Or if they did, they merely chuckled at the confidence of auditors who thought they could influence, in any way, the continued reckless spending of taxpayer money.

Here, for historical record at least, are just some of the suggestions and options to save money:

- Eliminate U.S. contributions to administrative costs in rogue states.

- End the U.S. capital subscriptions to the European Bank for reconstruction and development.

- Increase nuclear waste disposal fees.

- Recover federal investments in successfully commercialized technologies.

- Reduce the cost of the Rural Utilities Service's Electricity and Telecommunication Loan programs.

- Deny additional funding for commercial fisheries buyback programs.

- Further consolidate the U.S. Department of Agriculture's County Offices—of which there are four times more than are needed.

- Consolidate homeless assistance programs.

- Increase aircraft registration fees to enable the Federal Aviation Administration to recover actual cost.

- Eliminate the Essential Air Service program subsidies for small airlines.

- Eliminate flood insurance for certain repeatedly flooded properties.

- Improve fairness of Medicaid-matching formulas for states.

- Require all states to comply with the new rules about Medicaid's upper payment limit.

- Require competitive bidding for high-volume items of durable medical equipment for Medicare and Medicaid.

- Revise benefit payments under the Federal Employees' Compensation Act.

- Reduce improper payments to medical providers and middlemen for supplemental security income recipients.

- Prevent delinquent taxpayers from benefitting from federal programs.

- Improper benefit payments could be avoided if data from various programs were shared.

- Impose a fee on the investment portfolios of government-sponsored enterprises.

- Recapture interest on rural housing loans.

- Terminate land-exchange programs.

- Reexamine federal policies for subsidizing water for agriculture and rural uses.

Will we achieve any of these savings?
It's highly debatable. Why? Because the typical member of

Congress's political love is not for his or her country, but for the district that elects him or her every 2 years, a problem crafted by the Constitution that we probably can never change. Each of these cuts will in some way affect Congressional districts.

The only possibility for change is the spiritual evolution of our politicians, which is as likely as bringing heaven down to earth.

P

PERSONAL EXEMPTION

A Federal Inflation Trick That Hurts, Bad

To properly understand the personal exemption gimmick, it is best to compare politicians—from the Congress to the White House—to corporate executives. The latter seek larger revenues through sales so that they can pay themselves well and return maximum profits to their shareholders.

Washington politicians are in much the same situation, except that they have to be more devious in raising revenue for their pet projects because the money comes involuntarily out of the pocket of reluctant, sometimes bitter, taxpayers.

The very worst thing that politicians can do is raise the marginal tax rate, which is something taxpayers understand. When they raise the maximum rate from 28% to 39%, as several administrations have done, people know they are being hurt and exactly how. This can fuel anti-politician anger, resulting in the failure of some politicians to get reelected.

Politicians are usually ignorant of government realities, but they are not stupid; at least they are sage in ways of getting reelected by avoiding excessive resentment from their constituents.

Politicians instead seek covert gimmicks when they raise taxes, maneuvers that are difficult for citizens to understand and that can be used to raise still more money without appearing to do so. The personal exemption is one of the most effective tricks in bamboozling even skeptical citizens.

One of the most effective tax tricks is to play with the personal exemption, the amount of income immediately taken off your 1040 form, lowering your tax bite. Today that is $3,650 per person, which may seem reasonable until one examines its history. Then one realizes that it should be considerably higher— and, therefore, your taxes should now be considerably lower—if Washington were playing fair, which of course it isn't.

In 1950, the personal exemption was $600, which was considerable for a family of four. It represented an immediate $2,400 exemption for such a typical family at a time when the median annual family income in America was only $3,446. That single exemption left only a typical taxable amount of $1,006, which at a 25% rate, meant an IRS liability of $250, a beneficent tax rate of some 7%. Then, with additional deductions such as property and sales and state taxes, along with mortgage interest, the operating federal tax rate was a mere 2%.

That, of course, is one reason the nation was so happy under the presidency of Harry Truman—who left office with only a 30% approval rating, a reflection more on the American people than on President Truman, an American hero in more ways than one.

Even a quite successful family in 1950, which earned $5,200 a year, still had half their income taxes eliminated by the generous personal exemption.

What about today?

Today the government has played statistical games with the taxpayer, and manages to extract more and more taxes by the simple expedient of not providing the taxpayer with a fair personal exemption, historically speaking. The current exemption of $3,650 a person sounds reasonable, but it is a statistical fraud, one that over the years has been kept much lower than it should be by tax-hungry American politicians.

What should the exemption be after being adjusted for inflation?

First, the basic trick was to not index the exemption for inflation, a clever Washington gambit that existed from 1950 up through 1987. With that gimmick they gained more and more taxes each year as the value of the dollar was eroded through inflation. The official CPI shows that each dollar then now costs $9. A simple equation shows that the exemption should be $5,400 instead of $3,650 if we just use the official inflation figures.

A family of four now gets a personal tax exemption of $14,600. But that amount, using Uncle Sam's own numbers, should be $22,600. That is a current loss, each year, of $8,000 in exemptions, cumulatively a small fortune expropriated by Uncle Sam.

But that's only half the story. As most economic scholars believe, the CPI is a highly understated government statistic. Inflation in America since 1950 is much, much higher than 9 to 1. For example, in 1950 a movie ticket was $0.30. Today it is $8 or more, an inflation factor of some 25, not 9.

In virtually every comparison the CPI is shown to be understated. In 1950. a Ford four-door sedan cost $1,200. Today, it is $24,000, an inflation factor of 20. According to the government, the typical house in 1950 cost $7,354, while today it is still $180,000 despite the recent fall, an inflation factor of 24, not 9.

If we eliminate the extremes, such as a house or a car or a movie ticket, a reasonably accurate factor of inflation is 14 to 1. Thus $1 from 1950 is now worth some $0.07. This means that, to be fair, the personal exemption should be 14 times $600 (the 1950 number), or $8,400, or $33,600 for a family of four—not the present $14,000.

This honest number would, of course, expose the politicians' statistical trick and cut our IRS 1040 taxes in half, or less.

So how could Uncle Sam be honest and fair with the taxpayer when it has a $3.6 trillion annual budget, a bloated cost for a bloated government?

The answer, of course, is to cut the government at least 20% immediately, then increase the annual budget only by the percentage of inflation, historically about 3%. We will look at that goal carefully in the "Conclusion" (p. 324), if you will please follow my moving hand.

Meanwhile, we can be bold and raise the personal exemption somewhat back toward the honest, inflation adjusted figure of $8,400 per person, or $33,600 for a family of four.

And simultaneously we can also make believe that Harry Truman is still the president of the United States.

P

PRIMARIES, PRESIDENTIAL

INSTITUTIONALIZED POLITICAL MADNESS

On a cold January 3rd night in 2008 Iowans bundled up and trekked from their homes to the nearest public library or elementary school gymnasium or town hall or even a neighbor's home for the presidential Democratic and Republican caucuses, known locally as a "gathering of neighbors."

There was no crush at the meeting halls. Although the Iowa caucus was the first in the nation and was heavily covered by thousands of journalists, local Iowans largely ignored the event. Although all eyes of the nation were focused on that caucus for the first indication of who might be the nation's next president, Iowans were more interested in the $70 million in revenue it brought to the state than in the voting.

In fact, the turnout was pitifully light, as it is in most caucuses. Of the 2.2 million eligible to vote only 1 in 6 ever came out to the caucus, the first sign that the present primary system is more of a political joke than an exercise in intelligent democracy.

An average of only 100 people from each party gathered in the meeting halls in each of the 1,764 precincts throughout the state. They did not write out ballots or punch cards or use levers or sign in electronically. Instead, they voted with their bodies. They huddled together in small groups, each one indicating by their physical presence a choice of a particular presidential nominee. There even was a space assigned for the undecideds.

They shared their opinions with their neighbors and engaged in electioneering. Even a few of each flock were deputized to go from group to group, hoping to convert the others to their choice of nominee. After about 30 minutes, a preliminary vote was taken just to see if the groups were actually eligible to vote. By state law, each group backing a candidate in the room on primary night needed anywhere from 15% to 25% of the total present in order for any of their candidates to be eligible for the next round of voting.

After that was done, the sharing of opinions and the shuffling of bodies continued, changing once again the shape of the groups. Then a second vote was taken.

It wasn't truly a final vote, for all that body movement was not only temporary but not binding. All they had done was elect delegates to the county convention, which months later would elect delegates to the state convention, which would, in the case of Democrats, finally elect the 57 delegates to the national Democratic convention in Denver.

Of course, these delegates might even refuse to abide by the vote in all those meeting halls, which is quite legal.

The eight Democratic candidates spent millions on television advertising and set up dozens of offices throughout the state, hoping to make Iowa their first victory.

The nation waited with great anticipation. Who would emerge as the leader in the Iowa caucus and thus in the race for the White House? When it was all done, Barack Obama had 38% of the small Democratic vote. John Edwards received 30%, and Hillary Clinton 29%. With only 90,000 votes in a small state, Obama moved ahead of the pack and never looked back. It was, Obama himself mused, a moment for "history."

The caucus is a very poor gauge of public opinion, sampling only those willing to suffer the torture of a 2-hour meeting on a cold January night. Its only saving grace is that it usually requires that only members of a political party can vote, giving it some respectability.

But even that varies in the craziness of the season of presidential selection. There are also several "open" caucuses in which anyone can walk in and vote regardless of his or her party affiliation, as in the Democratic Party caucus in Idaho and Minnesota and Democrats abroad.

There were 17 caucus states during the 2008 primary season, most with much lower turnouts than seen in Iowa, highlighting the weakness, even the madness, of the system in choosing a presidential candidate. Most caucus turnouts are so low that they average only 5%, or 1 in 20 eligible voters, yet the press—and much worse the party—gives great credence to this abysmally small sample.

In the case of Nevada, one of the largest turnouts, only 1 in 10 of both Democrats and Republicans, showed up. It was only 5% in Colorado, and a ludicrous 2% in the Idaho Democratic caucus. It was the same minuscule turnout in Kansas. North Dakota came in at 6% for both parties, and Nebraska at only 3% for the Democrats.

Obama, through a masterpiece of organization, had won most of the caucuses by sending small groups of volunteers into the meeting halls in small states and walked away with extra delegates, an impressive piece of politicking. Clinton concentrated on the public primaries in the large states, most of which she won. But she ended up losing the nomination to Obama.

The caucus is the oldest form of presidential selection. From the early 1800s, state legislators and party leaders generally chose the senatorial and presidential candidates in nonpublic caucuses. But there was a clamor for more participation by voters in selecting nominees, plus the need for a secret, not public, ballot, as in the caucuses. As a result, the first statewide secret ballot presidential primary was developed in 1912 in North Dakota, the beginning of opening up a nominating process that had been dominated by party insiders.

A leader in this political movement was Republican Senator Robert M. La Follette, who won the first North Dakota primary in 1912, with former President Theodore Roosevelt finishing second. Roosevelt went on to win most of the 12 national primaries set up that year. But William Howard Taft had control of the party machinery and took the nomination at the convention.

It was in 1920 that New Hampshire's "first in the nation" primary began, one that has consistently been first ever since, a rather traditional but less than democratic operation. In 1932, although the bosses were still in control of the nomination, an increasing number of primaries were created, which FDR handily won. The primary movement progressed slowly, and in 1944 when Roosevelt was nominated for his fourth term, only 15 states held primaries.

On the Republican side that same year, World War II hero

General Douglas MacArthur won the early primaries in Wisconsin and Illinois in April. But at the convention, still controlled by bosses, the party nominated Governor Thomas E. Dewey. An important change in primaries took place in 1952 in New Hampshire, when the state altered its system of having its delegates unpledged. Instead, they moved strongly to choosing specific candidates.

On the Democratic side in New Hampshire that year, Tennessee's Senator Estes Kefauver beat President Truman 55% to 44%, and Truman decided not to run for another term. On the Republican side, General Dwight D. Eisenhower, a World War II hero, established his political base by defeating Ohio Senator Robert Taft, 50% to 39% in the New Hampshire primary. Even though Taft ended the primary season with more votes than Eisenhower, the convention named Ike as the nominee, and he went on to become the 34th president of the United States.

The presidential primary established itself in the public psyche in 1960 even though most states still did not have primaries. The Democratic contest was between John Kennedy, Hubert Humphrey, and Lyndon Johnson. Kennedy easily won the New Hampshire primary, then took Massachusetts as well. But he was considered at a disadvantage to Midwesterner Humphrey, who had substantial party boss allegiance. The next contest was in West Virginia, a heavily Protestant state. There had never been a Catholic president, and it was feared he'd lose. But when Kennedy took the West Virginia primary, the nomination was his.

Today, the party bosses are without sizable nominating power. All states have public primaries or caucuses, and together they determine the nomination. But we should not believe that the system makes sense or is democratic. It is, in fact, a system of uncoordinated contests with obtuse, differing state and party rules. It is more of a helter-skelter arrangement than a true contest determined by the people.

Instead of being a simple democratic method of choosing the presidential nominees, as was hoped, it has evolved into a system of institutionalized political madness.

We have seen how the caucuses make little sense and do not in any way represent the true opinion of the state's voters. Unfortunately, the same is often the case with public primaries, where rules are many and sometimes irrational.

There is not one uniform primary system, but three major types of primaries, and some with exotic twists. The first and most common is the closed primary, which makes the most sense. That is, no one can vote in that primary unless he or she is a member of the particular party. This fulfills the "party" part of a party primary. In the Republican Party there are 15 closed primaries, and the Democrats have 14.

The second type of primary is the "semiclosed," in which independents who are not registered in any party can change their party affiliation in the voting booth or with election officials, then participate on primary election day.

There is still another type of primary, the "open primary," which defies rational definition. In this case, anyone can vote in anyone's primary. That is, a registered Democrat can vote in the Republican primary and purposely distort it by voting for the candidate he thinks will be the easiest to defeat in the general election. This is called "raiding" and makes less sense than even the low-turnout caucus.

One would think this open voter trap would be uncommon, but it actually exists in either the Democratic or Republican primary in 16 states and territories, including Alabama, Arkansas, Georgia, Illinois, and Michigan. In a way, these open primaries logically nullify the value of the contests.

One of the most exotic, or ludicrous, primaries, depending on your viewpoint, is the so-called Louisiana primary, or "top two" primary, whose results can be surreal. As a result of this primary, the general election can end up being a contest between two members of the same party, while the opposition party has been knocked out of contention.

Voters in the Louisiana system can vote in either party, and instead of gaining victors in each party, it becomes a nonpartisan, or bipartisan, election in that the top two vote-getters, even if in the same party, go on to the general election. Then it becomes a runoff, in effect setting up two contestants for the general election regardless of party.

If one needed further proof of the madness of the present primary system, we can find it in what is known as "front loading." States are jealous of the peculiar political power that two small nonrepresentative states, Iowa and New Hampshire, have in the system.

As a result, other state legislatures are increasingly trying to jump ahead of them. In 2008, Florida and Michigan voted to create earlier primary dates, but two restraints came into play to protect the "traditional" advantage of Iowa and New Hampshire, no matter how misguided. First, New Hampshire, which has a state law requiring that it must always be first, moved its primary date up two weeks to January 9, and the Democratic Party voted to disenfranchise Michigan and Florida delegates because they tried to beat out New Hampshire as first in the nation.

It is becoming starkly obvious that the present primary system is a jumble that makes no sense and is ineffective and undemocratic in reflecting the people's choice for the presidential nomination. Several suggestions for change have been advocated, including holding four regional primaries instead of state-by-state voting. But this too misses the point of the inadequacy of both the caucus and various primary systems.

There is an obvious answer. The states are incapable of setting any universal parameters for a presidential race under the present system because of their competitive, even jealous, nature. Because we are dealing with a national office—in fact, the most important one—the rules must be set by the federal government.

This must be a function of Congress, which should establish new national primary rules instead of the present state-by-state jumble.

What is needed are national primary elections, done in stages, and interspersed with national debates among the contestants. One simple suggestion (mine) is as follows:

- All caucuses will be eliminated as being too narrow with too-small turnouts.

- On February 1, all states will simultaneously hold a semi-closed primary election in which only party members may vote. However, unaffiliated independents can choose to enroll in a party on the day of the primary, but can vote in only one party.

- The top five winners of that first race will enter a second national primary held on April 15.

• On June 30, the top two winners of the April 15 national primary will enter a third national contest. The winner of that contest will be the presidential nominee of that party, confirmed at the national convention.

There may be other methods of reforming the present primary madness, but in any case, we must have uniform rules and must eliminate the state caucuses, which are antiquated, undemocratic, and misleading contests. They can be captured by any candidate with a determined volunteer task force, resulting in the wrong nominee seizing a party nomination.

The present primary system is a shameful one that casts grave doubt on our ability to measure and provide for the political wishes of the American people.

It must be fully overhauled before the 2012 presidential election. Otherwise we'll keep electing presidents the people don't really want.

Q

QUESTIONABLE AND UNNECESSARY AGENCIES

Sunset Them And Build a Sunnier Union

Federal budgets are drawn yearly, but federal programs and agencies are actually created to live forever. They are designed to be nurtured and protected long after they are no longer needed. What is missing here, in federal parlance, is the use of a "sunset" provision, a time period, whether 5 or 10 years, in which a program is slated to live before it is closed or kept going.

The way federal laws are passed, the lifetime period for programs, of which there are thousands, is simply forever.

Today, more than ever, economy in government is paramount. Families are drastically cutting costs, but Washington has embarked, paradoxically, on a giant spending spree. This seems to negate the importance of spending less on a regular basis, something best done by cutting as many as possible of the useless federal programs that now choke the operation of government.

In the normal business world, companies are automatically sunsetted when they go bankrupt and more efficient companies take their place. In Washington, however, there is no such thing as bankruptcy. The worst performing programs and agencies just continue to perform poorly, robbing the taxpayers of their hard-earned money.

In my books on government I have made many sensible recommendations about which long-exhausted agencies and programs should immediately be sunsetted. There is often an initial enthusiastic reaction, even in parts of the federal establishment, followed by . . . nothing.

I will try once more. Perhaps I need some help, as per a bi-partisan commission appointed by the president to investigate the thousands of federal programs and make suggestions to Congress and the president on which to sunset permanently. Meanwhile, there are enormous savings to be made, many of which we have already covered, and others that are yet to be revealed in these pages.

Please follow me in this urgent pursuit of closing still more, some small and others sizable.

- Terminate corporate welfare, which runs some $75 billion a year. Some of the money is for research through the Advanced Technology Program (ATP) in which taxpayers take the risks, and companies like Intel and IBM get the profits. One report on ATP shows that often the research outlay is exceeded by the overhead.

- Close the Market Access Program of the Department of Agriculture, which subsidizes American corporations selling their products overseas through promotion and advertising in foreign publications. Costing taxpayers $1 billion over a decade, the money doesn't go mainly to struggling firms but to giants who don't need it to succeed—such as Gallo Wines, which grosses billions a year. Even Tyson Foods took in $500,000 from Washington to peddle their chickens overseas. No one can explain why Washington (us) should pay for their advertising.

· Close the Export-Import Bank, which makes and guarantees loans for foreign buyers of our products to ensure that they pay their bills, even when they may become insolvent. It makes no economic sense and the supposed bank has lost $8 billion in taxpayer money over 15 years.

· Close the consulting racket, which is costing us billions a year. Though the government employs some 15,000 lawyers, for instance, it also goes outside to hire legal consultants at some $1,500 a day! Years ago, I interviewed an auditor from the GAO who told me that agencies were supposed to check a box if they hired outside consultants. Many simply lied and said no when the true answer was yes, he explained. "They admitted to a few hundred million dollars of outside consultant use, but we learned the truth by checking the object class analysis number on each account. When the tally came in we found that in one recent fiscal year, they had spent $4.9 billion on outside consultants of every kind." The list was shocking. The Department of Energy had spent $99 million on consultants, $308 million for the Agency for International Development, $60 million by Education, and even $43 million by Treasury. It is time to make greater use of the giant underworked official bureaucracy and turn our back on even more expensive outsiders.

- Close the Maritime Administration, which has ruined our merchant marine fleet, and save some $600 million in the process.

- Stop federal support for political party presidential conventions.

- Stop the purchase of new lands by the Bureau of Land Management and the Department of Interior.

- Stop using federal funds to build U.S. Forest Service roads for lumber companies.

- With an enormous square footage of unused federal real estate, stop building new government buildings.

- Close the International Trade Commission.

- Close the Appalachian Regional Commission—or give every area in the nation its own expensive commission.

- Close the outmoded Rural Utilities Service, saving over $1 billion a year.

- Close the Legal Services Corporation, saving some $300 million a year, or give every American free lawyers.

- Close the Bureau of International Labor Affairs, saving some $100 million.

- Close the Government Printing Office, granting the business to private firms, and saving millions in the process.

- Eliminate the almost 1,000 federal advisory committees in 52 agencies.

- Close the Commission on Fine Arts, saving a few million.

- Close the East-West Center, saving $20 million.

- Close the U.S. Institute of Peace, pocketing $17 million.

- Stop farm subsidies for wool . . . mohair, lentils, and chick-peas.

- Stop the practice of paying more for drugs in the Medicare program than do other federal agencies.

- Close the ineffective Small Business Administration, saving $4 billion yearly.

- Close the Overseas Private Investment Corporation, saving $150 million.

- Sell much of the 1,200 civilian aircraft owned by the federal government.

- Sell half the government's 350,000 cars and do not buy new ones until they are at least 3 years old.

The list could go on seemingly without end, but this is a good sampling for any bipartisan commission seeking to sunset programs that may once have been valuable but have now lived beyond their time.

When all the agencies that need closing are identified, we will see a potential savings of several hundred billion a year, a greater contribution to the commonwealth than the enormous deficits the nation is now contemplating in the financial crisis.

Once that extravagant spending is completed, we must return to creating a nation that lives within its means. The best way to accomplish that is to stop fantasizing about what we can afford and instead cut our obligations to equal our revenue. One of the best ways to do that is to eliminate hundreds of useless federal agencies, which should have been sunsetted a long time ago.

Anything less is just yielding to the inevitability of national suicide.

R

RURAL AMERICA

ONLY 1,399 DIFFERENT FEDERAL PROGRAMS

Sometimes, the biggest problem with the federal government is its lack of diagnosis. It is impossible to correct the situation unless one knows what is wrong.

In Washington's case, the diagnosis is not easy. It is difficult to even locate and describe how many different programs in how many agencies are addressing a particular mission. Only with this diagnosis can you even attempt to correct the situation.

One problem Washington considers important is the poor condition of rural areas of the country. America was once mainly a rural nation, but those rustic areas have been shrinking regularly, replaced by towns, suburbs, and metropolitan centers. Still, Washington is concerned with the economic problems of this once romanticized section of the nation, which is now often made up of economically depressed small towns.

To ostensibly alleviate the pain, the federal government has put in what was once an unknown number of programs. The question is, is there a single or even a dozen federal programs designed to help rural areas survive the loss of population and economic strength? And how well are they doing?

It is surprising that someone in government asked the question. It was the Des Moines, Iowa, office of the Federal Home Loan Bank Board. For an answer, they hired SRI International, formerly the Stanford Research Institute, to conduct a survey. The finished survey, an 80-page report titled "Capitalizing on Rural America," tried to answer that difficult conundrum.

How much is Washington involved in the solution and how deeply? How many different programs and how many different agencies are attempting to help rural America?

The answer is in many ways a diagnosis of the federal government itself. It is a road map of its lack of design in understanding what is happening under its very nose. In fact, this time, as usual, it appears that Washington has no idea what it is doing.

The report first explains that rural areas are no longer necessarily farming communities. Says the SRI study: "Agriculture is no longer a major economic driver in the vast majority of rural counties. The nation's number of farm counties—defined as those where 15% or more of the county's total earnings or employment is derived from farming—decreased from 618 to 420 during the period 1990 to 2000.... Even in farm counties, an average of 80% of jobs are in non-farm sectors."

Poverty is more rampant in rural counties, which have a 14% poverty rate as opposed to the 12% poverty in urban areas.

This led the federal government to attack more vociferously. How much and how well?

First, how much? In 1989, the study found more than 88 federal programs in 16 agencies. But as the later SRI study indicates, that number has "grown considerably" since then. How much more?

It seems that the "key" federal funding programs for rural areas now totals 337, while the total number of programs is an enormous 1,399, spread out across 20 different federal agencies.

Can it really be 1,399? Yes. Unbelievable, but true.

The Department of Transportation has 58 programs for rural areas. The National Endowment for the Arts has 12. The Department of Labor has 49, the Department of Justice has 96, and the Department of Interior has 112. Housing and Urban Development has 102, while Health and Human Services had 307. There are 164 programs for rural areas in the Department of Education, and the Department of Commerce spends money on 90 programs, bested by the Department of Agriculture with 159.

Madness? What else?

This proliferation of programs is not just a matter of duplication, in which many agencies are doing the same mission— as when there are 160 different job-training programs spread throughout the bureaucracy. In this case, the villain is lack of coordination of the many different agencies dealing with a certain demographic or a geographic section of the country.

Coordination might require the use of various government agencies, but of course with a limit to the number of programs and with someone riding shotgun to coordinate the enormous and expensive overlap. In this case, the failure of coordination has created a masterpiece, a miasma of programs far beyond human interpretation.

How well do the 1,399 programs collectively do? Do they improve the economic development of these left-behind rustic towns and villages?

Hardly.

The opening statement of the report begins with a rather startling revelation: "The sheer number of federal programs for rural areas, spread across 20 government agencies, makes it difficult for rural communities to identify and access these programs." The report continues, noting that "federal rural development initiatives remain ill coordinated, difficult to use and poorly understood by rural residents and businesses."

In discussing the use of federal funds, the report is equally critical. It states that "there is no dearth of overall resources for rural areas," but that "the issue is whether financial resources have been so diluted that they are not having sufficient aggregate impact."

Overall, the report is critical and negative, indicating that a vast amount of money is being wasted by the scattershot operation, a failing of almost every federal program.

The 1,399 rural programs represent the history of the ills affecting the federal government as a whole: an uncoordinated forest of schemes with no one in charge and with no evaluation of how the money is being spent.

Perhaps this collection of failing legislation should be coordinated within a single agency, the "Rural American Aid" program, with its own inspector general and a goal of integrating this whirlwind into a usable whole, with a great savings of money. Then it should be examined and surely cut from 1,399 programs down to, say, 99.

Not only are these 1,399 programs poorly understood by the targeted recipients, as the study proves, but Washington is apparently equally confused.

Confusion seems to be the prime product of the Washington

establishment. Management consultants are hired to straighten out such confusion in large corporations. But it will take more than that to make Washington comprehensible even to itself. Then even more effort will be needed to clarify the cumbersome giant to its owners, the taxpayers, which is one of the goals of this book.

So, there are actually 1,399 federal programs just for rural areas. Believe it or not, Mr. Ripley.

S

SMALL BUSINESS ADMINISTRATION—AGAIN

CLEAN IT UP OR CLOSE IT DOWN

The Small Business Administration (SBA) has been examined by official watchdogs and has been reported by me with all its warts. But instead of reform, the agency keeps displaying its bureaucratic inefficiencies and, much worse, failing to block fraud of the people's money.

A few years ago, the inspector general of the agency, along with the Secret Service of the Treasury Department, concluded an investigation into a large group of defaulted loans. The operation, called "Clean Sweep," studied a sample of 3,352 defaulted SBA loans nationwide and found a most startling revelation.

It turned out that one in eight of these borrowers had criminal records. In fact, the borrowers committed still another fraud when they applied for the loan by claiming they had never been found guilty of a crime. The roster of businessmen who received SBA loans even included a murderer. One borrower received a

$700,000 loan even though he had a prior record that included five arrests for passing bad checks and resisting arrest.

Doesn't the SBA fully check their applicants for a criminal record?

In fact, no.

All the applicant has to do is state that he or she has no criminal record. The SBA used to make a criminal check of applicants through the FBI, but in 1987 the FBI decided that it would do complete investigations only if they received the borrower's fingerprints. Without that, a proper check was impossible.

The SBA refused to cooperate. Now, all the SBA can do is take the word of applicants that they are not criminals, a rather unsatisfactory, even foolish, method of screening.

The result is that criminal fraud continues to plague the SBA. In the summer of 2008, the Government Accountability Office revealed that the SBA had allowed itself to be involved in still another ludicrous scam. This time, the SBA was supervising a program called HUBZones, which is a federal policy to bring business to economically distressed areas by shifting many federal contracts to small businesses within the areas. In 2007, those contracts totaled a sizable amount, $8 billion.

The first problem, as the government learned, is that the SBA provided a map showing which areas were eligible for small business contracts from Uncle Sam. Unfortunately, the SBA map was just plain wrong.

"To help firms determine if they are located in a HUBZone area, SBA publishes a map on its web site," says the report. "However, the map contains areas that are not eligible for the program and excludes some eligible areas. As a result, ineligible small businesses have been able to participate in the program and eligible businesses have not been able to participate."

It turns out that this was an understatement. To be eligible, many firms just breezed past the maps and falsely claimed that they were located in HUBZones when they were not. Then they easily obtained loans from the SBA under false pretenses. The fraud was simply executed because, as says the GAO, "the SBA does not have an effective fraud prevention program in place."

That became obvious. The investigators used fabricated documentation and easily obtained HUBZone certification from the SBA for four bogus firms. The SBA wrote back on one that "your application for certification as a qualified HUBZone small business concern (SBC) has been approved."

To support one false application, investigators claimed their principal office was the same address as a Starbucks coffee shop that was in a HUBZone. But the SBA did not check. Two of the bogus applications used leased mailboxes in retail postal centers, a location that immediately disqualifies a firm from being qualified.

Investigators located 10 firms in the Washington areas which, although not qualified, received $105 million as prime contractors on government programs. Of the 10, 6 did not meet the requirement of a principal office in a distressed zone and 4 did not meet the requirement that 35% of the employees lived in such a zone. The investigators checked one supposed company headquarters and found it was a small room above a dentist's office. The building owner told them that nobody had worked there for "some time."

The SBA has been assigned as the principal agency to coordinate HUBZone eligibility and processing for all the government agencies involved in the program. In addition, they are supposed to monitor the results. And once again they failed.

One of the main requirements is that the company, to be eligible, had to fit the SBA definition of a small business. As of 2008, 12,986 firms participated in the program nationwide and over 4000 HUBZone firms received contracts in 2007. Not all, unfortunately, were truly small businesses. We learned this from a report issued by the inspector general of the Department of Interior, which participated in the program.

Checking the agency database, they found that incorrect information had been entered by many large corporations, which misrepresented themselves as small businesses. This fraud was no amateur operation. A total of 10 Fortune 500 companies, including Xerox and farm equipment maker John Deere, were involved.

The inspector general was quoted as saying that this was only "the tip of the iceberg" because the study was based on a review of only 0.3% of the contracts in which the department and small businesses were involved.

The American Small Business League stated that the problem of these contracts went far deeper than what the inspector general found. A spokesman noted that large corporations were getting these contracts not through error but by "intentional diversion of federal small business contract dollars to Fortune 500 firms."

John Deere, for example, which received $617,000 in small business contracts in two recent years, was listed in the government database as a company having only $2 million in annual revenues, when actually it is a multibillion-dollar firm.

The SBA has obviously done it again. Perhaps we should insist that they clean themselves up, or better still, simply close shop, with a great savings of billions for our mistreated taxpayers.

S

SOCIAL SECURITY

THE $4 TRILLION FEDERAL HEIST

Arithmetic is not the favored discipline of the American public, as our students regularly demonstrate in their failure in international math competition.

Simultaneously, arithmetic is the favorite tool of politicians when they are determined—as usual—to fool the American public. Social Security is a major case in point.

Since 1983, when Social Security was "reformed," meaning that the premiums were raised 25%, the program has been producing enormous surpluses each year, money that was supposed to be reserved for the time the boomers retire, which has already begun.

But by the year 2016, the surpluses will have vanished. Social Security will then operate in a deficit—that is, less money will be coming in than going out. In that system, it will eventually be impossible for the government to make full benefit payouts under present circumstances. Only by reducing the benefits, extending the retirement age, or raising the payroll taxes—or all three—can we keep the system going.

The reason is that, for decades, politicians have been playing duplicitous games with our Social Security money, spending it lavishly on other things, from welfare to highway construction, instead of hoarding it for the boomers. Meanwhile the FICA taxes for Social Security are being raised some 6% every year.

Since 1983, the payroll taxes have accumulated some $2.5 trillion dollars in surplus money over and above what was needed to pay Social Security recipients.

Where is that fortune? Very simply, it is gone. It is not in the bank, it is not in any real marketable securities, government or otherwise, that can be sold.

Then where is it?

Because there is no way for the government to save money—the budget is a yearly cash-in, cash-out operation—the surplus trillions have been put into IOUs that the government has given the Social Security fund. Of the more than $12 trillion national debt, almost a quarter of it belongs to Social Security.

The fund does get the interest on those government bonds, but they cannot be sold. And as far as cash is concerned, there is none. As everyone should now know, we can never pay back the federal debt, so the $2.5 trillion is locked up forever. It is just as if it were gone. The same will be true, even worse, in 2018 when the locked-up surplus will reach close to $4 trillion, the amount of Social Security money spent on everything except the aged.

The tragedy is that our politicians have treated Social Security funds as a piggy bank. The result is that we now have, in effect, to pay twice for those trillions in Social Security IOUs.

The surplus money is locked up forever in the national debt and not in the cash needed to pay benefits to the aged and disabled.

But isn't the surplus invested? Only theoretically. As the government states, these debt securities are an "asset," as if you could add your mortgage to your net worth instead of the other way around.

How did all this happen? Why this mess?

The reason is simple. It is called the "unified budget," which Lyndon Johnson put into practice in 1968 and which is now the villain of the piece. It means that the money from the rest of the government, which has a yearly deficit, is intermixed with the FICA funds, which for the last 26 years have been in yearly surplus. This results in the misuse and expropriation of our Social Security funds, which trickily are used to make the annual deficit look smaller than it really is.

It was this fake unified budget that, during the Clinton administration, was used to create a total surplus, which never really existed.

Former Senator Fritz Hollings (D–SC) made it all very clear. The Social Security money, he said, has been "looted." "For everyone crying 'Save Social Security,' the first order of business is to stop destroying it by looting the fund," he angrily explained.

How can this be righted for the future?

Simply by breaking the false unified budget now.

Instead we should treat Social Security as a true independent agency, separate from the general government, as is the Federal Reserve. If independent, then Social Security could refuse the government's desire to use its surplus money to spend in the general fund for anything it wants. Instead, we could use the surplus to help pay benefits and reduce, not raise, Social Security taxes every year until 2018.

There have been numerous bills in Congress to do just that, but most never even get out of committee.

Why? Because then Washington would have to face the awful truth—that they have been looting the fund for the past 26 years and will continue to do so until they have taken (read "stolen") not just the present $2.4 billion but more like $4 trillion.

But of course, if Americans could handle mathematics and politicians were honest, this swindle could never have taken place.

The history of Social Security has been a checkered and contentious one. Started by FDR in 1935, it has generally been praised for keeping the aged out of dire poverty, which it has done. However, it has gone through many variations, several of which have been harmful, leading to the present dilemma, in which only 3.3 workers support one aged person, while in 1935 it was a 16 to 1 ratio.

It has also led to much higher FICA taxes, plus a yearly increase, plus the frightening future of the boomer retirement, which will eventually bring the worker ratio down to 2 to 1 and make the program unsustainable without a massive tax increase. At the same time, the retirement age has been raised to 67 and is moving toward 70, a fact which could destroy the human capital of the program, making the gap between 67 and 70 perhaps untenable for the aged.

The costs have regularly been going up. In 1968, the unified budget—one of the major villains—came into being. In 1972, colas, or regular benefit increases to keep up with inflation, were instituted. But the formula, now based on prices rather than wages, has been excessive. In 2009, recipients got an increase of 5.9%, which is unsustainable.

It was in 1972 that the government made a large increase in benefits, raising them 20%. But in 1983, in typical political hanky-panky, they took back that increase by starting to tax Social Security benefits, breaking a lifelong political promise.

The year 1983 was the fateful one when Alan Greenspan was named to reform the system. That resulted in a 25% increase in FICA taxes, a tax that harshly reduced net benefits in the program.

Tax reforms, as we have seen, generally end up with less money in people's pockets, as this one did.

We can be proud that we have a retirement fund for our aged, which has kept millions out of poverty. But we can't be proud that we have manipulated, looted, and misspent the people's Social Security funds instead of finding a way to save them for the retired to come.

Only an independent Social Security, securely separated from our unstable politicians, can secure the future for our growing army of the retired.

If someone told FDR, the original architect of Social Security, that 75 years later American politicians would be treating his brainchild like a broken piggy bank, he would have tilted his cigarette holder a touch more rakishly and sadly shaken his head.

T

TAXES

WE REALLY MISS PRESIDENT
HARRY S TRUMAN

If one has lived long enough to remember Harry Truman and the nation he represented in 1950, the change in America is not just dramatic but overwhelmingly sad.

One of the saddest aspects of the change is the amount of money we pay in taxes to the hungry bureaucratic mouths of the federal government, the state government, the county government, the town government, the school districts, ad infinitum.

In 1950, the middle class, which grew in power and strength after the war, had tax bills that for most were virtually negligible. Let's take a typical family in that era, the truly good old days, especially when it came to taxation. A couple called the Stephens had two children and lived in the suburbs in a three-bedroom house on which they had a $10,000, 4% VA mortgage with a monthly payment of $55.

Their income was $3,300 a year, the national average. In the fashion of the day, Jack Stephens's wife didn't work, and more important, she didn't have to.

What were their federal income taxes?

After deductions of the property tax, $300 in mortgage interest, $2,400 in personal exemption deductions, $95 for interest on the car and other loans, $70 for sales taxes, and $9 in New York State income tax, their total deductions were $3,072. That put them in the 20% basic bracket, for a total federal income tax of $46, or less than 2% of their income. The national average at the time was 2%!

Jack's FICA payroll tax was only 1.5%, or $45. The Stephens's total federal and state tax was $100 out of $3,300, or just over 3%. Truly.

Next door were the Gordons, who were more prosperous, with an above-average income. They had an income of $5,000, and their deductions were about the same as those of the Stephens family. Their tax bite, federal, state, and local, was $465, or some 9%, less than one third of today's tax burden.

Today, those who typically earn anywhere from $50,000 to $150,000 per family of four are saddled with such excessive taxes that deprive them of the ability to live well. Meanwhile, Washington—and local governments—luxuriate if not in cash, then in wasteful expenditures on a mammoth scale.

In some metropolitan areas, such as New York, with federal, state, city, and property taxes, the tax bill can take more than 40%—perhaps up to 50%—of one's income, making life difficult even for the supposed successful family.

Under Truman, the government was almost frugal. The total expenditure, federal, state, and local, took only 22% of the gross domestic product. Today, government cost has reached the incredible level of 41%, almost double that of 1950. And taxation inevitably follows the spending.

Even Truman's relatively small expenditure was 50% higher than that of FDR, the supposed champion New Deal spender of all time.

The major difference between today and 1950 is that Washington has regularly cheated the middle class, year by year, until we have reached the present breaking point in both taxation and spending. Candidate Obama promised that he would give a middle-class couple a $1,000 a year tax break, which is childish considering what Washington has regularly taken from us over the years.

The final 2009 so-called middle-class tax break was actually only $400 a year per person, less than $8 a week, even less than the miniature promise.

In 1950, as we have seen, the personal exemption was $600, or $8,400 in today's inflation-adjusted money. That means $36,000 a year per family of four that wouldn't have to be counted as income. Instead, today, the exemption is only $3,650 a person, or $16,600 per family.

That has robbed almost $20,000 in exemptions for every family or what could be a cut in taxes of some $5,000 a year, a significant gain for the middle class, which has cleverly been taken away by a conniving, money-hungry Washington. And since state taxes are usually exempt from federal levies, that is another loss to the beleaguered middle class.

Today, the federal government has passed the political 4-minute mile, spending $3.6 trillion a year, while other governments, and there are thousands, take in and spend some $1.5 trillion more. This is more than sanity dictates and much more than taxpayers can afford. In fact, local and state taxes have tripled in real dollars since 1960.

The present tax structure is punitive, and alarmingly so. Years ago, the antitax movement in America was considered crackpot. Today, it is the federal government as well as the states and localities that have proven to be the crackpots. They have conjured up a bureaucratic spending orgy and tax system that threatens the stability of America and the ability of Americans to pay the exorbitant levies.

Every aspect of the tax code has been cleverly targeted against the middle class, with government having become expert at extracting the very last nickel from our bank accounts. This is especially true of the so-called payroll tax, which supports Social Security and much of Medicare and is taken out of your paycheck at the onset. Year by year, depending on how much money Washington wants to spend on other things, this tax goes up, like the sun rising in the morning.

Washington always low balls its projects to gain acceptance then forces reluctant taxpayers to pay the true freight. In 1950, the Social Security tax for employees was only 1.5% of the worker's wages. It went up inexorably year by year and reached 4% in 1968, then the present 6.20% in 1990, a fourfold increase since the glory days of 1950.

Suddenly, the payroll tax grew in another dimension. In 1966, a Medicare hospital tax was added, seemingly small, only 0.35%. But that too grew yearly, and by 1990 it had reached its present 1.45%, or 2.9% for employee and employer. This brought the total payroll tax up to its present 7.65% for employee and 7.65% for employer, a total of 15.3%.

The government's Medicare program for the aged has always been touted as not being "means tested"—that is every aged person pays a standard premium, rich, middle class, and poor, though the truly poor have free Medicaid. But no more for the successful middle class. Just in the last 2 years, if you make a substantial but not very high income of $160,000 for a two-wage-earning couple, you pay considerably more each month for Medicare coverage over and above the 1.45%.

Like all government promises to the middle class, no "means test" of Medicare turned out to be nothing more than political blather.

The government, which burns the midnight oil exploring new, more imaginative taxes for the middle class, also decided that self-employed middle-class people should suffer even more, by taxing them twice for Social Security and Medicare—once as an employee and another time as an employer, a failure of logic that is especially painful.

Today, the self-employed American, of whom there are some 14 million, pay a stunning 15.3% of their income just in payroll taxes. When the 15% is added to regular taxes, which can reach 39%, plus state taxes averaging 6%, plus local taxes of another 6%, the self-employed are not working for themselves, but for governments. (A very small relief in self-employed taxes was passed in 1984, which cut only a couple percent off the punitive rate.)

Where there's a way for Washington to increase taxes, they'll find it. In addition to higher payroll taxes, they have used another dimension to raise money. Regularly, Congress and the president increased the amount of salary subject to Social Security tax. In fact, the Medicare tax has no income limit—it goes all the way. The Social Security salary limit subject to tax was $53,000 in 1991, but it has since doubled to $106,800 in 2009, an easy if painful way to raise taxes despite political promises not to.

As taxes rise, Washington simultaneously uses its wiles to reduce taxpayer benefits and deductions. Over the years, they have secretly raised revenue by eliminating the ability of taxpayers to average their incomes over a 3-year period, which used to ease the tax burden of a one-time jump in income. But in 1986, the government removed this benefit, along with, as we have seen, the ability to deduct state and local sales taxes, and the one-time glory of deducting interest on loans and credit cards.

They gave taxpayers, temporarily, a lower (28%) maximum tax rate. But that—despite promises—soon disappeared and was replaced with the higher 35%, making the reform simply another gimmick to raise taxes on the middle class. That's the true aim of the government because that's where the real money lies. Not in the rich, as some falsely claim, and surely not in the poor, who pay almost no federal income taxes, but in the enormous middle class who pay two thirds of the entire bill.

Politicians know that the golden goose of political economics is the middle class, and the tax laws are written to wring it dry, a goal that borders on an obsession, and a successful one at that.

In 1993, Congress and the president, still seeking more revenue, once again deprived the middle class of tax deductions, some so petty that it is embarrassing.

Before the 1993 law, you could deduct a small office in your house where you did extra work. That was changed and now it must be your principal place of business. Before 1993, if you had to move for a new job, you could deduct the cost of scouting out a new home, temporary living for 30 days, plus meals, and going to and fro. Now you can deduct only the cost of moving and lodging on the one-way, mainly one-day trip.

Chintzy government? That's only the beginning.

The once valuable medical cost deduction has virtually been eliminated. Once it was all deductible, then the threshold was raised to 5% of your income. Then in the 1986 so-called reform, which eventually increased most taxes, it was raised to 7.5% of your income, which eliminated most medical deductions.

Until 1993, you could take your wife along on a business trip if she was valuable to the enterprise and deduct her costs. But no more. Now you travel alone or pay her freight.

Perhaps the greatest loss in valuable deductions for the middle class is the present law that forces you to partially renounce your deductions the more successful you become or if you live in a high-cost area. Today, you start to lose your deductions in two ways. The first is the inane formula of the "Alternative Minimum Tax" (p. 55).

The second is equally, if not more, insidious. Once your married but filing separately income reaches $79,975 a year (2008), you start to lose your deductions, as if you didn't earn and need them. When you itemize and you have reached that sacrosanct income ceiling, you lose 3% of your deductions for mortgage interest, property tax, state tax, and an even larger portion of your personal exemption.

Tax-greedy Washington perennially comes up with new taxes, using excuses and arguments that are ingenious. The latest proposed massive tax hike combines Washington's unproven theories of global warming (recall last winter's bitter cold nationally) and climate change ostensibly caused by our use of fossil fuels, two concepts that are far from scientifically accurate.

Federal thinkers, a profound oxymoron, have used pseudoscience to propose a new energy carbon tax that will raise our utility bills and add to the burden of the middle class and especially the poor. The theory goes like this: Because pollution from carbon, in the form of carbon dioxide and other pollutants, has ostensibly caused global warming and because humans are ostensibly responsible for the supposed change in climate, why don't we try to cure it by paying what is in effect a carbon tax, a hidden and expensive one at that?

Washington's new plan is to raise some $650 billion over a decade by auctioning off pollution "permits" that allow power plants, for example, to use coal for electrical generation. The system is called "cap and trade," in which these permits are actually traded like stocks.

If it sounds asinine, that's because it is, both scientifically and economically.

Who eventually pays for all this egotistical false theorizing used to extract still more money from the American people? Companies, not individuals, initially pay the freight, but naturally they will raise utility bills to pay for Washington's greed, extra taxes that no one can afford. In fact, Washington thinkers have already conceded it will cost the country more with each utility bill.

It may not be true science but it represents a true view of Washington and its lack of concern for the people.

The federal government avidly seeks the reputation of moral superiority when, in reality, its punitive tax policies show a failure of morality that permeates virtually all of its actions.

Yes Virginia, Uncle Sam is not only a meanie when it comes to taxes but a rather cold, hard, calculating one.

And don't continue to pray for another Harry Truman. That's futile. They stopped making that kind of politician a long time ago.

T

TRAVEL, GOVERNMENT EMPLOYEES

BILLIONS ON THE WING

No one, but no one, likes to travel more than government employees.

In addition to 5 weeks' paid vacation and almost 3 weeks of sick leave, which can easily, if illegally, be used as vacation time by healthy employees, they use every opportunity—and there are many—to leave their offices in Washington, or elsewhere, to take wing to somewhere else, a kind of extra vacation away from their desks.

Conferences are a simple and easy way to get away at enormous cost to taxpayers, and neither deficits nor a teleconferencing alternative can keep government help at home. In a recent 5-year period, federal government spending on conferences here and abroad rose 70%, reaching $1.4 billion in travel costs just for conferencing.

This is not just for top agency brass. Virtually anyone who is anyone is invited. The Department of Education sent 158 people to a gathering in New Orleans. No one can outdo the Department of Health and Human Services (HHS), which in one year sent at least 100 employees to 59 different conferences, including a record 1,000 bureaucrats to a confab in Orlando.

That same agency sent 236 staffers to a conference on AIDS in Barcelona, Spain, the cost of which could have instead paid for complete AIDS therapy for 1,500 patients.

Uncle Sam paid $19 billion in 2008 for travel, probably double the appropriate amount. That savings can only be accomplished by a revamp of the travel systems, with totally new controls.

The Department of Defense (DOD) is a common travel offender. Auditors found that in a recent 2-year period, the DOD paid twice for the same ticket. How many times? Only 27,000. They would buy the airline tickets directly, then strangely enough, reimburse the employee as if he or she had paid for it. One employee allegedly claimed he didn't notice that the DOD had falsely placed $9,700 in his bank account.

The Air Force Audit Agency checked up on a sample of travel vouchers and found that 142 airline tickets paid for by the DOD had also been reimbursed to government travelers for the same tickets.

The State Department, which does a great deal of traveling, was another major offender in the wasting of funds. As with other agencies, they dissembled, faked, and used any edge to fly their people the luxurious, expensive way, either business or first class, rather than by plebian coach, a cost that at least quadruples the cost.

A study of State's flying records showed a very wasteful travel budget. In a recent 18-month period, State made an enormous 32,000 first- and business-class bookings, costing $140 million.

Federal law generally requires cheap coach flight unless medical conditions or other urgent circumstances justify an upgrade. State got away with its giant luxurious booking because the underlings of the executives who were flying high created a "blanket authorization" that led to the fancy globetrotting. Of those 32,000 bookings, 67% was either not properly authorized or justified. In one case three senior-level employees spent $410,000 on premium-class travel, while flying coach or not at all would have been sufficient, auditors stated.

The disparity between the cost of coach and first-class flying is enormous. In one case, a family of four was flown by State from Washington to Moscow for $6,712 on a luxurious ticket when coach cost only $1,784. A study of the Foreign Agricultural Service of the Department of Agriculture found that employees took first- or business-class flights 30% of the time. Of the 112 premium-class flights studied, 79 were authorized not by a superior but by a subordinate of the traveler or by someone not permitted to authorize premium-class flights.

In September 2007, the first-class racket was revealed in depth by a report that covered all agencies, with startling results. During 2005 to 2006, federal agencies spent some $230 million on 53,000 premium-class airline tickets. Most important, $146 million of that was considered improperly authorized and spent on business- and first-class air travel.

Many agencies were even ignorant of the amount of their luxurious travel. That was the case in the Office of Management and Budget at the White House and at the General Services Administration, neither of which required any reporting of upper-class travel. One executive in the Department of Agriculture had a subordinate authorize 25 premium-class flights, claiming that 10 of them were "mission critical."

One Department of Defense executive flew premium-class 15 times, claiming a medical condition. However, on inspection, it was found that the medical condition was not documented by a physician but by a fellow DOD employee. It was also learned that a group of 21 employees from the office of the U.S. Trade Representative traveled from Washington, DC, to Hong Kong to attend an international trade conference with business-class tickets that cost some $100,000, compared to only $32,000 if they have flown regular authorized coach.

Flying perks are consistent with the present attitude of both employees and agencies, which is that Uncle Sam represents a wealthy organization that can afford the very best for its legions—if not for the taxpayers who foot the extravagant bill.

Washington bureaucracy has shown itself to be without a strong moral compass, and its honesty must be checked and verified at all times.

There needs to be a control agency that overlooks all government travel instead of the present corrupt system, which leaves it to individual agencies that would gladly bleed the nation for the convenience of themselves and their comrades.

I would estimate that of the $19 billion travel budget, we could save $9 billion a year with just a little horse, not bureaucratic, sense.

U

UNFUNDED MANDATES

WHATEVER HAPPENED TO
THE 10TH AMENDMENT?

Subterfuge has become a common modus operandi of the federal government.

In the case of welfare or poverty, as we have seen, Washington cleverly hides its enormous annual expenditure to quell criticism of how much it's spending on this mission, just as it does with other programs.

But hiding excessive and foolish spending is not always the preferred method of fooling the American public. Sometimes it's necessary to face it out, counting on the public's lack of knowledge of the true operation of their expensive government in Washington.

That is definitely the case with "unfunded mandates," the special expedient of a near-bankrupt federal government that forces states and localities to carry out Washington's programs without Washington paying for them. Instead, the states are obligated, by possibly unconstitutional laws, to carry out programs for Washington out of their own pocket with no federal renumeration.

Which of Washington's programs are forced not only on the states but on their bank accounts as well? The list is endless and growing annually. Here are some examples:

- Medicaid, in which the states pay anywhere from 20% to 50% of the $350 billion bill.

- The state and school district costs of No Child Left Behind, the national education program that Washington refuses to fully pay for.

- State enforcement of the Safe Drinking Water Act.

- The federal Individuals with Disabilities Act, requiring states and localities to provide ramps and other aids for the disabled out of their own pocket.

- State and local enforcement of the federal Clean Air Act.

- State costs of enforcing federal Homeland Security programs.

- Federal Environmental Protection Agency programs paid for by the states.

- State costs of enforcing the federal Endangered Species Act.

- The Emergency Medical Treatment and Active Labor Act, which requires all hospitals in states and localities to pay for the treatment of indigents, including illegal immigrants.

- Federal requirement to provide bilingual education in all schools, in which states have no say but must pick up the cost.

- Special education programs for disabled children.

- New federal laws requiring states and localities to buy updated voting equipment.

This truncated list does not include requirements to the states from federal court decrees, which raises the ante considerably. Senator Lamar Alexander of Tennessee says that these requirements include dictates on how to "run Medicaid in Tennessee, to run foster care in Utah, transportation in Los Angeles and how to teach English to children in New York City."

The big daddy of Washington commands, but junior pays. Of all Washington's schemes, this is the most egregious, resulting in higher state sales and income taxes, and rising local property taxes. Meanwhile, Washington pretends that no new money is being spent because they have passed off the costs to the states, a refusal of Washington to face the raucous fiscal music.

The cost of these unfunded mandates is at least $35 billion a year, says the National Conference of State Legislatures. It is actually almost four times that amount if Medicaid is included, which it must be.

Medicaid, which is required and basically controlled by Washington, costs the states $165 billion a year, which places the total cost of unfunded mandates at over $200 billion. That money should instead be paid back to the states and added to the increasing deficit and national debt, freeing the states from paying for still another Washington program. Why not also charge the states with the cost of Medicare as well?

In a piece of sophistry seldom equaled, Washington has tried to escape responsibility for the largest unfunded mandate. It has accomplished that by unilaterally ruling that Medicaid is not actually a federal unfunded mandate but rather a "partnership."

Obviously that's false, because the states have little say over major changes in its expensive content.

Medicaid is now as expensive as public education in most states and, with other unfunded mandates, the largest of state expenditures. This cripples states' tax policies, forcing a rise in property taxes, the fastest growing levy in America.

In an even worse case of sophistry, Washington declared that No Child Left Behind, a $24 billion program, is also not an unfunded mandate. But school districts throughout the nation complain bitterly at the cost of administering it, even prompting a lawsuit against the government by the National Education Association.

Rebellion against unfunded mandates reached such a fever pitch in 1995 that Congress passed the Unfunded Mandates Reform Act of 1995 (UMRA), which was supposed to slow down the proliferation of such laws. However, it left all existing unfunded mandates in place and offered no rescue for the states. All it did was allow a member of Congress to "raise a point of order" when the Congressional Budget Office estimated that the cost of the new mandate bill injured the states by $60 million or more.

The new law, by most observations, has been a failure. For example, since then, several new unfunded mandates have been passed, a few of which are here listed. According to the National

Conference of State Legislatures, the mandates from Washington to the states since 1995 include the following:

- A reduction in federal aid for states to administer food stamps.

- A prohibition on states to tax Internet services and transactions.

- A requirement that states issue and pay for special ID documents to improve national security.

- Elimination of federal matching funds to help states administer federal child support programs.

- A requirement forcing states to pay for extra security regulations on buses and railroads.

Many other mandates are not even mentioned above. Not only states but their localities are hard pressed by Washington's evasion of responsibility. The state of Ohio estimated it would cost $1.74 billion over a 3-year period to conform to federal unfunded mandates. That cost is then passed down to counties, cities, and towns. Often the mandate is not practical. Lake County, Ohio, was required to build a new $3.5 million landfill even though the current landfill was not filled and was environmentally sound.

It is much the same in other states. Candace Donoho of the Maryland Municipal League says that local governments in her state find it "hugely expensive" to fulfill federal mandates passed on to Maryland. "If the feds mandate a change in local regulations and there is no money associated with it," she said, cities often have no choice but to raise rates for services.

Are these unfunded mandates constitutional? Probably not.

Among the Founding Fathers, Thomas Jefferson was the most prescient about conflicts between the federal government being formed and the states, which as former British colonies, already existed in another form. Just as Madison predicted a "tyranny of the majority," in the form of a future monstrous Washington, Jefferson saw the possibility that the new Federal City would overwhelm the states, which he considered the fountainhead of our liberty.

When the Bill of Rights was being debated, Jefferson insisted that the 10th Amendment be adopted to protect the states and localities against what otherwise might be the total power of Washington.

The 10th Amendment, passed in 1791, reads in full: "All powers not delegated to the United States by the Constitution, nor prohibited by it to the States, are reserved to the States respectively, or to the people."

It seems clear that the responsibilities of the federal government and the states were divided by the Constitution and accentuated by the 10th Amendment. But over the years, Washington increased its reach into what previously had been considered the province of the states.

Congress used the Commerce Clause, with its stated control over interstate commerce, as a basis for Washington's extended reach into virtually every aspect of American life, stretching into areas normally reserved for the states and localities, and enhanced by the wording of the 10th Amendment.

As time went on, the 10th Amendment was quoted in cases

before the Supreme Court, but it became increasingly evident that it did not have the power it seemed to express, and little by little it lost its luster. Finally, in 1937, under the New Deal plan to alleviate the Depression by taking more power from the states and shifting it to Washington, it was finally tested before the Supreme Court.

In a lawsuit involving the National Labor Relations Board, which extended Washington's reach into management-labor relations—once the province of the states—the Court upheld the law. The result is that the 10th Amendment to the Constitution is no longer taken seriously and has become the stepchild of the Constitution, apparently ignored with impunity by the federal government.

Today, it is as if it had never been written.

A valiant but futile attempt to revive the 10th Amendment was recently made by the state of Oklahoma, which tried to recover some of its lost state sovereignty. The state introduced and passed a rebellious House Joint Resolution 1099, which in part reads: "Whereas, the 10th amendment defines the total scope of federal power as being that specifically granted by the Constitution . . . and whereas, the scope of power defined by the 10th Amendment means that the federal government was created by the states specifically to be an agent of the states . . . now therefore be it resolved . . . that the state of Oklahoma hereby claims sovereignty under the 10th Amendment to the Constitution."

Despite this futile effort by one state, the 10th Amendment is now almost totally discarded.

It certifies that Washington's power, even when used and abused by politicians, is in total control of the nation. It also makes possible the proliferation of unfunded mandates, which permanently establishes the states as totally secondary to Washington.

The death of the 10th Amendment has certified that not only is state sovereignty equally dead but that the states are now simple obedient servants, or colonies, of the federal government, all testifying to the prescient, if ignored, genius of Thomas Jefferson.

V

VICE PRESIDENT

In August 2008, before the party presidential conventions, the media was hypnotized as both presidential campaigns tantalized them and the country with false choices for the number two slot on their respective tickets.

The real choices, made personally by the head of the ticket, finally cleared the air. But why was the nation so concerned about the selection of a vice president?

Many years ago, John Nance Garner of Texas, the vice president during FDR's first term, cynically commented that the job "wasn't worth a bucket of warm spit."

Actually, events have proven him wrong. A total of 14 vice presidents in our history have assumed the presidency, either through the death of the president or by having been elected in their own right.

We've had some great veeps, and some downright failures, even some with a touch of evil. Jefferson's vice president was

Aaron Burr, who came within a few votes in Congress of beating Jefferson for the presidency. Later Burr killed Alexander Hamilton in a duel and was eventually tried for treason. Even though acquitted, he became a historic villain.

Spiro Agnew, Richard Nixon's vice president, was forced out of office when it was discovered that, while in office, he had received envelopes filled with cash from contractors in his home state of Maryland, where he had been governor.

Andrew Johnson of Tennessee, a former tailor who assumed the presidency when Lincoln was assassinated, was suspected of being a Southern sympathizer, and eventually was impeached by the House, but he was narrowly acquitted by the Senate. Lincoln's vice president in his first term, Hannibal Hamlin, served loyally for 4 years, but was replaced by Johnson, losing his chance to become president by just a few months.

Johnson was a political bet by Lincoln, who thought Johnson would attract some Democratic votes in his 1864 second term race against former Union Army commander General George McClellan, who now favored a rapprochement with the South. But the choice of Johnson later backfired.

Other vice presidents were colossal nonentities such as J. Danforth (Dan) Quayle. George H. W. Bush made this peculiar choice of a young, inexperienced, uncharismatic politician, noted for his misspelling of the lowly spud as "potatoe." In fact, Bush stubbornly kept him on as the vice presidential candidate for his anticipated second term, which failed at the polls.

But in other cases, the number two slot was a stepping-stone to historical greatness or at least to strong opinion and controversy. Vice President Theodore Roosevelt was elevated to the

White House when President William McKinley was assassinated in 1901. Lyndon Johnson, who came in second to JFK in the 1960 primaries, assumed the presidency after Kennedy's assassination, creating the Great Society, a now debated if historic period.

Harry Truman, who became the 33rd president after FDR's sudden death in 1945, has entered the tier of the great with his creation of the Marshall Plan and his successful work in stopping communism in Western Europe.

In selecting our presidents, the system is not fully democratic in that the people do not directly elect the chief executive. Rather he (or she) is chosen by the voters separately in each state, through the electoral college. It balances out in most cases, but several times—as recently as the Bush vs. Gore election in 2000—the popular vote went one way (for Gore), and the actual electoral college result another way (to victorious Bush).

What has varied greatly over our history is the method of choosing the vice president, which possibly accounts for the great variance in the quality of the veeps.

Originally, as established by the Constitution in 1789, the man who came in second for the presidency was named vice president, which made the office a consolation prize. This was the case in 1796, when Jefferson became vice president after his defeat by John Adams. Even though they were diametrically opposed politically (and disliked each other), Federalist vs. Republican-Democrat, Jefferson still joined Adams' administration in the number two slot.

This proved to be too conflicting. In 1804, the 12th Amendment to the Constitution changed the system so that the vice president was selected on the same ballot as the president and was therefore necessarily of the same party. It became the responsibility of the party to nominate the veep, which is still the system.

Within the party, the nomination method has changed since then.

For most of our history, the party chieftains, along with the presidential nominee, made the vice presidential choice. Because the party bosses generally made the presidential nomination before the primary system became commonplace, they also exercised power in naming the vice president. Sometimes, the party bosses even bypassed the presidential nominee's choice and named the vice president on their own.

The classic case of this was the nomination of Harry Truman to be FDR's running mate during his fourth term race in 1944.

The big-city bosses met in a hotel room in Chicago to name the vice president while Roosevelt was elsewhere. His only edict to them was "Anyone but Truman," whom he despised because of Truman's work in wartime waste and fraud. But the bosses overruled FDR, and Truman got the nod. Truman was virtually exiled by FDR during the few months the president lived during his fourth term, and he never told Truman that we were building an atom bomb.

Fortunately, as history has proven, the bosses had been much wiser than FDR.

In the past 30 years, the primary system has eliminated politicians as powers in the nominating procedure. Today, the naming of the vice president has settled conclusively in the hands of the party's presidential nominee, who has been granted full undisputed power in that choice.

This is, of course, the most undemocratic procedure possible, putting the fate of potential future presidents in the hands of one person.

In 1956, the Democratic Party nominee, Adlai Stevenson, whose grandfather had been vice president under Grover Cleveland, decided to democratize the nomination by throwing the choice to the convention itself. By coincidence, I served as a delegate at that convention and worked for JFK to become the vice presidential nominee. But we lost to Senator Estes Kefauver of Tennessee, who was of no help in the general election, in which Stevenson lost badly to General Eisenhower.

The vice presidential job, despite John Nance Garner's comment, is too important to be left to any single person's discretion, including that of the presidential nominee, as it now is. If we are to ensure better choices in the future than either Spiro Agnew or Andrew Johnson, we must leave that nomination to a larger group of people.

The grave danger of putting the vice presidential nomination at the discretion of the presidential nominee was demonstrated by FDR in his choice of Henry Wallace, a personal favorite, as his vice president in his third term. Wallace, we should remember, ran for president in 1948 against Truman as the head of the strongly left-leaning Progressive Party, which garnered only 1 million votes when it favored appeasement of the Soviet Union.

In reality, the vice presidential nomination should be left to the entire party, at the convention where it should be voted on by all the delegates, in a spirited debate. The presidential nominee should no longer hold the future of America in his or her hands.

No, we must change this new tradition and put the naming of the vice president—who one third of the time will become a future president—into the collective, wiser hands of the entire party, at their quadrennial convention.

Anything less is a violation of common sense, good government, and democracy.

By the way, could we have survived Henry Wallace as president in 1944?

WELFARE

How Washington's Antipoverty Programs Fail Both the Poor and the Taxpayers

As we have seen in detail, welfare is a mammoth, hidden portion of the federal government. (See "The Road to Oblivion" on p. 1.)

In fact, it is the largest of all federal programs, totaling some $700 billion a year for the 37 million Americans defined as poor.

It is so secretive that the Office of Management and Budget's pie chart of federal expenses, which is divided into seven portions from Defense to Social Security, doesn't even mention welfare or charity. One would think Washington is ashamed of the enormous and overexpensive effort, which exceeds both the separate costs of Social Security and Medicare, neither of which are welfare programs.

And ashamed they should be. The problem is that most of the money doesn't go to the intelligent support of the poor. Instead, the programs are ill-defined, duplicative, wasteful, and not well-directed to those for whom they were designed.

Most important, the amount of money spent is so enormous that if properly used, it would totally eliminate poverty in America with multibillions left over to reduce the deficit.

When I first began researching welfare, I learned that there is no category called "welfare" or "charity" in the federal budget. It would have been impossible for a citizen, a journalist, a congressman, or perhaps even a president to determine the total amount spent on the poor.

The true numbers are well hidden and scattered throughout the small print of the budget. They are so well hidden that I learned that there is no central computer accounting and no way to know how much any citizen was receiving and how many programs he or she was involved in.

Then how did I come up with the estimate of $700 billion spent each year on the poor, a number of citizens the government says is 37 million strong?

As we have seen in the opening chapter, we never would have known the truth except for the diligence, and courage, of one federal employee: Ms. Vee Burke of the small Congressional Research Service (CRS), who made this her chore for a number of years. In fact, every 2 years she pored through thousands of programs to learn the truth.

She came up with a 250-page encyclopedia of 85 different welfare programs emanating from six different cabinet agencies, and uncoordinated from one agency to the next. The name of her report was *Cash and Non-Cash Benefits for Persons with Limited Income*. The last volume was published in November 2003, covering the fiscal years 2000 through 2002.

Why isn't it published anymore? Because Burke retired and the government hasn't seen fit to publish an update yet.

The last volume showed that the cost of welfare in 2002 was $522 billion, including $373 billion in federal funds and $149 billion in state money. Most of the latter is in Medicaid, which is actually a Washington-designed and determined program, one of the unfunded federal mandates.

Then how did I arrive at $700 billion, one might ask? Easy. The programs keep rising in cost, but I used a very conservative increase per year of just over 4%, from 2002 to 2009. Actually, the $700 billion is surely much less than the actual figure, which might approach $800 billion, especially if we consider the rise just from 2001 to 2002 of $45 billion, an increase of a staggering 9.5%.

But the smaller increase will make the point as well. The math itself is frightening. If we take the government figure of 37 million poor, that means that we are spending $16,200 annually for each poor person in America, or some $65,000 in welfare for each poor family of four.

When this is added to the typical poor family's present estimated income of $13,000, we come to the astounding, and frightening, figure that each poor family could, in an ideal world, have $78,000 a year.

Of course that's not possible for many reasons, the most important being that we are dealing with the Goliath of waste and irrationality, the federal government of the United States, one of whose sacred principles is to protect the pet program of each and every member of Congress (and the president as well), no matter how fiscally ignorant he or she may be, as is usually the case.

The present system has 85 programs in eight categories: medical aid, cash aid, food aid, housing aid, educational assistance, social services, job and training services, and energy assistance.

Individually, the programs vary in importance and value, ranging from valuable to ridiculous. The uniting factor is that they are not united, or comprehensive, or generally intelligently designed. And as we have seen, they are horribly inefficient and wasteful. Let's look at one program, which has important value along with great liabilities, including vast fraud.

One of the major cash aids is the Earned Income Tax Credit (EITC) program that costs some $45 billion and sends checks instead of IRS bills to some 25 million Americans. Started in 1975, ostensibly to return $400 to poor taxpayers to help pay their payroll tax, it has since mushroomed in cost and inefficiency. Today, one can earn up to $42,000 a year and still receive a cash check from Uncle Sam. The program takes millions of people off the tax rolls, both from the IRS and from the FICA Social Security tax.

The title, of course, is deceptive. It is not earned, because one doesn't have to be working to receive the money. Nor is it a tax credit, in that many recipients pay no income tax. It does help millions of families, but it is simply welfare, another form of the same.

But the strangest part of the program is that you don't have to be poor to receive EITC. There is no means test, so a millionaire, with a Bentley, and a vacation home in Palm Beach, can get his EITC welfare check. Its only requirement is that you made less than $42,000 that year. The prior year you could have made a million, and the government will still send you a check, up to $5,000. In fact, they don't care.

It is a good program in some ways for the truly poor, although the $42,000 income limit is only $8,000 less than the typical American household income. You can be rich and still get your check, but there is one restraint: You can't have more than $2,950 a year in investment income. But you can live on borrowed money, or savings, and still get your check.

There is no doubt that EITC has helped many families to pay their bills on time, but its real failing is that it is a center of vast uncontrolled fraud. Millions of recipients lie to the government about their income. Government audits show that some $13 billion of the $45 billion is fraudulent, stolen from the Treasury by those receiving EITC. The truth is probably that this is an underestimate.

With so much complexity and frustration in delivering welfare intelligently, why not contemplate a totally different framework to help the poor?

Why not close all 85 programs, including such esoterica as Rural Housing Preservation Grant and Farm Labor Housing Loans and Section 236 Interest Reduction Payments? Instead, why not give every poor person in America enough cash rather than services so that he or she will no longer be poor?

What would that cost? Please go along with my math.

According to the U.S. Census Bureau report of 2008, there are 7,623,000 poor families in America. Each of them has 2.3 children, for a total of 26.5 million poor in family units. In addition, there are 10.7 million unrelated individuals and subfamilies, for the total of 37 million poor.

The first step is to get the families out of poverty. In 2008, the poverty threshold for families of four is somewhat less than

$23,000. If we assume that the typical poor family has an income of only $13,000, each would need $10,000 in cash to no longer be poor by federal definition.

What would that cost? Simple: 10,000 times 7.6 million families is $76 billion. We have now officially eliminated poverty in American families.

Let us assume that the 10.7 million poor individuals have incomes of only $5,000 a year. We add $5,000 a year in cash welfare, which officially takes them out of poverty as well. This costs an additional $54 billion. The total cost to eliminate poverty, officially, now totals $130 billion.

Because we are spending $700 billion now, that leaves a surplus of $570 billion, which we can put back in the federal Treasury.

But people can hardly live well at the poverty level. So let's give everyone in America a $40,000 family income and $17,000 for individuals. What would that enormous generosity cost? The bill to Washington would be another $17,000 cash per family, or $129 billion. Now the once-poor family is making only $10,000 less than the median family income of $50,000. They have become relatively financially independent and surely no longer poor. We have now spent $259 billion to create this nirvana.

Even with this amazing antipoverty result, we still have a surplus of $441 billion from our present $700 billion cost.

Don't stop me now, please.

To bring all once-poor individuals up to the $17,000 level would cost another $75 billion. Now, surely no one can claim that there is still poverty in America. We have spent a total of $334 billion, and have a surplus of $366 billion from our $700 billion, which we can begin to pay off our yearly deficit and chip away at the national debt.

But if $40,000 for families and $17,000 for individuals is still not enough for them to pay for their health insurance, let us close Medicaid and spend $300 billion on health plans for the poor. The first $75 billion will go to pay for nursing homes for former Medicaid patients and $225 billion for comprehensive health insurance policies for all 37 million poor.

That comes to an average of $6,000 per person and $24,000 a year in premiums for a full plan for a family of four. We'll save $50 billion a year because Medicaid now costs us $350 billion, and every poor person will have super-magnificent comprehensive health insurance much better than Medicaid.

Let's allot an additional $100 billion for miscellaneous welfare like college tuition and other overlooked needs. What could be more generous?

We have now spent some $384 billion on cash welfare, eliminated poverty, and put $316 billion back in the bank. Okay?

Obviously, it is money, not expensive, failed harebrained federal welfare schemes, that can eliminate poverty.

But don't worry. None of this will happen because of many reasons, including the stupidity of the federal government, which permits poverty despite spending a king's ransom on 85 mainly ineffective, even ignorant, antipoverty programs that threaten to bankrupt us.

But perhaps Washington likes failed antipoverty programs, after all. Surely some members of Congress have been made happy by having their names attached to what appears to be charity for the poor.

And as our little demonstration shows, there is one other reason why federal programs seem designed for failure.

We must remember the need for the government to have as

many poor people as possible to gain the glory of feeding and sheltering them at any cost, and ultimately to get their vote.

But my crackpot idea, I must admit, is still quite titillating, even revealing.

And just think—what if the present cost of welfare is actually $800 billion and not just a measly $700 billion a year?

X

X-PRESIDENTS

Too Cushy an End Game?

It was 1953. At the end of his term of almost 8 years, Harry Truman returned home to Independence, Missouri, and carried his own bags up to the bedroom of his wife's family home where he lived.

For the next 6 years, Truman lived frugally, relying partially on his $112-a-month army pension for his service as a decorated artillery captain in World War I. Because he had no presidential pension from Washington, he lived without much cash, not having enough, he told confidantes, to pay for his much increased personal mail.

Though he had many opportunities to cash in on his years as president, he refused to commercialize his service to the country, preferring to live modestly.

As ex-President Truman said: "I could never lend myself to any transaction, however respectable, that would commercialize on the prestige and dignity of the office of the presidency."

At the time, American presidents were a forgotten, overlooked class, and often, as with General Grant, were forced into poverty. In 1958, when Truman finally complained about his finances to Congress, they woke up and awarded him a $25,000-a-year pension and a small staff.

Today, things are absurdly different as America has turned about and created a new class of political rock stars—the ex-presidents, who splendidly and openly capitalize on their former positions, to the tune of many millions of taxpayer money a year. And unlike Harry Truman, they also have access to many millions the exes gain by blatantly commercializing on their past service.

Former president William Jefferson Clinton is the leader in that new political rock group.

Like the others, he receives a pension of $191,000 a year plus $96,000 for a staff, and an apparently unlimited amount for renting an office, plus equipment and travel. Clinton chose a large suite in Harlem at an exorbitant cost of $45,000 a month, more than the rental of some sizable American corporations. His phone bill from 2001 through 2008 was astronomical, some $420,000. All told he spent $8 million in the last 7 years, while his predecessors were more modest—$5.5 million for the elder Bush and $4 million for Jimmy Carter.

Clinton's office in Harlem is an 8,300-square-foot penthouse, but it is cheaper than his first choice, a large midtown spread that would have cost $811,000 per year in rent. Clinton moved to the Harlem penthouse when House Republicans complained.

Perhaps the largest upkeep of former presidents by taxpayers is the cost of the Secret Service for protection for all ex-presidents and their spouses for life. At last count that tab was some $23 million a year.

If they are two-term presidents, exes are entitled to a prepaid $10,000 health insurance premium, not available to one-termers. Reagan refused the benefit, but Clinton accepted.

As for commercialization, mainly from speaking engagements and memoirs, Clinton is also the leader. Mr. and Mrs. Clinton reported that in the last 7 years since they left the White House, they had a combined income of $111 million.

Again unlike Truman, all exes have brilliantly commercialized on their past service. Even George Herbert Walker Bush has received upward of $100,000 per speech.

The most recent ex-president, George W. Bush, is expected to rent an office in Dallas at a cost of $312,000 a year, which is less than Clinton's, but much higher then Carter's, who is among the most modest of exes, with a rent of only $102,000.

All of this is without the federal support of presidential libraries, which at one time were not on the taxpayer budget, but now cost us many millions a year to maintain.

The exes build their own libraries with private donations, as with the Clinton Library in Little Rock, which cost about $165 million. The library itself became controversial when Clinton accepted a large donation from Denise Rich before Clinton pardoned her fugitive husband, who had been wanted for fraud. He is still living in Switzerland for fear of being somehow prosecuted. despite the Clinton pardon, should he return.

There were seven presidential libraries built and maintained on their own—from Garfield through Lincoln to Calvin Coolidge—that were extant before Franklin Roosevelt donated part of his Hyde Park estate to the government for his presidential library. Today, from Hoover through Clinton, there are 12 presidential libraries built privately and now supported by the federal government agency, the National Archives and Records Administration (NARA). George W. Bush is planning to build his own, the thirteenth, on the campus of Southern Methodist University.

Washington is trying to ease the overall cost by asking the libraries to set up private endowments to handle part of the bill. But thus far, the private contributions are relatively small.

The upshot? Uncle Sam, or better still, the taxpayers, now spend some $46 million a year to maintain the presidential libraries. Harry Truman has one as well, in Independence, but I still believe he would turn over in his grave if he ever saw the extravagant bill.

Were he to come back as an ex-president today, Truman would surely have it better than he did, even as president of the United States.

Y

YANKEE STADIUM

Steinbrenner's New Castle, Courtesy of Uncle Sam

Let me make one thing eminently clear, as a former president was wont to say: I love the New York Yankees.

One of my fondest memories is that of my father, who finished work early each day, plucking me at the age of 11 from Junior High School 52 in the South Bronx and taking me to Yankee Stadium for a day game. I remember sitting in the bleachers—I think it cost 25 cents then—and roaring my approval of Jolting Joe DiMaggio, who was only a baseball's throw away in the outfield.

I love the current Steinbrenner billion-dollar club (even if I resent A-Rod's $30 million salary, especially with his impotence in the playoffs), and I will support them spiritually all the way until my dying day. But I have just learned that I am supporting them financially as well, something I had no intention of doing except through the purchase of the occasional ticket.

How? By contributing millions each year of my (and your)

federal tax money toward the construction of the new stadium directly adjacent to the old, seemingly ageless ballpark where they won 26 world championships.

In what form are we being touched for Steinbrenner's new castle in the Bronx?

By the use of federal tax funds for a private investment to be owned by the Yankees. The mechanism is simple. The city of New York, which is covering about 25% of the cost of finishing the new stadium, has a legitimate local economic rationale, which is their business.

But they have shaped a deal with the federal government to finance this private project with almost $900 million in federal tax-exempt bonds, the same mechanism usually reserved for public schools, highways, bridges, and so on—using something called municipal bonds.

This is money the U.S. Treasury will never get from taxes on the interest paid to bondholders, money the Treasury needs and should get. On your 1040 form there is a box where you are supposed to enter income from tax-exempt bonds. It's there, but you pay no taxes on it, so Uncle Sam loses on that type of income.

In this case, the bond is not for a public but for a private— very rich capitalist—enterprise. I'm a strong believer in capitalism, but just as strong a believer that our tax money should not support private enterprise, no matter how colorful. The rationale for the federal government's involvement—stimulated by the City of New York—is weak at best and, like many unnecessary federal projects, is part of a largesse we surely cannot, and should not, afford.

Private is private, city is city, and federal is federal. This is a lesson that members of Congress, with their pork earmarks, and the White House itself insist on ignoring at huge cost to the taxpayer.

The pain to taxpayers for the new Yankee Stadium is substantial, a loss of about $40 million a year in federal taxable revenue. But that is only the beginning. This same tax-free mechanism has been used to build some 40 new private sports stadiums in the nation at a cost of some $8 billion in federal tax-free bonds. Houston alone used $700 million in these bonds to build baseball, football, and basketball stadiums.

The overall cost to taxpayers in lost taxable interest is over $400 million a year, or $4 billion every decade. As late Senator Everett Dirksen of Illinois once informed us: "A billion here and a billion there and soon you're talking about real money."

Senator Byron L. Dorgan (D–ND) has correctly called the program "a subsidy for millionaires who own these teams and the millionaire athletes who play on them." He's right, but living in the glass house of giant farm subsidies in his home state, Dorgan would be better off keeping his political mouth closely shut.

Meanwhile, every time I watch A-Rod strike out in a vital postseason game, I not only shudder but remember that it's costing us thousands of dollars a swing.

Z

ZIP CODES

Washington Is Blatantly Unfair, Geographically Speaking

One of the greatest lies in national government is that Uncle Sam is fair with all its citizens, whether they live in Manhattan or Mississippi. A person's ZIP code is supposedly something that only helps the post office deliver your mail.

An American is an American, the myth goes. But the reality is quite the opposite. Your federal taxes are collected uniformly—someone from the Bronx pays the same as someone in Boise, Idaho. Someone who has a local low cost of living pays the same on his 1040 IRS form as someone from Manhattan, where living costs might be three times as high.

But outside the IRS, the exact opposite can be true. Washington is generous or chintzy with Americans, depending on where they live. Their ZIP codes, by state, can determine who is going to get a good financial break from the federal government and who will be penalized for where they live. The equation is simple—tax money out to Washington, federal aid in.

For example, citizens of certain states receive Washington's bounty while others are forced to pay exorbitant federal taxes to support the citizens of those certain states, a basically unfair system of give and get. The prime example is Washington, DC, itself—ZIP code 20001 and up.

Washington, DC, is a case of poor federal judgment, in fact, catastrophically. For every dollar that citizens of the capital pay to the IRS, they receive $6.17 in government aid, making the city the center of American government charity. The top 10 "getters" or "winners from the federal government include North Dakota, which receives $2.03 for every dollar its citizens pay in federal taxes, followed by New Mexico, Mississippi, Alaska, West Virginia, Montana, Alabama, South Dakota, and Arkansas, which receives $1.53 for every dollar paid to the IRS.

How come this disparity? The answer is that Washington likes poorer states and sends them much more money, taking it from the supposedly richer states. The result, of course, is that the supposedly richer states, like New York, pay exorbitant federal net taxes, eventually making them less rich, by a country mile.

The so-called "richest" states are the losers in this geographic federal game, topped by New Jersey, which sends a fortune to Washington but gets back only $0.62 on each dollar its residents pay in federal taxes, a loss of almost 40%. Other losers in this federal roulette game are, in order, Connecticut, New Hampshire, Nevada, Illinois, Minnesota, Colorado, Massachusetts, California, and New York, which receives only $0.81 back for every dollar it sends to Washington.

The government manages this state preference business in

many ways, including how they pay for Medicaid, health insurance for the poor, which now costs $350 billion a year. The federal government calls it a "partnership" between the states and Washington. But in actuality it is really an unfunded mandate in which the states operate the system, but Washington has total control of the matching fund.

The states are forced to pay a portion of the giant bill according to a complicated federal formula (Federal Medicaid Assistance Percentage), which once again sets up winners and losers, helping some states and penalizing others, mainly according to the state's per capita income (PCI).

As a result, the final dollars received from Washington are even more unfair. States get much more or much less than they should if the state's poverty level is involved, especially because Medicaid is only for poor people. For example, New York with only 8% of the nation's poverty population received almost 13% of federal Medicaid dollars, while Texas, with a higher poverty level, 10%, got only 6% of federal dollars.

In this roulette game, the supposedly richer states have to pay up to 50% of their Medicaid costs, which fiscally cripples wealthier states like New York and Connecticut while Washington gives giant subsidies to poorer states, with subsidies of up to 84% of their Medicaid bill. New York City, based on the punitive federal formula, pays a staggering $6 billion bill annually for Medicaid.

There is, of course, a fallacy in this entire business of rich and poor states. Mississippi is surely poorer than New York according to the PCI, but at the same time the federal government doesn't take into account that living in New York might cost double or triple that of Mississippi.

So the next time you write your ZIP code on a letter, think twice. It's not just a matter of a $0.44 stamp but billions of dollars coming your state's way—or billions lost in Washington's irrational game of financial roulette.

INSTRUCTIONS FOR THE PRESIDENT

How to Better Govern America

It should now be apparent that Congress is the very last organization to accomplish a reformation of the American government, reform that is necessary if we are to reverse Washington's present suicidal course.

The presidency is the only possible instrument of reform, if it should so choose. The executive branch has the opportunity to make a thorough examination of the federal government, and then devise a reconstruction plan, which it will submit to Congress. With enough public pressure, Congress should accede to the changes that are necessary.

The difficulty is that although there are constant claims of undertaking reform, never in the last 50 years has there ever been a serious attempt to clean up the Augean stable of Washington, DC, the nucleus of America's anguish and intellectual corruption.

If such a reconstruction of Washington is seriously done and completed, we should have a savings of some $600 billion a year and a reformed organization that operates much better with less waste and overlap, and with far greater integrity. And perhaps most important, our government would then be less subject to political motivation and more based on reasoned intelligence in the day-to-day operations.

The present government is too ignorant and too heavily based on failed political tradition and partisanship.

In this chapter, I advocate a detailed plan for change, including methods and specific recommendations, as follows.

- There are more than 1,000 programs that are duplicated in the federal government, spread throughout scores of bureaus and several cabinet agencies. All programs with the same mission should be assigned to a single agency rather than being dispersed and effectively hidden, as they now are.

Once they have been identified, those programs that are duplicated should be closed, leaving only a core of one or two programs to accomplish the mission. For example, there are 10 different federal agencies promoting American exports. Take these programs out of 9 of the agencies involved and place only the main components in the Department of Commerce, eliminating all duplication.

Take the 70 drug abuse programs for young people out of 13 different federal agencies and put them all in one place, in the new Department of Health. We should close most of the 70, saving both money and juvenile health. Do this throughout the government, eliminating some three quarters of the 1,000 duplicated programs, now spread out and hidden. The savings will be in the scores of billions.

- Reduce the number of government employees by 20%, saving $120,000 a year for each in salary and benefits, plus a substantial savings in overhead. This is an easy task for it requires that no one need be discharged. There is a 7% turnover each year. By not rehiring 5% a year, within 4 years the objective will be achieved.

Anyone who has done business with the federal government knows this will have a positive effect on the efficiency and work habits of Washington. After the bureaucracy has been reduced 20%, we should evaluate the possibility of reducing it by still another 10%, again through attrition.

- Simultaneously, eliminate the federal credit card and travel card programs for all employees. Employees have proven they cannot handle such temptations on the honor basis, nor are they properly supervised. These programs have tempted many bureaucrats into criminal activity. Again, a massive annual savings.

- Close some 25 of the 50 independent agencies. These are no longer necessary but have continued for decades without examination. Examples are the Maritime Administration, the Small Business Administration, the Export-Import Bank, the Overseas Private Investment Corporation, the Appalachian Regional Commission, and the Federal Railroad Administration.

In addition, among the thousands of lesser federal programs, some 150 others—as listed by the Office of Management and Budget—should be severely cut back or closed, including Ameri-Corps, Rural Utilities Service, Market Access Program for food companies, ethanol tax subsidies, farm subsidies (except for the few small farmers), international enterprise funds, metric program, and sugar subsidies. The savings will be in the multibillions.

- Change the present permissive atmosphere among bureaucrats, and prosecute those involved in any criminal activity, which has become epidemic.

- Reorganize the present 15 cabinet agencies by first defining the purpose of each, then reform them so that their missions are clear, moving functions that do not belong into other agencies.

Many cabinet agencies are an incoherent collection of missions. The Department of Energy, for example, handles atomic energy and provides heating aid for the poor. The Department of Agriculture, which has dozens of extraneous missions, including providing electricity for large cities, must be reduced to its true mission, caring for our farmers.

Subsidies should be maintained only for poor, struggling farmers, if such still exist. All aid to farmers earning over $100,000 a year should be discontinued, as well as all subsidies to part-time gentlemen farmers. Two thirds of the enormous network of farm offices should be closed as the number of independent farmers continues to decrease.

Close the Department of Agriculture, making it a small agency within a new Department of Natural Resources, which will include a closed Department of Energy, leaving all nuclear work to a separate Bureau of Atomic Energy, which will be more targeted and effective. The Forest Service should also be transferred to the new Natural Resources department, as should several aspects of the Department of Interior.

We should combine the Department of Commerce and the Department of Labor, creating greater harmony between capital and labor, helping our industries grow.

Take the $700 billion now spent on the poor in federal and state money, and transfer all 85 welfare programs from six cabinet agencies and from throughout the government into one new Department of Welfare. That agency will be fully computerized and able to know which poverty services and how much cash are going to any one recipient. Most important, the emphasis of the program will shift from services, which may not be valuable in raising people out of poverty, to cash. By issuing sufficient cash from the present $700 billion cost to the 37 million poor, we will be able to raise everyone out of poverty level and save anywhere from $250 billion to $400 billion a year.

To continue with our cabinet reformation: Close the Department of Housing and Urban Development and close the Department of Transportation. Create a new cabinet department of Urban, Suburban, and Rural Affairs to consolidate thousands of various programs under one roof, including highway construction. Separate out the Civilian Air Agency, without cabinet status, to control air passenger travel and safety throughout America.

The present Health and Human Services (HHS) is another grab-bag organization that has too many functions, including various welfare programs. With Welfare separated out as a cabinet agency, HHS's title should be changed simply to the Department of Health, handling Medicare, Medicaid, the Surgeon General's office, public health, and all medical research of the federal government. It should be headed not by a politician but by a renowned physician from civilian life.

When the president's cabinet reform is completed, we would have only 12 cabinet agencies, instead of 15, and arranged in a more logical distribution of functions; as follows:

- Department of State

- Department of Defense

- Department of Homeland Security

- Department of Commerce and Labor

- Department of Natural Resources

- Department of Health

- Department of Welfare

- Department of Urban, Suburban, and Rural Affairs

- Department of Justice

- Department of Treasury

- Department of Veteran Affairs

- Department of Interior

With the new, more logical system, we would also save scores of billions a year.

To clamp down on excessive spending, we also need greater control, as follows:

- Establish a National Inspector General's Office, an independent group answering directly to the president that will appoint inspectors general for various agencies but not be responsible to those agencies, but to the central IG. At present, the inspectors general are hired by the same agencies they cover and can be fired by them, which greatly inhibits their objectivity and desire for reform action. (Incidentally, I'm available for the job.)

- This new IG group will mesh with the Government Accountability Office in ensuring that recommendations for change are publicly announced on a regular basis, then actually accomplished. Cost cutting and reform will actually take place instead of being ignored, which is usually the case at present. This move will also cut down considerably on rampant bureaucratic corruption.

- This IG oversight group should hire a private management consulting firm to evaluate all programs in the federal budget and publicly suggest which to cut, or reduce.

- The IG should also concentrate on waste and fraud in the Medicare and Medicaid programs, which now run an astronomical $150 billion a year. In fact, the inspector general should have a large group of accountants working in every agency and, in the case of Medicare and Medicaid, in major medical institutions as well to reduce fraud. Doctors and hospitals that cheat should be prosecuted with the full force of the law.

- Establish a joint executive-legislative screening board, approved by both Congress and the president that will report to the nation on all projected legislation, evaluating whether it duplicates a bill on the books, whether it is needed, and whether it has a reasonable cost–benefit ratio. This work should be done and disseminated to the public before the bill is voted on and becomes law.

- Establish a law, or a constitutional amendment, that sets a 4-year sunset limit on all legislation, requiring the Congress and the president to review the programs every 4 years. After review, the programs will either be extended or closed.

- Establish new legislation to make government more efficient and responsible.

- Pass a constitutional amendment stating, as Jefferson proposed, that no borrowing could be done year to year by the federal government, except in times of a declared war. Budgets should be adjusted yearly to make them dollar neutral, enabling the government to create a surplus in good years, which must be used to pay down the national debt.

There are many more methods and actions that will lead to a better and more equitable government. They include:

- Eliminate all corporate welfare, which will save some $60 billion a year.

- Eliminate the China trade imbalance by a new equalization tax on their goods based on the value of their underpriced yuan.

- Return all mineral rights to the states on their federal lands so they can produce for the nation.

- Put in a true ethics law requiring that all federal employees and all members of Congress be restricted from lobbying for a period of 5 years after leaving government employ. End the revolving door of lobbyists returning to federal service in all circumstances.

The following list includes several more suggestions for cutting expenditures:

- Eliminate the AMT.

- Eliminate all support for bilingual language.

- Eliminate the birthright citizenship of children of illegal immigrants.

- Restrict Community Development Block Grants to poor communities.

- Cut at least half of the present federal contractual workers and consultants.

- Close the No Child Left Behind program and use the money to reconstruct the present K–12 system as proposed in "Education" (p. 142).

- Eliminate all earmarks, subjecting members of Congress to ethical charges if they propose extra funds for their localities.

- Track down and eliminate the present documented $13 billion a year fraud perpetrated by recipients of the IRS Earned Income Tax Credit welfare program for the working poor.

Perhaps most important, reduce the exorbitant amount of money spent on discretionary items, such as the recent 8% growth in discretionary funds in the Omnibus Bill of 2009.

Spending has become a compulsive activity in Washington, and must be cured if we are to survive. For the 2010 budget, the administration proposed $18 billion in discretionary spending cuts, as it increased overall spending by $600 billion—a laughable budgetary gesture, with no guarantee that Congress would pass even that small reduction.

The best way to control discretionary spending is to declare a budget holiday and have no increase beyond inflation in the following year's budget, then attempt to repeat that for 4 years. The savings will be almost $100 billion a year.

On taxation, follow the new knowledge that indicates that on certain gradient taxes such as capital gains, that tax income will—especially in bad economic times—rise with a lower rate. In the present stock market, for example, very little capital gains taxes are being collected. By lowering, not raising, the capital gains rate from 15% (and the new 20% rate) to 7.5%, the Treasury will gain billions, and the stock market will quickly change directions, in a positive way, leading to greater prosperity.

To control expenditures in general, we should consider requiring that any increase in the discretionary federal budget beyond inflation will require a super majority in both Houses of Congress, perhaps a 60% vote instead of a simple majority. The temptation of legislators to spend money to impress their constituents is potent and can be curbed only by new legislation.

For the sake of comprehensive reform, we should consider acting on all cost-savings and reform found in the pages of this book.

The federal government's break with reality, in purpose and fiscal cost, has become its unfortunate hallmark. No piecemeal reform is meaningful at this stage. The nation must face up to its challenge.

We are now headed on a suicidal path of taxes, spending, deficits, and debt. To reconnect us to a healthy government and thus a nation of renewed optimism will require dispensing with partisan concepts and mustering a new patriotic emotion, one that has saved us from past calamities in wartime and could do the same again in times of peace.

In the final analysis, the future of America is not in the hands of its present or future politicians but is totally in the province of all American citizens. We can either remain indolent in the face of crisis or react strongly against the policies of our most irresponsible elected officials.

Final note to the president:

> *There is no other course if we are to save America from national suicide.*

ABOUT THE AUTHOR

Educator, columnist, and investigative reporter **Martin L. Gross** is the author of a dozen nonfiction works on subjects such as government, education, national culture, psychology, and medicine.

His phenomenal bestseller, *The Government Racket: Washington Waste from A to Z*, reached number 3 on the *New York Times* bestseller list and opened up a still-raging bipartisan debate on the failings of the federal government in Washington, DC.

Martin L. Gross has discussed his often controversial works on such national television programs as *Larry King Live*, *20-20*, *Good Morning America*, and *CBS This Morning*, as well as news channels such as CNN, Fox News, C-SPAN, and many others.

He has testified before House and Senate committees six times, and has received praise from both sides of the aisle for his researched revelations.

Martin L. Gross's syndicated columns have appeared in the *Los Angeles Times*, *Newsday*, *Chicago Sun-Times*, and *The Dallas Morning News*. He is the author of more than 100 magazine articles, which have been appeared in publications such as *The New Republic* and *Life*.

His critique of American tax policy, *The Tax Racket: Government Extortion from A to Z*, was another *New York Times* bestseller, and his examination of education, *The Conspiracy of Ignorance: The Failure of American Public Schools*, received plaudits from leading educators intent on reform.

He is also the author of *The Brain Watchers: An Analysis of the Psychological Testing Industry*, a critical examination of psychological testing; *The Doctors: A Penetrating Analysis of the American Physician and His Practice of Medicine*, a study of American medicine, which received praise from the head of Massachusetts General Hospital and contributed to needed reforms; and *The Psychological Society: A Critical*

Analysis of Psychiatry, Psychotherapy, Psychoanalysis, and the Psychological Revolution, a critique of Freudian theory.

Mr. Gross is a member of the National Association of Scholars, was on the faculty of the New School University, and was an adjunct professor of social science at New York University. He has received awards for his work frm the American Heritage Foundation and the National Education Association.